Coleridge's Poetics

For J.R.H. and P.J.R.H.

Coleridge's Poetics

PAUL HAMILTON

Basil Blackwell

© Paul Hamilton 1983

First published 1983
Basil Blackwell Publisher Limited
108 Cowley Road, Oxford OX4 1JF, England

British Library Cataloguing in Publication Data
Hamilton, Paul
    Coleridge's poetics.
    1. Coleridge, Samuel Taylor—Knowledge—
    Literature
    2. Criticism—Great Britain—History
    3. Poetics—History
    I. Title
    801'.951'0924   PR4487.L5

ISBN 0–631–13364–X

Typesetting by Freeman Graphic, Tonbridge
Printed in Great Britain by
Billing and Sons Ltd, Worcester

Contents

Acknowledgements

I am grateful to many people who have encouraged or usefully taken issue with this study at various stages of its production. My thanks are due to the Master and Fellows of Balliol College for the Junior Research Fellowship which allowed me to complete a large part of the basic research. My work at that time was commented on with helpful trenchancy by, among others, Anthony Kenny, Patrick Gardner, Mary Warnock and Stephen Prickett. Christopher Cordner, David Doyle, Bob White and David Norbrook provided argumentative backing; Naomi Segal taught me the value of abstract words. My greatest single obligation is to Roy Park, so generous in sharing knowledge and offering support. Like all who write on Coleridge I am much indebted both to the editors of the *Collected Coleridge* and to the imaginative work of the Coleridgeans with whom I have agreed or disagreed. At least the remaining mistakes and infelicities are my own.

Abbreviations

Coleridge

A   *Aids to Reflection* (London, 1825).

BL   *Biographia Literaria*, ed. with his Aesthetical Essays by
        J. Shawcross (London, 1907, corrected 1954), 2 vols.

C&S   *On the Constitution of the Church and State*, ed. J. Colmer
        (Princeton and London, 1977).

CIS   *Confessions of an Inquiring Spirit* (London, 1840).

CL   *Collected Letters of Samuel Taylor Coleridge*, ed. E. L. Griggs
        (London, 1956–71), 6 vols.

CLL   *Coleridge on Logic and Learning*, ed. A. D. Snyder (New
        Haven, 1929).

CSC   *Coleridge on the Seventeenth Century*, ed. R. F. Brinkley
        (Durham, NC, 1955).

EOT   *Essays on his Own Times*, ed. D. V. Erdman (Princeton and
        London, 1978), 3 vols.

IS   *Inquiring Spirit*, a new presentation of Coleridge from
        his published and unpublished writings, ed. K. Coburn
        (London, 1951).

Log   Unpublished MS 'Treatise on Logic' in the British Library's
        Egerton Collection (Egerton, 2825, 2826), 2 vols.

LPR   *Lectures 1795 on Politics and Religion*, ed. Lewis Patton and
        Peter Mann (Princeton and London, 1971).

LR   *Literary Remains of Samuel Taylor Coleridge*, ed. H. N.
        Coleridge (London, 1836–39), 4 vols.

LS   *Lay Sermons*, ed. R. J. White (Princeton and London, 1972).

M   *Marginalia*, ed. G. Whalley (Princeton and London, 1980), 1 vol. published.

MC   *Coleridge's Miscellaneous Criticism*, ed. T. M. Raysor (London, 1936).

NB   *The Notebooks of Samuel Taylor Coleridge*, ed. K. Coburn, 3 vols. published (London, 1957, 1961, 1973). Where a reference is made to Miss Coburn's edition followed by the letter 'n', this signifies a reference to Miss Coburn's volume of notes accompanying each volume of Coleridge's entries. References to Coleridge's still unpublished notebooks are to the originals in the British Library.

PhL   *The Philosophical Lectures of Samuel Taylor Coleridge*, ed. K. Coburn (London, 1949).

SC   *Coleridge's Shakespearean Criticism*, ed. T. M. Raysor (London, 1930), 2 vols.

TF   *The Friend*, ed. Barbara E. Rooke (Princeton and London, 1969), 2 vols.

TM   *Treatise on Method*, ed. A. D. Snyder (New Haven, 1934).

TofL   *Hints towards the Formation of a More Comprehensive Theory of Life*, ed. Seth B. Watson (London, 1848).

TT   *Specimens of the Table Talk of the late Samuel Taylor Coleridge*, ed. H. N. Coleridge (London, 1835), 2 vols.

TW   *The Watchman*, ed. Lewis Patton (Princeton and London, 1970).

Wordsworth

W   *The Prose Works of William Wordsworth*, ed. W. J. B. Owen and Jane Smyser (Oxford, 1974), 3 vols.

WLC   *Wordsworth's Literary Criticism*, ed. W. J. B. Owen (London, 1974). When quoting from the 1802 'Preface' to the *Lyrical Ballads* I have used *WLC* because this version of the 'Preface' is printed there as an integral text and not, as in *W*, in the form of one set of the many variations between the printed 1800 and 1850 texts recorded only in footnotes.

Introduction

This book studies the place of poetry in Coleridge's thought. In doing so it is forced to explain schemes that never quite work, to draw out the implications of arguments that Coleridge never fully expressed, and to point up the importance of his lines of thought which subverted his stated intentions. This method is the only one which fits the material, but amongst Coleridgean scholars it tends to produce quite polarized results. At one extreme, the critic, supported by a knowledge of innumerable fragments, preserves an Olympian indifference to the contradictions in Coleridge's major writings which upset the ordinary reader. Coleridge's incompleteness is really complete: to the initiate his failures are successful ironies. In the gaps and incoherencies of *Biographia Literaria* we find his encouragement to watch the enlargement of our own minds as we piece out, supplement and imaginatively verify the theory of imagination he has promised, and then has artfully failed to supply: a mutually flattering solution, this one, reflecting to the credit both of Coleridge and his reader. At the other extreme, Coleridge is found to be simply intellectually disreputable. Thomas Carlyle's portrait in his *Life of Sterling* sets the tone, later echoed by Matthew Arnold, Walter Pater, Leslie Stephen and others, and plainly heard in F. R. Leavis's verdict that Coleridge's 'currency as an academic classic is something of a scandal'. However, this approach frequently represents not only a distaste for the whiff of scandal which has always surrounded Coleridge — the mixture of laudanum and transcendentalism; the aura of the philosophical mountebank always about to produce the great scheme, provided we subscribe to a belief in its success in advance – it also often amounts to a straightforward opposition to the notion of literary theory. The felicities of Coleridge's practical criticism are to be prised from their theoretical dross and exhibited in a pure form.

The claim I advance here is that a proper understanding of Coleridge's practical criticism cannot detach it from theory, any more than it can remove Coleridge's theories intact from the problematic way in which they are expressed. The idea of a pure essence of either is an illusion, for in his critical thought, theory and practice are only fully comprehended in one another. How is this collaboration to be explained?

Coleridge's poetics rationalize the most ambitious assumptions behind English Romantic poetry. If we imagine a composite statement – an English Romantic manifesto – then Shelley might begin by declaring that 'A poem is the very image of life expressed in its eternal truth', while 'poetry', for Wordsworth, 'is the impassioned expression which is in the countenance of all Science': *all* science, in case we were tempted to underestimate. 'It is', Coleridge would continue, 'the blossom and the fragrance of all human knowledge, human thought, human passions, emotions, language.' William Hazlitt would only be revealing the prevailing assumptions when he asserted that 'Poetry is the most perfect language men can use.' Arnold reiterated this almost verbatim, calling poetry 'the most perfect speech of man'. More recently, I. A. Richards described poetry as 'the completest mode' of utterance; and for Leavis, literary language was simply 'the language we can't do without.' The exaggerated, Romantic tone is still recognizable, but we need to make an effort to recover the argument which was thought to justify it.

These defences of poetry, unlike literal statements, reiterate the poetic context they attempt to justify. They are not simply poetry, but passages that define themselves as poetry, apparently confident that it is self-recognition which unravels the nature of poetic significance, and explains the extravagance of the Romantic poet's claims. This performative defence is reticent. But again it is a mistake to believe that this proves the absence of any theoretical content to the Romantic argument. Rather, what is needed is an understanding of how poetic self-consciousness can be thought to constitute a defence of poetry.

This Romantic defence of poetry with an equally poetic description of the language poets use aligns a native, English tradition, which accords philosophical significance to the poetic use of language, with another tradition. This second, German tradition was introduced to England mainly by Coleridge, and was little developed after his death, although much recent criticism, calling itself poetics, has revived the theoretical implications of poetic self-consciousness as if this could be done without considering the historical constraints upon the original Romantic theory. The first tradition consisted in a conservative belief in the value for the philosophy of mind of a practical understanding of linguistic propriety, an understanding fostered by the sensitivities of poetry. Ordinary-language philosophers from Thomas Reid to J. L. Austin opposed various philosophical theories by pointing out the offences they commit against standard linguistic usage – as Gilbert Ryle calls it, 'the informal logic of the employment of expressions'.

Coleridge lived at a time which was still registering the effects of an upsurge in ordinary-language philosophy in reaction to the scepticism of David Hume. And in his case, this common-sense trust in the contribution of the study of language to the concept of mind was enriched and refined by an awareness of the development of German thought in the work of Immanuel Kant, F. Schiller, J. G. Fichte, Friedrich Schlegel, and others. Within this second tradition he could participate in a defence of poetry based on poetry's awareness of its own aesthetic status. It is this tradition which is felt most strongly in literary theory today. The English Romantics' poetic affirmation of the importance of poetry could be seen to point to self-consciousness as an essential constituent of poetry and the key to its philosophical consequence. Poetry presents itself as fully aware of its own fictional status, possessing a consciousness which automatically places it in relation to other forms of thought. Its typically ideal significance for science, politics and religion is to set standards of completeness or insightfulness which are then ironically eroded by the melancholy recollection that they are, after all, the products of artificially-arrested conditions. The heuristic, exemplary quality of poetry dwindles into feeling, symbol and play. Yet the fictional distance to which poetry removes itself still allows it to exist in relation to the sciences in the form of an ambitious imperative. Poetry's imagined fulfilments are the only ideas permitted us of that harmonious development of self for which the progressive sciences ought to strive. Its artificial conditions mime the limitations of knowledge, but the perfections it achieves within its own conventions create the notion of a normative ideal with, in Schiller's words, 'every right to command'.

Coleridge believed that the self-consciousness utilized by the Romantic poet's poetic defence of his art both disqualifies poetry from prosaic reality and indicates its unique power. His quarrel with Wordsworth in *Biographia* mostly arises from the fear that Wordsworth was doing away with the devices and conventions which signal this awareness, although Coleridge also used this accusation of literalism to defuse the political implications of Wordsworth's applications of their shared radical aesthetic. The degree to which Coleridge participated in this self-conscious defence can be measured by his own failure to achieve the transcendental deduction promised in volume I of *Biographia,* along with the continuing philosophical relevance he attributes to the criticism of volume II. There, he painstakingly draws out the theoretical implications of the poetic use of language. His practical criticism reveals the philosophical effects arising from poetry's self-awareness.

Coleridge's use of the common-sense tradition in British philosophy leads him to treat linguistic usage as philosophical evidence, letting the language '*think* for us'. However, he moves beyond the conservatism of the common-sense philosophers to use language as a model for the progress of knowledge. He explains this by his theory of desynonymy – a largely neglected area of his thought. Desynonymy is meant to illustrate how knowledge advances: it uses the example of the proliferation of language through the discovery that words we had thought were synonymous in fact have different meanings. If we keep this in mind, Coleridge's most notable act of desynonymy –

intuitively distinguishing fancy and the two imaginations from within his critical practice early in *Biographia* – suggests that the original direction of his thought was obscured by its much-heralded but unsuccessful attempt to deduce rules of criticism from the philosophical character of imagination. In contrast to this, his desynonymizing encourages us to understand his philosophy by understanding his critical usage. His appreciation of the logic of modern, 'sentimental' poetry prompts this act, and his criticism of Wordsworth implies that the secondary, poetic imagination is one whose activity imbues its products with an awareness of their own aesthetic status. It places them as poetry, and therefore needs to be differentiated from the imagination in perception, and from the fancy which can appear in art, but whose function is not necessarily aesthetic. It is Coleridge's increasing anxiety about the specific political form which radicalism supported by his poetics in method and conclusion might take – an anxiety which eventually led him to write *On the Constitution of the Church and State* – which accounts most economically for his repression of the argument from desynonymy in *Biographia* in favour of the ill-fated transcendental deduction.

Coleridge's interest in desynonymy shows that there is a method behind his practical criticism: that in the finer discriminations released by his critical understanding he could have regarded himself as doing something philosophically important, something which even provided a model of philosophical discovery. This reading of Coleridge means that we can concur in Leavis's judgement that, in *Biographia,* 'the master of theoretical criticism who matters is the completion of the practical critic', without also agreeing that this implies the irrelevance of theory to the activity of criticism. On the contrary, Coleridge's theoretical definitions and defences of poetry and poetic imagination are produced by his practical understanding of poetry's responsible awareness and considered exploitation of its own nature.

The first chapter of this book looks at different approaches to the problem of Coleridge's failure in *Biographia* to achieve what he set out to do. The second deals with the mixture of native and German philosophical traditions from which Coleridge's ideas on language and poetry derive. In the third chapter, I discuss his theory of desynonymy; and in the fourth I trace his related habit of criticizing unprogressive philosophies of human nature by criticizing the language in which they are written. His poetic openness to human potential, however vague its political tendency, promotes a radical philosophy which desynonymy can be seen as intended to rationalize. Chapter 5 explores the logic of his practical criticism in order to understand the need he felt to desynonymize the poetic imagination from uses of the imagination not consciously aesthetic. Finally, there is the different direction taken by his later political and religious thought. According to the predominant, orthodox strain in Coleridge's ideas, art must become the expression of religious and political certainties we already possess if its radical potential is to conform to Coleridge's conservatism. This contradicts the vestiges of his earlier radicalism, which now take the extravagant form of imagining that religious truth unburdens itself by perceiving history as a vast cyclical poem – a progressive movement which obviously threatens the claims of any political or religious establishment already to embody truth. Chapter 6 suggests that the more influential orthodoxies of Coleridge's *On the Constitution of the Church and State* distract from the radical quality of his poetics; and that this neglect is paradoxically encouraged by his fudged presentation of his theory of poetry in *Biographia*. The main effect of the failure of the transcendental deduction in *Biographia* was to lead later English critics to think they could dismiss his theorizing, while appropriating his practical criticism. We are still suffering from this false separation. The lasting importance of Coleridge, historically understood, is to show that the theory and the practice of criticism are not alternatives.

CHAPTER ONE

The Integrity of
Biographia Literaria

To say it once more: today I find it an impossible book: I consider it badly written, ponderous, embarrassing, image-mad and image-confused, sentimental, in places saccharine to the point of effeminacy, uneven in tempo, without the will to logical cleanliness, very convinced and therefore disdainful of proof, mistrustful even of the *propriety* of proof, a book for initiates, 'music' for those dedicated to music, those who are closely related to begin with on the basis of common and rare aesthetic experiences, 'music' meant as a sign of recognition for close relatives *in artibus* – an arrogant and rhapsodic book that sought to exclude right from the beginning the *profanum vulgus* of 'the educated' even more than 'the mass' or 'folk'. Still, the effect of the book proved and proves that it had a knack for seeking out fellow-rhapsodizers and for luring them on to new secret paths and dancing places.

> F. Nietzche, 'Attempt at a Self-Criticism', *The Birth of Tragedy,* trans. W. Kaufmann (New York, 1967), 19

'THE MAIN RESULT'

Deep in the heart of English critical theory, at the centre of Coleridge's exposition of his own views on the relation which philosophy bears to a proper understanding of poetry, there is a disabling gap in the argument. In' the first volume of his literary biography Coleridge declares his aim of investigating 'the seminal principle' of poetic composition. He intends to expose, by transcendental deduction, the nature of the imaginative faculty which the poet characteristically employs. After deducing what the faculty of imagination is, he will show what defines poetry as its recognizable product. For a moment the plan seems straightforward: the first volume of *Biographia Literaria* will provide a philosophical theory of imagination; the second will explain how the imagination expresses itself. And the philosophy of the first volume and the literary criticism of the second will complement each other.

However, Coleridge fails to 'proceed to the nature and genesis of the imagination', and contents himself with 'stating the main result' of the missing chapter. The statement of 'the main result' is the short descriptions Coleridge gives of the primary imagination, the secondary imagination, and the fancy. These are certainly tantalizingly suggestive; but they are, on Coleridge's own admission, not conclusions drawn from a preceding line of reasoning. After referring the reader to a 'future publication', Coleridge moves on briskly to the literary criticism of the second volume. Without philosophical arguments, both for what the imagination is and for how the imagination informs poetry, the two volumes of *Biographia* slide inexorably apart.

The result is that the most famous, self-professed attempt in English literature to exhibit the relation of philosophy to poetry disintegrates. The abstruse, technical discussion towards the end of the first volume becomes increasingly disreputable with the accumulation of more and more unacknowledged borrowings, mostly from the German philosopher, Schelling. With little warning, and for no apparent philosophical reason, the argument halts. On opening the second volume the reader is plunged into a lucid practical criticism of poetry, mostly that of Shakespeare, Milton and Wordsworth. Coleridge, as George Whalley concedes, 'renounces the effort of providing an adequate transition'.[1] The lively, engaging nature of his literary criticism makes the philosophical difficulties seem even further removed from a concern for understanding poetry.

[1] See G. Whalley, 'The Integrity of *Biographia Literaria*', *Essays and Studies*, new series, 6 (1953), 87–102.

Nevertheless, Coleridge's criticism of Wordsworth, Shakespeare and Milton retains a considerable philosophical resonance. The original design of *Biographia* would have made the practical appreciation of poetry the necessary correlate of a philosophical understanding of the role of imagination in human experience. In the absence of any argument explaining the nature of this correlation, the literary example of poetry has to carry a large weight of philosophical significance on its own.

The history of the writing of *Biographia* shows that once he had decided to expand the 'Preface' to his poems into a work in its own right Coleridge most likely completed most of volume II before returning to what is now chapter 4 of volume I. He then tried to complete his account of the philosophy of which he must have hoped his later practical criticism would appear to be the natural result.[2] At this stage *Biographia* was still conceived as a one-volume edition. It was the printer who discovered that its length would not match that of its intended companion volume, *Sibylline Leaves*. And it was he who decided that *Biographia* would have to be published as two volumes. The division, then, was an accident of typography cruelly exposing the already existing gap in the argument which Coleridge's last efforts, as the printer's deadline approached, failed to bridge. The practical criticism could not have been intended to have the individual consideration we are now inclined to give it as we read it at a safe distance from the earlier volume. The biography of *Biographia* suggests instead that the attempted transcendental deduction of the imagination was inserted by Coleridge into the middle of a chapter which was 'a natural antecedent to chapter xiv', the first chapter of volume II.[3] The philosophy is therefore surrounded by the framework of an argument which it was supposed to expand discursively – an argument based on the intuitive power to identify and discriminate,

[2]I am relying on the conclusions of Daniel Mark Fogel, 'A Compositional History of the *BIOGRAPHIA LITERARIA*', *Studies in Bibliography*, XXX (1977), 219–94.
[3]*Ibid.*, 231. See Fogel's conclusion: 'That Coleridge spent two months adding the metaphysical part to a work which he could have passed off as finished demonstrates that from his standpoint the philosophy of volume I of the *Biographia* was an essential foundation for the assessment of Wordsworth's poems, theory, and poetry in volume II', 233.

to *desynonymize* the uses of fancy and imagination in poetry.

Coleridge's public failure to unite philosophical theory with the practical criticism of poetry has had a momentous effect on subsequent literary criticism. It helped critics from Arnold to Leavis to overestimate the importance of a pure practical criticism, and even to believe in the possibility of its self-sufficiency. In their work practical criticism retains an air of philosophical seriousness, along with the tacit belief that we need not bother to explain the philosophy. Until very recently this has been the tendency of much literary criticism in this country. Arnold's emphasis on the power to identify 'touchstones' of literary value is the hidden support of many finely persuasive readings by T. S. Eliot, I. A. Richards, Leavis, Empson, and American 'new critics'. Good criticism in this tradition tends to disregard the philosophical context of Romantic criticism, while clandestinely retaining in the appreciation of, say, Shakespeare, an unargued conviction of profundity which could only have derived from the context which has been ignored.

Since a quotation from Shakespeare is usually regarded as incontrovertible proof of excellence, it is hard for somebody working in the English literary tradition to see why it need be explained philosophically. Shakespeare's stature has not only been a burden on the genius of later English poets trying to create an original style, it has also rendered critics speechless from Arnold to Harold Bloom, escaping all their explanatory theories: 'Others abide our question. Thou art free.'[4] Shakespeare's virtues seem to transcend argument, and his universality to defy definition. As a consequence, the phenomenon which E. P. Thompson, that most professedly English of historians, calls 'the old Adam of the English idiom' reasserts itself.[5] Drawing attention to the full exploitation of the rhythms and structures of ordinary language becomes sufficient critical argument,

---

[4]'Shakespeare', *Poetical Works of Matthew Arnold* (Oxford, 1950), 2–3. See Harold Bloom, *The Anxiety of Influence, A Theory of Poetry* (Oxford, 1973): 'Shakespeare is the largest instance in the language of a phenomenon that stands outside the concern of this book . . .', 11.

[5]'An open letter to Leszek Kolakowski', *The Socialist Register* (1973), 14; see R. Williams, 'From Leavis to Goldmann', *New Left Review*, 67 (May–June 1971), 3–18.

and an inability to say more is presented as the highest criticial accolade. A deep respect for poetic language itself rejects the contribution of philosophy to the critical debate.

The problem at the heart of *Biographia* is therefore central to any critical theory which lays claim to philosophical respectability or to any critical practice which claims to say anything on its own account. The composition of *Biographia* shows that Coleridge believed that practical criticism, the gift of close reading, was a necessary but not a sufficient condition of critical accomplishment. There still remains a need to amalgamate practical sensitivity with the theoretical ability to justify it. From criticism it seems reasonable to want to *know* why understanding poetry is philosophically important, as well as *feeling* that power of self-renewal liberated in us by an interpretative reading which then disappears into the text which prompted it. The best practical critics make themselves invisible, which is to say that they explain nothing. They aim to become superfluous, to let us step through their looking-glass into the text itself; to render their own paraphrase transparent, speechless. Felt life, presence, immediacy of experience – these are the guarantees that criticism has put us in touch with the text. A work of literature has been most effectively recommended when it can be enacted or relived in as spontaneous and natural a manner as the reader's own existence. In Leavis's words, this assumes that 'A language *is* a life', brought into being by 'the non-Urizenic activity, that which creates a language.'[6] Leavis argues by quotation, and by touchstone, evoking a vital figure of Romantic imagination which he refuses to demythologize: no explanatory theory is allowed to come between critic and text.

The problem of providing an intuitive response with a discursive explanation is the one Coleridge faced but failed to solve directly. The consequences of his evasion are still with us. He saw most clearly the lack of a philosophical explanation of the critical activity and gave to English literature its most memorable expression of this need, but he apparently failed to answer it. The modern critic has to return to *Biographia* both to recover the clear statement of the central critical

[6]F. R. Leavis, *Nor Shall My Sword* (London, 1972), 183, 23.

ambition, and to press the historical question of what went wrong in Coleridge's case.

This book aims to establish that Coleridge did have the means at his disposal to resolve this problem, and that his ideas on desynonymy, repressed in *Biographia*, are the clue to the missing theory which he could have drawn out of his expertise as a practical critic. Had he done so he might have had a more constructive influence on the present criticial dilemma in England where theory and practice are often unhealthily polarized, and where linguistic structuralism and its epigones so rarely impinge on the literary imagination. Coleridge was a practical critic who wrote voluminously on the philosophy of language.[7] The contention here is that his views on the language of poetry reveal a helpful theoretical perspective which was not fully articulated for specific, historical reasons.

WAYS OF READING

When Agent Behrend had lost a silk umbrella he advertised for it, and described it in the advertisement as a cotton one; for, thought he, if I call it a silk umbrella, the finder will be more strongly tempted to keep it. So also thinks, in all probability, the systematist: 'If on the title page and in the announcements I call my production a persistent striving for the truth, alas! who will buy it or admire me? But if I call it the System, the Absolute System, everyone will surely want to buy the System' – if only the difficulty did not remain, that what the systematist sells is not the System.
S. Kierkegaard, *Concluding Unscientific Postscript,* trans. D. F. Swenson and W. Lowrie (Princeton, NJ, 1968), 99

Because the project of *Biographia* is so important for critical theory it has attracted unusually strong and definitive reactions. Briefly, these divide into the responses of philosophers, critics and sympathizers. The philosophers are rightly impatient of Coleridge's prevarications

[7]For Coleridge's modern relevance see, amongst others, G. Steiner, *Extraterritorial* (London, 1972): 'it is Coleridge's presence which stands out most vivid and premonitory when the modern "language revolution" gets under way at the turn of the century', 183; also R. Scholes' claim, in *Structuralism in Literature* (New Haven and London, 1974), that Coleridge's differences from Wordsworth on the subject of language show 'precisely the shift in linguistic thought which marks the beginning of structural poetics', 177.

and plagiarisms; the critics find enough meat in the practical criticism to justify ignoring the philosophy altogether; and the sympathizers try to reveal a connecting thread running through the whole book which shows its argument to be complete. These readings are equally unsatisfactory, for *Biographia* is an incomplete attempt to relate philosophy to criticism, while its value lies in its formulation of a perennial problem to which it may indirectly suggest a solution.

Approaching *Biographia* by means of Coleridge's ideas on language is the indirect solution tested here. Coleridge did not leave us a systematic exposition of his views on language, although he probably did intend to publish these views in the part of his proposed *Opus Maximum* to be called 'Elements of Discourse', which he frequently mentioned in his letters.[8] The 'Treatise on Logic' in the British Library contains material which would have been relevant, as do notebooks, letters and almost all his other writings. This lack of system could be a good sign: when Coleridge presents his own thought systematically there is always a great danger that he may be plagiarizing, but his scattered ideas on language appear to be his own, or to be within a tradition which he may develop, but which is itself insufficiently formulated for him to be able to reproduce as he does ideas from Kant in the 'Treatise on Logic', from Schelling in *Biographia,* and from A. W. Schlegel and others in his *Shakespearean Criticism.* Perhaps that is why Norman Fruman, while identifying Coleridge's unacknowledged borrowings, could encouragingly concede that a study of Coleridge's ideas on language 'might prove a worthwhile project'.[9]

But we can be too sympathetic towards Coleridge's intellectual disorderliness. Coleridge once announced, somewhat airily in a letter to Thomas Allsop of 1820, that he possessed a list of theoretical works 'requiring only to be put together, from the loose papers and numerous Common-place or Memorandum Books, & needing no other change whether of omission, addition, or correction, than the mere act of arranging & the opportunity of seeing the whole

[8]See especially *CL* V 275 and n., 281, 323, 337, 427–8; VI 967, 1067 for a complete list of references.
[9]N. Fruman, *Coleridge, The Damaged Archangel* (London, 1972), 471 n. 157.

collectively' (*CL* V 25). He presents the possibility of his research yielding a coherent argument almost as an afterthought, the icing on the cake. Some of his sympathetic modern critics have exonerated Coleridge beyond his wildest dreams. The most impressive of these, Thomas McFarland, argues that this lack of formal organization in Coleridge's thought itself indicates a philosophical standpoint, and that his deliberate openness to all kinds of ideas precludes his commitment to any one system. His huge philosophical receptivity shows a theoretical concern which has a definite method despite having no encompassing formal expression. McFarland calls this the 'reticulation' of Coleridge's thought, 'a concern for as many inter-connexions as possible' requiring a 'mosaic' method of composition. [10]

Walter Pater was perhaps the first to defend Coleridge's lack of system in this way when he claimed that 'what is lost in precision of form is gained in intricacy of expression. . . . His very language is forced and broken lest some saving formula should be lost.' [11] But both Pater's aesthetic relish for an intricate style, and McFarland's enthusiasm for Coleridge's intellectual resistance to systems of pantheism identify Coleridgean qualities, but do not succeed in dealing with major problems. Unfortunately, it is what McFarland describes as failures in reticulation, flaws in the web-like structure of Coleridge's thought, which occur at critical moments such as the gap in the argument of *Biographia*. [12] More recently it has been argued that Coleridge's incompleteness, even in *Biographia*, expresses a phil-osophical stance. *Biographia*, more than most texts, asks any critical approach to define itself and show its credentials. The gap in Coleridge's argument seems to force the sympathetic critic to complete it with the recognizable substance of his or her own theory. The danger is then that this unveiling of the reader's own assumptions tends to distract attention from what he or she is reading. Could this have been Coleridge's intention?

The thought behind some of the more recent readings is as

---

[10]T. McFarland, *Coleridge and The Pantheist Tradition* (Oxford, 1969), xl, 27.
[11]W. Pater, *Appreciations* (London, 1889, 1910), 69–70.
[12]McFarland, *Coleridge,* 40.

follows.[13] Coleridge's argument is intentionally incoherent, or at least incomplete, because of his profound scepticism regarding the sufficiency of any transcendental deduction of the imagination. His approach is instead rhetorical. The fragmentary progress of the final chapters of volume I exemplifies the constraints belonging to another kind of philosophical explanation. Truth, according to this view, is not a fixed essence to be seized as the last link in a chain of deductive argument; rather it is becoming, a process which can only be experienced, not an object to be pinned down in a dead reckoning. The strategy appropriate to the philosopher who believes this is the rhetorical one of soliciting the participation of his reader. The ironic failure of the philosophical deduction impresses upon the reader the inadequacy of this method of defining imagination. He is involved in an alternative logic: the reality of imagination has to be experienced in order to be comprehended philosophically. In keeping with some of Coleridge's theological statements, we must, in this instance, believe before we can understand. The famous 'letter from a friend' of chapter 13 written by Coleridge himself to forestall the need for a conclusion, and even the obtrusive plagiarisms from Schelling, can then be seen as counters in a rhetorical argument. They are ironic gestures which draw attention to the failure of the philosopher to achieve a deduction which he has reason to think is impossible anyway. His reader only grasps this thought through experiencing the lacuna in the deductive argument.

This response to the problem of finding unity in *Biographia* is implicitly based on a recent and sometimes exhilarating scepticism

[13]See M. G. Cooke, 'Quisque Sui Faber: Coleridge in the *Biographia Literaria*', *Philological Quarterly*, 50 (1971), 208–29; R. Mallette, 'Narrative Technique and Structure in the *Biographia*', *Modern Language Review*, 70 (January 1975), 32–40; J. C. Christensen, 'Coleridge's Marginal Method in the *Biographia Literaria*', *Publications of the Modern Languages Association*, 92 no. 5 (1977), 928–41; 'The Genius in the *Biographia Literaria*', *Studies in Romanticism*, 17, no. 2 (1978), 215–31; D. Simpson, *Irony and Authority in Romantic Poetry* (London, 1979), 96, *passim*; K. Wheeler, *Sources, Processes and Methods in Coleridge's "Biographia Literaria"* (Cambridge, 1980). For clear discussions of modern reading theory see W. Iser, 'The Reading Process', in *The Implied Reader* (Baltimore and London, 1974), 274–95; *The Act of Reading* (London, 1978); J. Culler, 'Literary Competence', in *Structuralist Poetics* (London, 1975), 113–31.

regarding the claims any piece of writing may make to say what it is. The apparently central concern of *Biographia* to produce and exemplify a theory of imagination is put to one side, decentred, and otherwise marginal details, irrelevant or even embarrassing to the declared purpose of the work, are found to be of crucial explicative importance. This new perspective does draw attention in an original way to the mechanics of Coleridge's text – its eccentricities, fictions, jokes, allusions – but in order to claim for them the power to reorientate the direction of the argument. *Biographia* is variegated enough to tempt this kind of critical cubism, but the central problematic gap remains visible from all angles.

To place responsibility for the coherence of the argument of volume I on the experience of the reader at first seems to provide an unanswerable defence for Coleridge. However, Coleridge mimes confusion and disruption so convincingly in his presentation that we seem in this case to have lost any criteria for distinguishing an incoherent text from one that demands an ironic reading. Furthermore, the possibility of an ironic reading is parasitical upon the knowledge of a philosophy which would be a reasoned alternative to a transcendental deduction. As a model of philosophical argument the transcendental deduction obviously derives from Kant. It is against the standard of Kant's *Critiques* that Coleridge's deduction is found wanting and his plagiarism from Schelling misguided, as will be explained in the next chapter.

Which philosophical model might the deductive failure gesture towards as an alternative? Above all it is a philosophy which Coleridge never wrote. *Biographia* presents itself as a test case of coherence: 'the statement of my principles in Politics, Religion and Philosophy, and an application of the rules, deduced from philosophical principles, to poetry and criticism' (*BL* I 1). *Biographia* is not an autobiography which happens to allude to a system expounded elsewhere. But perhaps Coleridge had not written it yet, or was hinting at the theory of another philosopher? However Coleridge always, and not just in *Biographia,* envisages his main philosophical project as a transcendental deduction of sorts, and nowhere gives us grounds for thinking he had in mind a radically different philosophical stance from which he could parody the deductive method of Kant and Schelling. Coleridge sells *Biographia* as a system, even if it is not systematic. To save the possibility of an alternative method we have to imagine something like this: Coleridge had thought through in his head, without bothering to write it down, a philosophy as innovatory as that of Hegel, Kierkegaard or Nietzsche.

Irony certainly played a large part in the philosophy of Coleridge's German contemporaries. Friedrich Schlegel once suggested that 'the classification of works of art into naïve and sentimental might perhaps be fruitfully applied to criticism as well.' The possibility of *extending* Schiller's distinction from poetry to criticism, suggesting an artful, ironic, sentimental criticism which publicizes its own artificiality, is discussed (one wonders how unironically) by Schlegel in various places. [14] Coleridge, I shall argue, assumes Schiller's distinction in his own criticism. But nowhere in Coleridge's writings is there a justification for attributing to him Schlegel's extension of Schiller's distinction to criticism itself – other, that is, than the practice in *Biographia* which was the thing to be explained in the first place. Coleridge's borrowings from Schelling lack the extra context of his own thought which could absorb Schelling's philosophy into a stage of the movement of an Absolute Spirit, as recounted by Hegel, or which could transform plagiarism into an ironic 'repetition' in the manner of Kierkegaard. Nor do we have evidence for detecting the embryonic technique of a Nietzschean discussion deliberately 'presented in the context of *art*' in the reasoned belief that 'the problem of science cannot be recognized in the context of science.' Yet it is a solution of this degree of originality which is required. There is a world of difference between Schlegel's 'system of fragments', which looks ahead to these later philosophers through its ironic admission of philosophical limitation, and the fragmented system of *Biographia*. [15]

[14]F. Schlegel, 'Lyceums-Fragmente', 31, in *Kritische Friedrich-Schlegel-Ausgabe* (Munich, 1958–), ed. E. Behler and H. Eichner, II, 150 (trans. in *Friedrich Schlegel's 'Lucinde' and the 'Fragments'*, trans. P. Firchow (Minneapolis, 1971), 145–6). See also Schlegel's review of *Wilhelm Meisters Lehrjahre*, *Kritische Ausgabe*, II, 126–47.
[15]*Hegel's Phenomenology of Spirit*, trans. A. V. Miller with an analysis by J. N. Findlay (Oxford, 1977), 488–90, 591; S. Kierkegaard, *Repetition*, trans. W. Lowrie (Oxford,

In other words, we have to postulate an enormous unspoken and unwritten effort on Coleridge's part in order to believe in a philosophical standard supporting his irony, and rescuing his reader's experience from being one of pure incoherence. So imaginatively sympathetic a reading is forced to create its own ideal object, *scriptible* rather than *lisible,* since the text can only point towards something its author may have planned, but never disclosed. To read *Biographia* as a parody of deductive philosophical method we have to supplement imaginatively the argument of volume I with a completely different frame of philosophical reference; and then, by a further stretch of imagination, we must attribute this awareness to Coleridge, otherwise the irony of Coleridge's gesture dissolves. Lacking any direction, it becomes indistinguishable from a parody resulting from ineptness and incompetence rather than art: a parody in the sense of travesty and caricature. But the redemptive activity required of the reader's supplementing imagination also eclipses the philosophical effort of *Biographia* itself. Its virtues now become rhetorical or even poetical rather than philosophical. *Biographia* becomes a vast trope of desire, a patchwork, extended metaphor for the kind of certainty which the text cannot provide literally.[16] The argument is distilled into poetic pointers to seek enlightenment elsewhere, and to ascribe even this to Coleridge through a final act of imaginative charity.

Over-ingenious sympathy for the broken argument of *Biographia* condemns Coleridge's work to a sadly vicarious existence. We should accept that the absence at the centre of *Biographia* is a genuine hiatus in his thought, and not the mask worn by his supersubtle philosophy. It is not an ironic gesture towards the true philosophy: in view of Coleridge's further failure to provide a coherent account of this elsewhere his irony could only be self-lacerating. Nor is volume I of

1942); F. Nietzsche, *The Birth of Tragedy . . . With an Attempt at Self-Criticism,* trans. W. Kaufmann (New York, 1967), 18; *Schlegels Briefe an seinen Bruder August Wilhelm,* ed. O. F. Walzel (Berlin, 1980), 336. For Friedrich's 'system of fragments', see 'Lyceums–Fragmente' (1797); 'Athenäums–Fragmente' (1798); 'Ideen' (1800).
[16]Christensen, 'Coleridge's Marginal Method': 'in the *Biographia* . . .Schelling's words furnish plausible certainties that are the pretext for the author's own desired certainties', 939 n.21.

Biographia a kind of poetry, in line with Friedrich Schlegel's remark that 'Poetry can only be criticized by means of poetry' – perhaps an extreme example of the rhetoric of the Romantic sublime in which the 'absence of a signified itself assumes the status of a signifier, disposing us to feel that behind this newly significant absence lurks a newly discovered presence.'[17] Poetic relish for the rhetoric of *Biographia* would certainly obviate the need for a systematic body of thought elsewhere, somehow denoted by *Biographia,* on whose existence an ironic response to the work is parasitical. To insist on that would lead to the heresy of paraphrase, and show a blindness to the constitutive character of *Biographia's* poetic language in symbolizing an area of sublime experience beyond systematic understanding. The sublime *is* present in the 'letter from a friend' of chapter 13, where Coleridge's pseudonymous contributor calls a halt to the philosophical exposition. He does so in the name of an experience which is frightening, confusing and ultimately unnameable, reversing, so he claims, the traditional hierarchy of philosophers, and upsetting conventional criteria of knowledge. When reading Coleridge's text, he tells us:

The effect on my *feelings,* on the other hand, I cannot better represent, than by supposing myself to have known only our light airy modern chapels of ease, and then for the first time to have been placed, and left alone, in one of our largest Gothic cathedrals in a gusty moonlight night of autumn. 'Now in glimmer, and now in gloom;' often in palpable darkness not without a chilly sensation of terror; then suddenly emerging into broad yet visionary lights with coloured shadows of fantastic shapes, yet all decked with holy insignia and mystic symbols; and ever and anon coming out full upon pictures and stone-work images of great men, with whose *names* I was familiar, but which looked upon me with countenances and an expression, the most dissimilar to all I had been in the habit of connecting with those names. Those whom I had been taught to venerate as almost super-human in magnitude of intellect, I

[17]Schlegel, 'Lyceums–Fragmente', 117, *Kritische Ausgabe* II, 162; T. Weiskel, *The Romantic Sublime* (Baltimore and London, 1976), 28; see also Fruman on Coleridge's famous philosophical passages in *Biographia* as 'prose poems celebrating an abstraction . . . a glorious hymn of praise to man's creativity', *Coleridge, The Damaged Archangel,* 189; or L. S. Lockridge's mysterious claim 'that one will find a great amount of material better described as Coleridge's than as Kant's or Schelling's or Jean Paul's if one develops an ear for the Coleridgean rhetoric of intellectual exploration.' 'Explaining Coleridge's Explanation', in *Reading Coleridge,* ed. W. B. Crawford (Ithaca and London, 1979), 34–5.

found perched in little fret-work niches, as grotesque dwarfs; while the grotesques, in my hitherto belief, stood guarding the high altar with all the characters of Apotheosis. In short, what I had supposed substances were thinned away into shadows, while everywhere shadows were deepened into substances. . . (*BL* I 199)

In this twilight of the idols great men of intellect succumb to the apotheosis of grotesques, and shadows presume over substances. The response produced in the pseudonymous reader is the poetic one provoked by an 'orphic tale'. However, the ascendancy which poetic appreciation seems to have gained over philosophical understanding is suddenly removed when the pseudonymous author next claims that he 'Look[s] forward anxiously to your great book on the CONSTRUCTIVE PHILOSOPHY' and 'your announced treatises on the Logos or communicative intellect in Man and Deity'. The sufficiency of a poetic response to Coleridge's philosophical fiction is further undermined when he himself takes up the pseudonymous reader's words and contents himself 'for the present with stating the main result of the Chapter, which I have reserved for that future publication, a detailed prospectus of which the reader will find at the close of the second volume' (*BL* I 202).

Another false hope raised. The 'prospectus' is not there, an omission which this time is hardly calculated to raise sublime feelings. There is no poetic content in this broken promise, yet if we read *Biographia* as the ironic gambit within a larger philosophical solution we must take the promise seriously. *Biographia,* then, contrives its own *reductio ad absurdum*: even if we willingly suspend our disbelief, Coleridge's sublime is precarious; and if we don't, his philosophical irony is bound to disappoint us.

Modern theories of reading, therefore, try to reconstruct the unity of *Biographia* as ironic gesture or poetic trope by deconstructing its declared aim of producing and exemplifying discursively a theory of imagination. This approach devalues it as a philosophical project in its own right, and is ultimately unsatisfying in its pretensions to provide a coherent alternative. It is also unacceptably anachronistic. As we saw above, according to this approach the narrator solicits a constructive response in which his reader fills gaps, completes arguments and generally finds meaning and significance where they seem to be most obviously fragmentary or absent. The reader gains a specifically ironic orientation from the work because it deliberately frustrates his normal expectations of a deductive argument. But Coleridge's own opinion of the reader was too low for such co-operation between himself and his audience to be plausible. We must remember that he conceived of his reader as a member of the reading public, and not as an ideal figure. To idealize this figure is to put history to one side and ignore the entire political dimension of his discussion of reader-response. He presents difficulty in *Biographia* as a means of enhancing his own philosophical authority, not as an incentive for the reader to take over and start producing his own text. He describes his public as a dismal entity, produced, like the French Revolution, by 'the magic of abstraction', divided in opinion and despotic in judgement.[18] He deplores the diffusion of literature and the growth of the reading public because of what he takes to be the resulting decline in the status of the book, and in the authority of the writer. Books which once 'were as religious oracles' are now 'degraded into culprits' because of the quality of the reading to which they are subjected (*BL* I 41-2). In a footnote, Coleridge berates the reading public for not having expectations worthy of the name of reading (*BL* I 34n). For Coleridge, the phenomenon of 'the critic still rising as the author sunk' (*BL* I 41) would certainly not encourage any new kind of

---

[18]See Thomas Love Peacock's satire on Coleridge's views of the reading public, in *Nightmare Abbey* (1818) and *Melincourt* (1817), and Marilyn Butler's discussions in *Peacock Displayed* (London, 1979), 87–90, 110–39; and in *Romantics, Rebels and Reactionaries* (Oxford, 1981), the chapter on Coleridge. She has revived, single-handed, Peacock's awareness of the organizing political principles behind *Biographia*. I try to modify her account by arguing that Coleridge's conservatism is rendered unstable and contradictory in its presentation because of Coleridge's allegiance to a radical theory of poetry whose obvious political implications he tries to keep undifferentiated. In her most helpful book, *The German Idea* (Cambridge, 1980), 1–104, Rosemary Ashton argues that English prejudices regarding, first, the immorality, and later, the obscurity of German literature and philosophy rubbed off on Coleridge rather than vice versa. He therefore hid his sources as part of his efforts to protect himself from these stock reactions. This adds still more to our understanding of the difficulties Coleridge encountered in trying to establish his philosophical authority.

writing which took advantage of the reader's growing pre-eminence. He condemns the new subservience he sees in the attitudes of authors to their readers, and instead is devoted to raising literary expectations to a more sophisticated level than that expressed in contemporary criticism. Education must come from above, from the prescriptions of an intellectual elite like the Clerisy of *On the Constitution of the Church and State*. Finally, he lacks the political confidence to start tampering with the authoritarian structure of writer and reader. He would scarcely be likely to entrust responsibility for the ultimate, unstated meaning of *Biographia* to the ingenious reading ability of his audience.

It is only to be expected, therefore, that Coleridge would be critical of authors who use their authority in irresponsible ways. At the end of chapter 4, before embarking on the philosophical discussion occupying the rest of the volume, he anticipated his reader's difficulties, but insists that these arise from his need to provide 'deductions from established premises' without which he could not 'present an intelligible statement of [his] poetic creed' (*BL* I 65). Coleridge asks for his reader's faith in his enterprise by defining reader-expectations. The suggestion is that even if the reader gets lost in obscurities, he can believe in the ultimate rationality of what he is reading: Coleridge, at least, is in control. In an important footnote only a few pages earlier Coleridge had rebuked the kind of writer who tries to make his point by frustrating his reader's expectations (I 52–3n). Here, his adverse criticism – to be elaborated in the second volume – of certain 'peculiar opinions' of Wordsworth's 'Preface' could equally apply to *Biographia* considered as new, ironic philosophical technique. Coleridge describes how Wordsworth trifles with his readers' trust in his authority by telling them 'that they had been all their lives admiring without judgement, and were now about to censure without reason.' But in his 'very judicious letter' in chapter 13 Coleridge pseudonymously concedes that his *own* reader, even if he 'had comprehended [his] premises sufficiently to have admitted them, and had seen the necessity of [his] conclusions', would still have been in the same frustrated state of mind as the reader of Wordsworth's 'Preface'. The earlier rebuke administered to Wordsworth's 'perverseness' surely now applies to Coleridge. Coleridge describes both experiences as the 'antithesis of a bull'. In a 'bull' or contradiction we feel 'the *sensation* without the *sense*' of the connection between two incompatible thoughts. In the opposite of a 'bull' we have 'a distinct sense' without the '*sensation*' of connection. This bewildered reaction which Coleridge attributes to the reader of the 'Preface' is also referred to by the pseudonymous reader to express his own feelings, and could be ascribed to any readers of *Biographia* as they struggle to feel the connection they are assured is meant to hold between the incomplete theory of imagination in the first volume and the practical criticism of the second. The letter of chapter 13 only avoids admitting Coleridge's débâcle through the self-abasement of a reader who volunteers his own incompetence, the length of the explanation required, and the resulting increased expense for the public as excuses for Coleridge's abandonment of the transcendental deduction. The reader's suggestion that it will appear elsewhere more appropriately – in Coleridge's 'great work' – props up an authoritarian structure that has been badly shaken.

Biographia challenges critical preconceptions to an unusual degree, and any account of it must acknowledge this quality. Part of the experience of its modern reader is to feel invited to supply a standard of coherence which will solve its riddle and restore its integrity. *Biographia* draws out its 'fellow rhapsodizers', of whom I am one; and if I seem to protest too much, this arises from my attempt to do justice to the fact that Coleridge is intensely conscious of the effect upon his reader of the language and terminology he chooses to employ. He is as aware in *Biographia* of the expectations he raises in writing as his reader is made conscious of the expectations he brings to his reading.

Recent critical approaches, otherwise historically misleading, have highlighted this in a useful way. The pseudonymous contributor is the figure of this mutual preoccupation of reader and writer in whom both sets of expectations seem to meet. But the figure is Coleridge's own invention, and is there to get him out of a scrape by disappointing the real reader's expectations, without eroding his own authority. Coleridge is fascinated by the process of reading, although he never for a moment deliberately surrenders the initiative to the reader. His interest in reading is rather part of his general interest in language. In raising the project of a transcendental deduction he frequently doubts whether it is intelligible or readable. Authority is preserved – but at what cost? His doubts usually take the form of remarks on language, and the intermittent stream of digressions and asides on this throughout the first volume creates an informal link with the criticism to come, the close reading of poetry, more effectively than the projected deduction itself. The reader seizes on these hints towards a reconstruction of what the argument of volume I should have been in order to illuminate volume II. These hints lead to a vast number of statements about the nature of language and poetry from which a theory of imagination could have been constructed. The reader's dilemma is perhaps best expressed by saying that in the first volume Coleridge constantly wanders in the right direction, but away from the main point.

Look at the opening of *Biographia:* within the first few pages Coleridge devalues the interest of his narrative, already undermining the title of his book: 'the least of what I have written concerns me personally.' The narrative is to exist primarily as an introduction to Coleridge's statement of his 'principles', and in particular to the now familiar project of deducing from philosophical principles the rules he intends to apply to poetry and criticism. Yet it is the philosophical deduction which next gives way to Coleridge's desire to settle 'the long continued controversy concerning the true nature of poetic diction' – as though this were something different from (or in addition to) the deduction. The inevitable footnote on the second page refers to another set of principles, 'the principles of Logic or universal Grammar'; and the apocryphal anecdote concerning Coleridge's schoolmaster, Bowyer, following soon after, suggests that philosophical insights can be gained from an appraisal of uses of language, such as poetic diction, rather than vice versa.

Bowyer figures in Coleridge's parable[19] as E. P. Thompson's 'old Adam of the English idiom' who can inculcate 'plain sense and universal logic' by turning his pupils into good practical critics.

[19]Fruman casts considerable doubt on the truth or the originality of Coleridge's anecdote, *Coleridge, The Damaged Archangel*, 215–16.

Practical criticism facilitates philosophical discrimination: 'I learnt from him that Poetry, even that of the loftiest and, seemingly, that of the wildest odes, had a logic of its own, as severe as that of science.' Coleridge has stood his original argument on its head; it is the practical understanding of poetry which now reveals philosophical principles distinguishing it from science. We have, in miniature, started to read the plan of *Biographia* in reverse. Argued in this direction *Biographia* starts from a confidence in ordinary language quite inimical to the elitist, transcendentalist terminology to which Coleridge gives formal approval.

Of course, the original order of the project of *Biographia* continually reasserts itself. But we are now alerted to the traces of a politically subversive reading which Coleridge could not have squared with his distrust of the reading public, and so had to repress. For example, when Shakespeare is cited for his 'consummate judgement . . . not only in the general construction, but in all the *detail*, of his dramas' (*BL* I 22n), we feel again the pressure of Coleridge's perpetual interest in language: the magnetic force of his belief that a discriminating appreciation of the common language, 'the *detail*', is more effective in releasing a philosophical understanding of the untranslatable significance of poetry than protective, mystifying statements about 'the depth' of the author's 'philosophy'. This primary orientation towards language surfaces again and again in *Biographia* as though part of a private, subliminal attempt to pull together the argument of the two volumes despite their public, formal differences. The suppressed rationale is Coleridge's theory of desynonymy. In his lectures on Shakespeare, the division in *Biographia* becomes the difference between Coleridge's immediate response to Shakespeare's text recorded in his marginalia, the product of his close reading, and the fascinating, although largely derivative, medley of critical and philosophical opinions found in the transcriptions by ammanuenses of his public lectures. In T. M. Raysor's edition of the *Shakespearean Criticism,* marginalia and transcriptions appear in separate volumes and thus reflect a divergence similar to *Biographia.*

In conclusion, the reader of *Biographia* should recognize the gap in its argument, while still wanting to know as precisely as possible the nature of the philosophical burden which has been forced on the practical criticism of the second volume, and which is hinted at throughout the first. The aim should be to find a way of reading *Biographia* which justifies the sense of momentousness attributed to the literary example. This alternative reading is made possible by studying how Coleridge's ideas concerning the nature of language and poetry assumed and expressed a philosophical standpoint. This gives an idea of the integrity Coleridge could have provided for the work. By revealing the philosophical implications of Coleridge's practical criticism we can expose the theory of imagination which the second volume could have produced for the first, and suggest the historical reasons for why Coleridge did not argue in that more profitable direction.

CHAPTER TWO

British Common Sense and German Sublimity: Theories of Language, Imagination and Poetry

THE DESPOTISM OF THE EYE

The basic assumption of the approach to *Biographia* which I am recommending is that Coleridge's views on language and poetry are most usefully considered as generating the kind of philosophy with which he sympathized rather than, as he would have us believe, things being the other way round. This polemical view of language and poetry was already a feature of eighteenth-century thinkers who opposed the empiricist tradition in British philosophy represented primarily by Hobbes, Locke, Berkeley and Hume. This tradition had culminated in the tough-minded scepticism typical of what has been aptly called 'the grand paradox' of British empiricism – 'its hostility to experience'.[1] Succeeding philosophers argued that the faculty of imagination escaped the restrictions imposed by the empiricist philosopher's model of knowledge, which likened the mind to a *tabula rasa* on which we receive impressions of the outside world. Out of these impressions our knowledge is compounded. Hume's more sophisticated version of this model allowed for a distinction between 'impressions' and the 'ideas' we use to think about them. Hume's opponents resisted what they took to be the predominantly visual character of this model in which the basic items of knowledge, ideas, are justified as such by their derivative quality of resembling or

---

[1]A. D. Nuttall, *A Common Sky – Philosophy and the Literary Imagination* (London, 1974), 23.

representing the basic particulars of our experience, impressions. This was the 'despotism of the eye', attacked by Coleridge in the first volume of *Biographia* as attributing 'to causes a susceptibility of being *seen,* if only our visual organs were sufficiently powerful' (*BL* I 74). The opponents of the empiricists' model of knowledge used other elements of Hume's philosophy, his theories of sympathy and the association of ideas, to undermine the model's claim to sufficiency. They argued that the sympathetic imagination gives us access to kinds of experience which cannot be explained by reference to the empiricist model of knowledge. Poetry, as the expressive language of this sympathetic, imaginative insight, was then cited as evidence for the need to find a philosophical alternative to the empiricist tradition.

Furthermore, our use of language in general, and not just poetry, was taken as evidence against the sceptical conclusions of Hume's philosophy. Many British philosophers' reaction to Hume's scepticism concerning our knowledge of a world external to our experience took the form of a renewed trust in the criteria for that knowledge: criteria to which our human limitations inescapably bind us. They thought that a prime example of our confinement to such criteria was our use of language. Though deficient in the face of demands for scientific perfection, it was the basic index of how we are constrained to make sense of our experience in a certain way. One such constraint was our assumption that we know of the existence of a world external to our experience. The extremes of Hume's scepticism were seen as a distortion of language, where language exhibits and patterns the form our thinking has to take.

The British reaction to Hume pales before Kant's awakening from dogmatic slumber in Germany. It is important, though, to realize the extent to which in Coleridge's own country language and poetry had already been regarded in a polemical light – as standing on one side of the philosophical fence rather than the other. Throughout the eighteenth century the gradual formulation of an alternative to Hume's sceptical empiricism reveals a growing interest in the nature of language. What is relevant to our interpretation of Coleridge is not simply the obvious fact that the period teems with treatises on the origin, history and progress of language; but that such an interest could also be a consequence of trying to find an alternative to the empiricist tradition in philosophy. Disillusion with empiricist metaphors for how we acquire knowledge leads not only to new metaphors, but also to a discussion of metaphor in general. Coleridge's remarks on the philosophical character of language emerge from this kind of argument. The authority of the empiricist metaphor, the 'despotism of the eye', is undermined by revealing that it is language as a whole, and not any particular usage, which exhibits the true shape of our knowledge. The empiricist model or metaphor is only one instance of a more pervasive condition under which any philosophy must labour.

There is, then, a way of reading the development of eighteenth-century philosophy which provides a preface to a discussion of the philosophical importance of language and poetry in the second volume of *Biographia*. Coleridge's polemical regard for language and poetry is in the interests of a philosophy which will provide him with a theory of imagination. He develops the eighteenth-century attempt to emancipate theories of imagination from the 'despotism of the eye'. This attempt claims that the language of poetry is philosophically significant in exemplifying an exception to the empiricist model of knowledge. Coleridge wrote *Biographia* at the end of a philosophical debate in which poetry had forcefully participated.

In his papers in *The Spectator* of 1712 concerning 'The Pleasures of the Imagination', Joseph Addison describes the imagination as a mental faculty whose materials and methods were exhaustively explained by showing their dependence upon the sense of sight.[2] In this respect, Addison's aesthetic is a typical product of the prevailing British empiricist philosophy. The British empiricists never satisfactorily defined the nature of the correspondence between the basic items of knowledge and the basic particulars of experience. The language used to gloss over this difficulty was, as already indicated, primarily visual. Hobbes' theory of imagination was visual, and subject to the same

[2] *The Spectator,* ed. D. F. Bond (Oxford, 1965), 5 vols, III, no. 411; Addison's papers on imagination are nos 411–21.

limitations as the rival Cartesian philosophy. Locke's theory of perception was a representative one, and the tendency to regard all mental contents as images was strengthened by the assumption that perception was the underlying model for the explanation of all knowledge, 'having ideas and perception being the same thing'.[3] What may first have been conceived of as a useful metaphor for dealing with a highly abstract relation seems eventually to have assumed control of the investigation which employed it, and dictated the terms in which the rest of the investigation was to be conducted. Hume defined an idea through its relation to an impression. That an idea was genuine is guaranteed by our ability to derive it from an impression; and this derivative relation was openly characterized as pictorial – 'our ideas are images of our impressions.' This was Hume's 'first principle'.[4]

Of course, many of Hume's examples of impressions – tastes, smells, heat, passions – show that he could not have thought that the representations of these impressions were always visual. But the danger in his terminology, which was fastened on by his critics, was his habit of describing different kinds of experience under one heading: 'For philosophy informs us, that every thing, which appears to the mind, is nothing but a perception.'[5]

Hume's psychology – his theories of sympathy and the association of ideas – is used by succeeding aestheticians in a way that suggests alternatives to, rather than extensions of, his basic empiricism. Hume's philosophy was never happy with itself. His scepticism produced 'a philosophy against the philosophers . . . a series of reasonings turned against reasoning itself.'[6] The threat of paradox haunting so many of Hume's fundamental doctrines inspired the vigorous reaction against him by the philosophers of common sense;

[3]R. Descartes, 'Meditation VI', in *Works*, trans. E. S. Haldane and G. R. T. Ross (Cambridge, 1967), 2 vols, I, 185–6; John Locke, *An Essay Concerning Human Understanding*, ed. A. C. Fraser (Oxford, 1894), 2 vols, I, 127; T. Hobbes, *Leviathan*, ed. J. Plamenatz (London, 1962), part I, chapter 3.

[4]D. Hume, *A Treatise on Human Nature*, ed. L. A. Selby-Bigge (Oxford, 1888, 1968), Book I, part I, §i.

[5]*Ibid.*, Book I, part IV, §iii, 193.

[6]E. Halévy, *The Growth of Philosophical Radicalism* (London, 1928, 1972), 10.

and his ambiguities also allowed writers less explicitly opposed to him and still using his methods – Kames, Gerard, Duff, Blair, Adam Smith, Alison and others – to begin the process of showing how the poetic imagination might escape the visual paradigm of an empiricist theory of knowledge.

Kames, on occasion, can sound like Keats. However even he explained how one thing can mean another thing in language by referring to a visual model. The empiricist metaphor is still at the heart of the following passage.

The force of language consists in raising complete images; which have the effect to transport the reader as by magic into the very place of the important action, and to convert him as it were, into a spectator, beholding everything that passes. The narrative in an epic poem ought to rival a picture in the liveliness and accuracy of its representation: no circumstance must be omitted that tends to make a complete image.[7]

The escape of the expressive poetic imagination from the representational requirements of the 'spectator' cannot take place within the empiricist tradition. Berkeley, Burke and later Payne Knight all argued against judging the force of language to be primarily visual in this way. 'Critics,' writes Payne Knight, 'have been led into the notion that imagery is rendered sublime by being indistinct and obscure, by mistaking energies for images, and by looking for *pictures* where *powers* only were meant to be expressed.'[8] Blake showed the degree of emancipation to be achieved by this revolt against empiricism when he claimed in his annotations to Reynolds' *Discourses* that 'Obscurity is Neither the Source of the Sublime nor of any Thing Else.'[9] To think so, in Blake's opinion, would be to measure the

[7][Henry Home], Lord Kames, *Elements of Criticism* (Edinburgh, 1762, 1788), 2 vols, II, 329; see I. A. Richards' attack on Kames' 'appeal to *imagery* as constituting the meaning of an utterance', in *The Philosophy of Rhetoric* (Oxford, 1936, 1965), 16–17.

[8]R. Payne Knight, *An Analytic Enquiry into the Principles of Taste* (London, 1805), 387; see G. Berkeley, *A Treatise Concerning the Principles of Human Knowledge* (1710), ed. G. J. Warnock (London, 1967), 59–60; E. Burke, *A Philosophical Enquiry into our Ideas of the Origin of the Sublime and Beautiful* (London, 1757), part V, 167ff.

[9]W. Blake, *Complete Writings,* ed. G. Keynes (Oxford, 1966), 473; see also his annotations to Reynolds, p. 52 (457) and p. 102 (464) dated c. 1808.

imaginative discrimination of the artist on the wrong scale. Visionary particularity is not the same as visual particularity. Blake asserts the independence of imaginative language from empiricist criteria of perception.

'What,' it will be Question'd, 'When the Sun rises, do you not see a round disk of fire somewhat "like a Guinea?" O no, no, I see an Innumerable company of the Heavenly host crying "Holy, Holy, Holy is the Lord God Almighty." '[10]

We detect imagination in Blake by identifying an informed, quasi-biblical reading of the world, not by calculating the size or intensity of sense data.

Payne Knight's remark captures a distinctively Romantic tone, similar to Coleridge's and Hazlitt's discussions of Milton's sublime characterizations of Satan and Death. But he also differs in emphasis from these two thinkers for whom the proper interpretation demanded by poetic language immediately suggests an alternative or new philosophical tradition. This radical exercise is not as important a part of the argument for Payne Knight. It is for the same reason that Dr Johnson was curiously irrelevant to any attempt to define Romantic theory, whether he is viewed as opponent or precursor of the new movement. Johnson's critical pronouncements can certainly be placed within a philosophical context, but they are not unique contributions to any contemporary philosophical argument. He wrote about poetry; but the Romantic theorists wrote about philosophy *by* writing about poetry. The Romantic reaction to empiricist metaphors of knowledge suggests how this unusual complicity between philosophy and poetry could come about. For if the Romantics were to break away from the visual predominance in the 'force of language' described by Kames, then, since it is right at the root of language, they would have to adopt a peculiarly creative attitude towards the use of language and metaphor. And their characteristic concentration on the artistic process, the growth of a poet's mind, highlighted the one place where the explanation of epistemology on the visual model had proved especially limited. The

[10]*Ibid.*, 617.

doctrine of sympathy, finally used by Hume to guarantee objectivity in taste and morals, was commandeered by his followers in its earlier mechanical form to provide an alternative source of experience: the conversion of an idea into an impression.[11] In this model, ideas generate impressions instead of being the derivative images of impressions – a considerable paradox in Hume's philosophy. The sympathetic imagination functions independently of the sanction and authority of the resembling relation between ideas and impressions cited as the paradigmatic explanation of the possibility of knowledge and experience on all other occasions.

Thus, Adam Smith's *Theory of Moral Sentiments* shows the sympathetic imagination able to do what the senses cannot do, and the whole empirical structure is threatened: 'our senses . . . never did, and never can, carry us beyond our own person, and it is by the imagination only that we can form any conception of what are his sensations.'[12] The imagination can generate passions on its own and is, for Smith, to this extent subjective and expressive: we can blush for the shameless, pity the happy unfortunates, and even feel for the dead.

In finding an expressive language for the power of imagination, the Romantics would therefore be attributing to poetry a theoretical importance already implied in the writings of many theorists concerned with sympathy, and the problem of explaining how we come by our knowledge of other minds. From Kames to Hazlitt, the main proof of the success of the epistemology of sympathy is the infectious power of language harnessed by the artist for the benefit of

---

[11]D. Hume, *Essays, Moral, Political and Literary* (1741–2, Oxford, 1963), 245; *An Enquiry Concerning the Principles of Morals,* ed. L. A. Selby-Bigge (Oxford, 1962), 272–3; *Treatise,* Book II, part I, §xi.

[12]A. Smith, *The Theory of Moral Sentiments* (London, 1759, 1790), 2 vols, I, 2–3; see J. Beattie's critique of Addison's visual theory of imagination, and his conclusion that 'the common use of language would warrant a more comprehensive definition. The anxiety of a miser, and the remorse of a murderer, are not corporeal objects; and yet may be *imagined* by those who never felt them. Shakespeare, who was neither a murderer nor a miser . . . has expressed these feelings in such a manner, as will satisfy every reader, that his conception of them was equally just and lively.' *Dissertations Moral and Critical* (Dublin, 1783), 2 vols, I 88–9.

the spectator through a method transcending mere empirical observation. The language of Shakespeare becomes the most popular example appealed to as evidence that we can sympathetically breach the barrier, impenetrable within an empiricist philosophy, excluding us from a knowledge of other minds. Even empiricist followers of David Hartley, like Joseph Priestley and William Belsham, cited Kames and held that 'nothing less than a genuine expression of passion can awaken the attention or sympathy of the spectator.' It is Shakespeare, therefore, who displays 'the most perfect knowledge of the human mind'.[13] The power of his language gives the lie to any claims empiricism might make to be an exhaustive philosophy. William Richardson noted, as Francis Jeffrey was to do later, that the philosophy of mind was retarded by the inability of empiricist philosophers to conduct appropriate 'experiments'. Richardson believed he was pointing to a deficiency in methods of empirical 'scrutiny'[14] which must be supplemented by a different kind of activity altogether. He wanted to show how 'that class of poetical writers that excel by imitating the passions, might contribute in this respect to rectify and enlarge the sentiments of the philosopher.'[15] Philosophical method is in this case inferior, and must give place to poetical insight. This way of thinking presages the Romantic claims for the philosophical status of the poet, and for the importance of the poet's language as irreplaceable philosophical evidence.

Nevertheless, the primacy of the visual metaphor as paradigm of empirical knowledge, was not to be got rid of so easily. A novel theoretical and linguistic approach is needed from those trying to escape its limitations if these are inseparable from the 'force of language'. John Jones points out that

Keats, like many other writers, is put into difficulties by the poverty of our language of sensation; but what is an occasional problem for them has

[13]W. Belsham, *Essays Philosophical and Moral, Historical and Literary* (London, 1789, 1799), 2 vols, II, 470, 468.
[14]W. Richardson, *A Philosophical Analysis and Illustration of Some of Shakespeare's Remarkable Characters* (Edinburgh, 1774), 14–15, 16; F. Jeffrey, 'Review of Stewart's Account of Reid' (January 1804), in *Contributions to the Edinburgh Review* (London, 1844), 4 vols, III, 325–7; and see his reply to Stewart's rejoinder, *ibid.*, 378ff.
[15]Richardson, *A Philosophical Analysis*, 25–6.

become omnipresent and cardinal for him. In the first place it is easier to talk about the look of things than about their physical feel, and Keats's focus upon touch and a highly idiosyncratic innerness of contact means that he approaches sensation the hardest way.[16]

But this hardness in Keats' self-imposed task would especially oppress any poet who, after the empiricists, concentrates on the expression of his own powers and modes of apprehension. Kames himself, when trying to describe a poem's 'ideal presence', complained how 'lamentable is the imperfection of language, almost in every particular that falls not under external sense.'[17] The expression of the poet's sympathetic understanding, in opposing the visual core of language, requires great resourcefulness in the face of linguistic poverty. Blake's militantly visionary art shows the lengths to which Romantic poets were forced to go in order to establish clearly their originality.

To summarize: the sympathetic imagination of the poet and his expressive language expose the limitations of empiricist philosophy by implying an alternative to the traditional model of empirical knowledge. But since the empiricists' visually-based account is deeply rooted in the nature of language itself, any poet who wishes to use or describe the alternative account of apprehension implied by the process of poetic imagination will have to be peculiarly inventive. Since he is breaking new linguistic ground, the metaphors which he must forge in his account of his experience will themselves constitute the main significance of his efforts. Pictorial images will be replaced by self-sufficient symbols. The poet's originality will measure his departure from empirical explanations and models of knowledge. Original linguistic creation will embody a rival philosophical method. The 'great poet' will have proved Coleridge's dictum, and become 'a profound philosopher'.

THE DECEITFUL MEDIUM

The competition between the visual metaphor of empiricist epistemology and emergent alternatives was a live issue of the time. In the

[16]J. Jones, *John Keats's Dream of Truth* (London, 1969), 27.
[17]Kames, *Elements of Criticism*, I, 90.

work of the Scottish common-sense school the philosophy of language was seen as the key to finding an alternative to the restrictions of empiricism. The status of the visual metaphor was vigorously attacked by Thomas Reid, James Beattie and Dugald Stewart. Reid's first main work, *An Inquiry into the Human Mind on the Principles of Common Sense,* was published in 1764, and Stewart carried the movement on into the nineteenth century, having among his pupils Francis Jeffrey and James Mill.

Reid characterized the empiricist error as the misuse of an analogy. We apply physical descriptions to mental processes; we think of the object as stamping an impression of itself on the mind, or leaving us with an image, both of which resemble the object. This use of analogical language is acknowledged by Reid and his followers to be inevitable. As Locke and Condillac had already established, there is no natural language of the mind, so we do not have any alternative.[18] But philosophers let these analogies impose upon them and set the conceptual boundaries of discussions of mental phenomena. At this point the analogy becomes pernicious – a deceitful medium: 'we contemplate the operation of our minds, only as they appear through the deceitful medium of such analogical notions and expressions.'[19] In the case of the empiricist's habit of thinking of 'meaning or idea' in terms of images, the use of this visual metaphor involves the deceits of scepticism. An idea is an act of the mind, not a thing,[20] and to look on

---

[18]T. Reid, *An Inquiry into the Human Mind on the Principles of Common Sense* (Edinburgh, 1764), 535–7; *Essays on the Intellectual Powers of Man* (Edinburgh, 1785), 55, 363, 406; J. Beattie, *Essays on Poetry and Music, as they Affect the Mind* (Edinburgh, 1776), 252–3; D. Stewart, *Account of the Life and Writings of Thomas Reid* (Edinburgh, 1802), 49; *Elements of the Philosophy of the Human Mind* (London, 1792–1827), 3 vols, I, 13–14. For a good discussion of Locke and Condillac, see H. Aarsleff, *The Study of Language in England, 1780–1860* (Princeton, New Jersey, 1967), 32–3.

[19]Reid, *Essays on the Intellectual Powers,* 206.

[20]Reid is partly anticipated by Abraham Tucker, admired and edited by Hazlitt, for whom the 'queen-like mind . . . perceives not what it contains' but whose 'mental organs are . . . the immediate instruments of perception', *An Abridgement of The Light of Nature Pursued by Abraham Tucker,* ed. W. Hazlitt (London, 1807), 50–1; and Reid is followed by, among others, R. Price, in *A Review of the Principal Questions and Difficulties in Morals* (London, 1758, 1769), 54–5 and n. The later edition acknowledges Reid's 'great merit' in this discovery.

it as an image which more or less resembles objects or other ideas is to push the visual analogy or metaphor further than it can legitimately apply. Reid thinks that the standard of this legitimacy is common sense, and its 'medium' ordinary language. His notion of common sense is not meant to be a crude appeal to vulgar opinion, but a claim that the structure of language reveals how we are obliged to think about the world. Because, for example, language is fitted for social purposes, solipsism is absurd: 'To see without having any object of sight is absurd. I cannot remember, without remembering something.'[21] The abuse of language is the hallmark of the deceitful medium and the pointer to philosophical error: 'there is reason to distrust any philosophical theory, when it leads man to corrupt language.' and this describes the distortion which the paradigmatic visual metaphor imposes 'in giving the name of *perception* to the bare conception of things'.[22]

The appeal to the authority of ordinary language over the analogical language of philosophers could be a clear and precise way of dealing with misleading philosophical theories but for one thing: the problem is that Reid admits that the common language with which we describe acts of the mind is of course equally analogical and metaphorical. Like Kames, Reid finds that the visual analogy is ineliminable, 'interwoven with the structure of language'.[23] He has to accept that philosophy necessarily has an interpretative role, elucidating rather than condemning the analogical and expressive character of human apprehension. The philosopher's task is therefore hermeneutical: he is primarily concerned with providing a convincing interpretation of the language we are obliged to use in understanding the world. The most basic level of philosophical explanation is that which construes the metaphors in which any existing theory is necessarily presented, and which registers any new analogies which a new theory will introduce. Nevertheless, caught within the world of

---

[21]Reid, *Essays on the Intellectual Powers*, 43, and see 44, 73.
[22]*Ibid.*, 361, 365; Monboddo shows the same approach at the start of his massive work on language [James Burnett, Lord Monboddo], *Of the Origin and Progress of Language* (London, 1773–92), 6 vols, I, 6.
[23]Stewart, *Thomas Reid*, 90–1.

language, the philosopher still has to adjudicate between the conflicting claims of different usages. Since Reid's philosophical criterion of common sense is bound to one such usage he never manages to provide an impartial and universal standard of certainty.

Reid has inadvertently left the way clear for metaphor to become the proper object of philosophical scrutiny. He does seem to realize this in his aesthetics, where he recognizes that in the realm of imagination the medium, the metaphor and the analogy have pride of place.[24] The figurative language peculiar to the imagination is irreducible. This is confirmed by Reid's follower and admirer, Archibald Alison, who believed that the imagination consists in the association of ideas of emotion which possess a uniform principle of connection. This amounts to the claim that if I were to describe an object of aesthetic experience scientifically, I would remain unintelligible. If, on the other hand, I were to tell someone 'that it was expressive of Melancholy, Gaiety or Tenderness, [I] would make him understand at once the reason of [my] Emotion.'[25]

However, aesthetics is a safe place to let metaphor predominate. Alison did not apply his insight to the rest of philosophy as he might have felt encouraged to do from reading Reid. Even in common-sense aesthetics a deep conservatism persists. Reid and Alison wished to leave things as they are; to explain existing usages certainly, but not in the interests of original criticism or innovation. Coleridge said of Alison's kind of originality that, 'It is an excellent charm to enable a man to talk *about* and *about* any thing he likes, and to make him self and his hearers as wise as before' (*BL* II 222). By the beginning of the nineteenth century this conservatism was being condemned by Jeffrey. The Scottish tradition of introspection in philosophy, of employing self-consciousness as the instrument of observation is

[24]Reid, *Essays on the Intellectual Powers*, 746–7.
[25]A. Alison, *Essays on the Nature and Principles of Taste* (Dublin, 1790), 99, 180; R. Wollheim makes the same point more clearly in *Art and its Objects* (Harmondsworth, 1970), 49–50, 'For it is not at all clear that, in the cases where we attribute emotions to objects . . . we have any other way of talking about the objects themselves. There is not necessarily a prior description in non-emotive terms, on which we superimpose the emotive description.'

bound to result in nothing more than documentary. Jeffrey worries that because this philosophy of mind fails to result in a practical psychology philosophers have become grammarians, mere recorders of usage.[26] But he had little to offer in its place, and failed to recognize that poets who invented new symbols for their own imaginative activity obviously did.

The philosophy of common sense was described by Sir James Mackintosh as 'efforts of the conservative power of philosophy to expel the mortal poison of scepticism'.[27] The political equivalent is Edmund Burke's belief in an essential humanity constituted by 'the common feelings of men'. This common essence is obvious to those who 'have chosen our nature rather than our speculations, our breasts rather than our inventions, for the great conservatories and magazines of our rights and privileges.'[28] However, it is more someone like Richard Price – attacked by Burke, but as much an opponent in his own way of Hartley's and Priestley's picture of human nature – who anticipated the Romantic pattern of argument. He maintained a due deference to common-sense humanism, while not allowing this to compromise his progressive philosophy of man.[29] It is this kind of amalgam of dissenting radicalism and anti-empiricism which prefigures the later humanism of Coleridge. Burke's humanism, though, displays a strategic trust in language much resented by his opponents. Sir James Mackintosh, in *Vindiciae Gallicae,* contemplating the task of refuting Burke, complains that 'no man can be expected to oppose arguments to epithets.' Tom Paine attacks the Burkean rhetoric as being that of people who 'hold out a language which they do not

[26]Jeffrey, *Contributions to the Edinburgh Review,* III, 326–7.
[27]Sir James Mackintosh, 'Dissertation on the Progress of Ethical Philosophy, Chiefly during the Seventeenth and Eighteenth Centuries', in *Miscellaneous Works* (London, 1846), 3 vols, I, 214.
[28]E. Burke, *Reflections on the Revolution in France* (1790, Everyman edn, 1967), 77, 32–3.
[29]*Ibid.*, 9–11, 51 for Burke's attacks; see also the controversy between Price and Priestley in their *A Free Discussion of the Doctrines of Materialism and Philosophical Necessity* (London, 1778), and Price's *A Review of the Principal Questions and Difficulties in Morals* for his objections to educational schemes which lack 'somewhat natural as their foundation', 282–8; and his own description of such a 'natural' but infinitely improvable category 'capable of increase and advancement without end', 376.

themselves believe.'³⁰ The young Coleridge had to find a way of
excusing his delight in Burke's language in a manner consistent with
his own radical sympathies.

Within the common-sense tradition in British philosophy the
activity of imagination in producing the analogical character of
language is recognized; but its linguistic conservatism was not
capable of providing a radical alternative to empiricism. The
predominant character of analogical language is visual and physical,
and therefore particularly suited to an empiricist reduction. What
was needed was an innovatory attitude quite opposed to the
conservative temper of common-sense philosophy – new metaphors
and analogies opposing those which empiricism so ably rationalized.
But common-sense philosophy is a much underestimated part of the
explanation of how the Romantic poet could be thought to have a
significant philosophical role to play. We can see now that the
English Romantics wrote expressly imaginative poetry at the end of a
tradition in British thought which cried out for a new kind of
philosophy of mind fostered by the creative use of language.

The last views within Reid's immediate tradition come from
Dugald Stewart in his *Philosophical Essays* of 1810 where he comes
close to seeing the need for this essentially creative alternative to the
old analogies. For Stewart, the explanations of human nature given by
Hartley, Erasmus Darwin, Priestley and Horne Tooke are 'the sorry
mechanism that gives motion to a puppet.' The remedy offered by
Stewart for such distorting caricatures is not only the patient
introspection typical of Reid, but also a creative attitude: 'to *vary,*
from time to time, the metaphors we employ, so as to prevent any one
of them from acquiring an undue ascendant over the others.'³¹

³⁰Sir James Mackintosh, 'Vindiciae Gallicae' (1791), in *Miscellaneous Works,* III, 47;
T. Paine, *The Rights of Man* (1791–2, Everyman edn, 1969), 73. Paine had also
reversed the predominantly conservative meaning of the term 'common sense',
making it stand for the scepticism with which he reviewed all positive political
institutions and hoped to encourage people 'generously [to] enlarge [their] views
beyond the present day', *Common Sense* (1776) ed. I. Kramnick (Harmondsworth,
1976), 82.
³¹D. Stewart, 'Philosophical Essays' (begun 1810), in *Works,* ed. Sir William
Hamilton (Edinburgh, 1854–60), 11 vols, V, 175–6, 157, 173.

However, Stewart objects to treating 'metaphorical expressions as solid *data* for our conclusions in the science of Mind'. In his opinion Reid had 'been led, in various instances, to lay greater stress on the structure of speech, than . . . can always bear in a philosophical argument.' Nevertheless, Stewart is still fundamentally committed to a hermeneutical philosophy concerned with the interpretation of language – 'the History of the Human Mind, as exemplified in the figurative mechanism of language'.[32] He thus provided a confused conclusion to the philosophical tradition deriving from Reid. He seems finally bewildered by 'the deceitful medium', sensing its philosphical significance, but unable to accommodate this within a strict philosophical framework containing 'solid *data*'. Coleridge is only able to show the relevance of poetry to philosophy by appropriating elements of German aesthetic theories, especially from those of Kant and Schiller. A passage in the *Philosophical Lectures*, contending that Hume contradicts beliefs 'interwoven in all languages', shows that he felt the force of Reid's argument; but he realized that the final bankruptcy of the common-sense tradition demanded an infusion of new blood.[33] Stewart and Jeffrey never appreciated the Germans, and neither thought of the Romantics as suggesting a way out of the failed common-sense theory of mind. They furnish late examples of that paradox of the Scottish Enlightenment: a deep interest in the philosophy of language to the neglect of the best in current literature.[34]

HUME ON IMAGINATION

There is now an exalted philosophical role made available to the poet wishing, in true Romantic fashion, to describe his own imaginative activity. However, the background to Coleridge's idea of the philosophical significance of poetry is still crucially incomplete. For while the anti-empiricist and common-sense traditions in eighteenth-century British philosophy have shown how poetry and philosophy

[32]*Ibid.*, 157–8, 154, 185.
[33]*PhL* 375.
[34]This is part of David Daiches' argument, in *The Paradox of Scottish Culture: The Eighteenth-Century Experience* (Oxford, 1964).

could be related, they have perhaps gone too far. Philosophy now needs poetry so sorely in its revolt against empiricist metaphors that it threatens to absorb poetry completely. The logic of the argument we have been following seems to lead to the conclusion that we could philosophize simply by writing poetry. For the common-sense philosophers, all uses of language to refer to mental acts and emotions are equally analogical, whether those uses be found in poetry or in philosophy. A use of language embodies beliefs which philosophy can rationalize; and it is a matter of indifference whether the use of language is poetic or not: its utility for the common-sense philosopher is not affected by such a distinction.

Coleridge may sometimes sound as if he thinks that poetry is a kind of philosophy; but this is a confusion to which he is fundamentally opposed. Philosophy is for him a kind of science: its theories can be true or false, proved or disproved. Poetry may contain apparent statements of philosophical positions; but the truth or falsity of these are considerations distinct from the poetry. As the most casual student of Coleridge knows, he opposed science to poetry throughout *Biographia*. Science, unlike poetry, 'proposes *truth* for its immediate object'. The dispute with Wordsworth in *Biographia* reveals Coleridge arguing that the poetic use of language is of a different order from quotidian usage. For Coleridge, the expression of the poetic use of imagination could never become the common sense of Reid and his followers; it could never express merely the constraints language puts upon knowledge and still remain poetry.

Coleridge wants to be able to show the relevance of poetry to philosophy without collapsing one into the other. He thinks that poetry can only exist under the dispensation of a certain kind of philosophy which it supports against the conclusions of opposite philosophical systems. The background sketched in the last two sections is thus most germane to Coleridge's position. But it reached a dead end with its inability to articulate the crucial distance which separates poetry from a sympathetic philosophy, and so allows it to furnish an independent support for that philosophy.

Another way of expressing this takes us back to 'the main result' of Coleridge's missing theory of imagination and his distinction between primary and secondary imagination, which suggests that poetry and the exercise of imagination are not entirely commensurate. Poetry is created, according to Coleridge, by the imagination; but there are uses of the imagination which are not poetic. The exercise of imagination is a necessary but not a sufficient condition for the existence of poetry; therefore, we need a more discriminating definition of imagination. The primary imagination will account for the use of imagination in perception and knowledge; the workings of the secondary imagination will then explain the exertions of the poet's imagination in making poetry. Already we have gone beyond the fragmentary definitions which Coleridge gives us. Coleridge's criticism in volume II will be found to assume that the poet's use of imagination and the secondary imagination are meant to be identical; but we have to supply the missing explanation.

We have, then, to study Coleridge's predecessors in his native tradition in order to feel the strength of the idea that the poetic expression of imagination can take up arms against British empiricism. But in arguing for the philosophical power of poetry, this tradition raised a problem which it could not solve on its own. It is from the Germans, chiefly Kant, that Coleridge takes the argument for how poetry and the poetic imagination could inform philosophy without becoming philosophy.

As a preface to Kant, Hume's philosophy must be understood in more detail than was needed for our discussion of the British common-sense philosophers' reaction to his scepticism. It has been seen how British thinkers writing soon after Hume developed some elements of his philosophy at the expense of others. In particular, they adapted Hume's concept of the sympathetic imagination as a faculty which, since it was capable of generating impressions on its own, was an independent source of experience – independent, that is, of experience received through the senses and subsequently thought of by means of ideas. The sympathetic imagination does not simply order experience by grouping our ideas of impressions in a significant way. It supplies us with what are for Hume the basic particulars of an experience – with impressions. Without the imagination we would not have the experience.

In this case, Hume thinks that the impressions in question are passions. The sympathetic imagination is our means of appreciating the mental and emotional life of others. Hume also claims that when the imagination acts on certain customary and habitual principles – resemblance, contiguity and cause and effect – it creates the experience which leads us to believe in the existence of an external world. Its transitions between ideas, in accordance with these principles, themselves constitute impressions and so create experience.[35] The fiction of an external world which the imagination creates is something to which we are compelled by 'principles which are permanent, irresistible and universal.' If we try to do without such principles 'human nature must immediately perish and go to ruin.' Hume defines the understanding as 'the general and more establish'd properties of the imagination'. The imagination, he confesses, has now become 'the ultimate judge of all systems of philosophy'.[36] This means that we may, as sceptical philosophers, discount the illusions of the imagination; but if we do so we also abandon any attempt to describe human experience.

The common-sense philosophers thought that this is a choice which is simply not open to us. In their own philosophy the dictates of common sense, rather than the principles of imagination, became the foundation of thought and action. Common sense did not mean for them ordinary gumption, but rather a group of beliefs assumed by any description of experience. They argued that we cannot use language without thereby expressing these beliefs. Hence their appeal to language is an appeal to what is understood to be a repository of the beliefs which Hume's philosophy of scepticism tries to discount and his philosophy of imagination finds essential.

This is a very crude reply to Hume's scepticism. Questions arise immediately about the nature of these dictates of common sense. What does it mean to say that we have to have certain beliefs in order to think or act as we do? Is this compulsion psychological, or is it a logical necessity? The common-sense philosophers do not make clear the nature of the requirements of common sense. For Kant, a much

[35]Hume, *Treatise,* Book I, part III, §xiv, 165.
[36]*Ibid.,* Book I, part IV, §ii, 200–1; §iv, 225.

greater philosopher, this need for clarification is only the beginning of a proper refutation of Hume. Kant believes that Hume's scepticism must be mistaken; but the problem that his scepticism raises is not solved by showing that we *are* compelled to believe in the existence of an external world. This, as he explained in his criticisms of common-sense philosophy in the *Prolegomena*, is to miss the point.[37] Hume is perfectly aware of that belief and has given his own explanation of how it arises. The proper answer to Hume would be to show that our compulsion to such belief is of a nature which logically precludes scepticism. As Kant saw, Hume argues consistently from his adopted premises. His successful opponent must be able to show that Hume's premises are mistaken, or at least incomplete. Kant argued that Hume failed to consider that *a priori* principles might operate in our understanding – principles which yield knowledge independently of our experience, whether that experience be composed of impressions and ideas received through the senses, or produced by the imagination. Kant, in accounting for our compulsion to believe in the existence of an external world, thus introduced new premises not found in Hume's philosophy.[38]

This innovation was beyond the power of Hume's philosophical opponents in Britain. But before going on to examine the role played by imagination in Kant's philosophy we have still to consider the role played by poetry in Hume's *Treatise*.[39] Since the imagination occupies a pre-eminent position in Hume's philosophy he has to comment on the poetic use of imagination. The poetic use of imagination is, in his opinion, different from the use of imagination in understanding and sympathy. However, when the imagination is detached from the 'permanent, irresistable and universal principles' of these faculties, it can degenerate into 'madness and folly'.[40] Hume thinks we tolerate poets because 'they profess to follow implicitly the suggestions of their fancy.' This self-consciousness allows their readers to put up

[37]I. Kant, *Prolegomena to Any Future Metaphysic* (1783), trans. L. W. Beck (Indianapolis, 1950), 6–8.
[38]*Immanuel Kant's Critique of Pure Reason* (1781, 1787), trans. Norman Kemp-Smith (London, 1929, 1970), B 788ff.
[39]See Hume, *Treatise*, Book I, part III, §x; part IV, §iii, iv; Appendix, 630–2.
[40]*Ibid.*, Book I, part III, §x, 123.

with poetic inventions in the way they would condone a child's world of make-believe.[41]

However, there is another strain to Hume's thinking about poetry which at first glance appears to grant it more importance. 'Poets themselves,' writes Hume, 'tho' liars by profession, always endeavour to give an air of truth to their fictions.' The manner in which poets try to convince us is regarded by Hume 'as a very strong confirmation' of his own 'system'. Poetry not only shows that the imagination, acting on principles different from the understanding, 'can be satisfy'd without an absolute belief or assurance'. Respect for poetry can be more than praise of folly. Poets often use the names of historical personages, and take the actions of their tragedies from history, because they know that this will gain for their productions a greater influence over the imagination. For Hume, this means that poetry illuminates his philosophy of belief. He seems to think that poetry affects us just in so far as we can mistake it for something else, a product of the understanding. It is the transitions of the imagination which produce beliefs in matters of fact, and Hume thinks poetry shows the corollary of this. A belief in a matter of fact 'gives vigour to the imagination'. In responding to poetry we experience the mutual assistance which belief and imagination give to each other.[42]

But on closer examination poetry is no better off than before. Belief, fact, understanding and imagination all define each other in Hume's philosophy. He has no conception that poetry and the poetic imagination might have a purpose different from that of the understanding which produces beliefs in matters of fact. Hume's description leaves poetry either as make-believe or 'a counterfeit belief'. He measures the impressions which are produced by the transitions of the imagination in poetry on the same scale as he measures the impressions produced by the imagination in the understanding. He is the perfect target for Blake's visionary polemic. Coleridge's secondary imagination, the 'echo' of primary imagination, is distinguished from its original by 'co-existing with the conscious will'. This independent motivation can now be understood

[41]*Ibid.,* Book I, part IV, §iii, 225.
[42]*Ibid.,* Book I, part III, §x, 121–3.

as intended to relieve this use of imagination of the otherwise
unavoidable burden of producing belief in an external world
constituted by 'all human Perception'. The 'willing suspension of
disbelief' which Coleridge thinks produces 'poetic faith' describes an
experience which conspicuously proffers its own artificiality. The
object of poetry no longer competes with the real world, but defines
itself by not submitting to the same realistic criteria. The difference
between this and Sir Philip Sidney's *Apologie* is the implication that
the definition of poetry has become part of the consciousness it
expresses.

Coleridge's alternative to Hume's views presupposes a Kantian
argument. In Kant's philosophy the imagination is not the sole
authority for beliefs in matters of fact, and can therefore have a poetic
function which does not prejudice our understanding of the world;
hence it indirectly rehabilitates the poet's use of imagination.

KANT ON IMAGINATION

The critique of aesthetic judgement of the beautiful

Hume believed that without imagination there could be no belief in
an external world. For Kant the supreme principle of all employment
of the understanding is no longer the imagination.[43] Nevertheless,
despite this difference, within Kant's *Critique of Pure Reason* the
imagination at first seems as bound to the task of giving us knowledge
of the objective world as it was bound in Hume's *Treatise* to produce
belief in the external world. If the imagination is still fundamentally
committed to a scientific role, then its employment in poetry will
once more appear as a distraction from its proper function. Poetry will
play the inferior or suspect role which was allotted to it by Hume. But
in the *Critique of Judgement* – 'the most astonishing of his works', as
Coleridge told Crabb Robinson (*MC* 386) – Kant argues that the
poetic use of imagination has significance in its own right.

In his critique of the aesthetic judgement of the beautiful, Kant
does not distinguish strictly between the act of imagination in

---

[43]It is the principle of the synthetic unity of apperception – Kant, *Critique of Pure Reason*, A 105–7, B 132–9.

creating a beautiful object in art, and the imagination as it functions in our aesthetic judgement of a beautiful object in nature or art.[44] Poetic creation and critical definition are beginning to merge. In both cases, what is all-important is the reading of a meaning into a sensuous representation of the object independently of any concept of the understanding which would determine it as an object of knowledge. In both cases, therefore, the mediating imagination does something impossible for it to achieve in the determinant judgements of the understanding. As well as this distinction, there is another very important point to be made which is a consequence of Kant's discussion. In Kant's critique of aesthetic judgement the imagination is brought to *consciousness* in a way in which it is not in the synthetic unity of apperception described in the *Critique of Pure Reason*. There Kant found imagination's activity hard to describe, and something 'of which we are scarcely ever conscious.'[45] He accounted for it only in terms of the necessity of its formal contribution to the unity of representations required for knowledge to be possible. But in the *Critique of Judgement* imagination is raised to the level of conscious appreciation. Kant's discussion of imagination may appear as cerebral and purely formal as before, but there is a difference: the autonomy of imagination in aesthetic judgement, in giving a law to itself, means that in judging an object to be beautiful we are judging how the imagination works. The unity or order we then read into a painting or a poem, or our appreciation of a scene in nature, reveals only the pattern of imaginative activity. This pattern defines what we are conscious of in aesthetic experience. Imagination is no longer just a formal requirement for some kind of experience, but constitutes the objects of that experience. This will be crucial for understanding Coleridge's criticism of Wordsworth, and for explaining the self-conscious, reflective, sentimental quality which Coleridge, like Schiller and Schlegel, ascribed to modern poetry. Poetry's critical or self-defining consciousness of itself as poetry, as the product of what Coleridge, referring to 'The Rime of the Ancient Mariner', called 'pure' imagination, is part of its subject-matter.

[44]See M. Warnock, *Imagination* (London, 1976), 41.
[45]Kant, *Critique of Pure Reason*, B 103.

Kant thinks that in aesthetic experience we are conscious of how we apprehend objects over and above our knowledge of the objects themselves. In being conscious of the imaginative pattern in a representation we become aware of the co-operation of our cognitive faculties.[46] Imagination, as it functions in aesthetic judgement, may not yield knowledge, but it does give a sense and feeling of that harmony between our cognitive faculties which makes knowledge possible. Although this harmony is necessary for knowledge, the *consciousness* of the harmony is not specifically given in knowledge.

Kant sometimes calls our sense of this harmony 'common sense'. 'Common sense,' for Kant, 'is not to be taken to mean some external sense, but the effect arising from the free play of our powers of cognition.'[47] It is therefore different from the common sense championed by the British philosophers opposed to Hume. It is not a specific body of knowledge which sceptical philosophers like Hume were accused of ignoring. Kant argues that common sense is a necessary presupposition for knowledge to be possible; and that the imagination can allow us an appreciation of common sense not given in knowledge.[48] The imagination, as it works in aesthetic judgement, gives us a sense and awareness, which we otherwise would not have, of how we must apprehend things prior to knowledge. We are in this way given a feeling for the order which the imagination must confer on its representation in its efforts to secure the co-operation of the cognitive faculties of sensibility and understanding. But our feeling, our conscious sense of this harmony, is not a feature of our knowledge of objects because it is generated by the imagination alone, without the aid of a concept of the understanding. Because poetry enjoys the free play of the imagination, something we can feel but not know,[49] it is distinct from knowledge. The common-sense philosophers similarly claimed that knowledge has a human character: it is because *our* cognitive faculties are of a certain limited kind

---

[46]I. Kant, *Critique of Judgement* (1790), trans. J. C. Meredith (Oxford, 1952), part I, 33–4.
[47]*Ibid.*, 83.
[48]*Ibid.*, 151–3.
[49]*Ibid.*, 86, 59–60.

that we have the knowledge we do. But they were incapable of seeing how it could be argued that this truth expressed a universal logical requirement for all knowledge, and not merely a mysterious prompting of our natures. Also, they could not see, as Kant did, that such a requirement, whatever its philosophical status, might be a concern separate from how we could feel, appreciate and express this human character of knowledge. Kant's distinction of the function of imagination in understanding from its function in aesthetic judgement creates the distance needed for poetry, art and all aesthetic experience to remain independent of philosophy. Yet they are still most closely and deliberately interrelated. Kant can only describe the pleasurable feeling arising in aesthetic judgement in terms of a condition necessary for the possibility of knowledge. And poetry independently gives a feeling for our powers of apprehension which philosophy would be incapable of supplying on its own. Poetry and philosophy, within Kant's critique of aesthetic judgement, inform each other, while each remains separate and significant in its own right.

The critique of aesthetic judgement of the sublime

So far we have been discussing Kant's critique of the aesthetic judgement of the beautiful. This judgement consisted in finding an order, pattern or form in a representation which has been freely discerned by the imagination without applying a concept of the understanding. As a definition of all aesthetic judgement this is obviously inadequate. Aesthetic pleasure can equally be derived from objects which appear formless, random, disorderly, things which we could never conceptualize; and an explanation of aesthetic judgement has to take account of this range of experience as well. Kant carefully maintains a symmetry between the pattern or 'finality' which the imagination finds in a representation, and the concept of the understanding which could be applied to that representation to transform it into knowledge. But he thinks this need not always be so: as well as aesthetic judgements of the beautiful, he thinks we make aesthetic judgements of the sublime, in which the aesthetic feeling is for the free play between imagination and reason, rather than imagination and understanding. Here the reason and not the understanding furnishes the blueprint for the rule imagination gives to itself: 'the beautiful seems to be regarded as an indeterminate concept of understanding, the sublime as a presentation of an indeterminate concept of reason.'[50] Kant extends the jurisdiction of aesthetic judgement by finding another model on which imagination can create its own law: an idea of reason. This in turn enables him to accommodate appreciation of the formless and the logically incoherent within his account of aesthetic judgement, because an idea of reason belongs to a faculty superior to understanding and beyond its grasp. It is therefore a faculty which we may employ in trying to make sense of experiences which remain totally incoherent to the understanding. Kant believes that an idea of reason can never be placed under a concept; but it may be 'indeterminately indicated' by the imagination.[51] We may therefore find an imaginative expression for an experience which has confounded all our attempts to understand it. If we feel aesthetic pleasure in this kind of representation of the imagination, we are judging not of the beautiful but of the sublime.

What is important for Kant's critique of the aesthetic judgement of the sublime is not so much what the ideas of reason are, but that we have a faculty of reason which remains untroubled by particular failures of the understanding to comprehend the world. The feeling of the sublime may seem 'to contravene the ends of our power of judgement, to be ill-adapted to our faculty of presentation, and to be, as it were, an outrage on the imagination, and yet it is judged all the more sublime on that account.'[52] It is just this failure to grasp the object of aesthetic experience in knowledge which is represented by the imagination.

For the sublime, in the strict sense of the word, cannot be contained in any sensuous form, but rather concerns ideas of reason, which, although no adequate presentation is possible, may be excited and called into mind by that very inadequacy itself which does admit of sensuous presentation.[53]

[50]*Ibid.*, 90–1.
[51]*Ibid.*, 104.
[52]*Ibid.*, 91.
[53]*Ibid.*, 92.

Kant avoids the mimetic fallacy. He does not think that the aesthetic experience of the sublime consists in wallowing in and miming our own sense of inadequacy. It is, as Schiller was to elaborate, a *mixed* feeling of failure and exaltation. It is only as we can see the feeling of incoherence as suggestive of a higher order at the level of reason that the experience of the sublime becomes significant: 'the Subject's very incapacity betrays the consciousness of an unlimited faculty of the same Subject, and that the mind can only form an aesthetic estimate of the latter faculty by means of that incapacity.'[54] In the experience of the sublime, the imagination reaches towards reason, but the feeling this gives is only of an *aesthetic* idea of reason. The imagination can frame an idea of reason only through a representation 'which induces much thought, yet without the possibility of any definite thought whatever, i.e. *concept,* being adequate to it, and which language, consequently, can never get quite on level terms with or render completely intelligible.'[55]

It is because it escapes the strict conditions necessary to determine knowledge of objects that Kant thinks the imagination can possess its peculiar power to provide an indeterminate concept of reason. Yet the sublime feeling of the inadequacy of the understanding to grasp the ideas of reason is only produced by the 'completeness' of the imaginative representation of these ideas. He writes:

The poet essays the task of interpreting to sense the rational ideas of invisible beings, the kingdom of the blessed, hell, eternity, creation, &c. Or, again, as to things of which examples occur in experience, e.g. death, envy, and all vices, as also love, fame, and the like, transgressing the limits of experience he attempts with the aid of an imagination which emulates the display of reason in its attainment of a maximum, to body them forth with a completeness of which nature affords no parallel; and it is in fact precisely in the poetic art that the faculty of aesthetic ideas can show itself to full advantage.[56]

Kant is careful to stress that this ability to represent ideas of reason 'is properly no more than a talent [of the imagination]'.[57] In judgements

---

[54]*Ibid.,* 108.
[55]*Ibid.,* 175–6.
[56]*Ibid.,* 176–7.
[57]*Ibid.,* 177.

of the sublime we only feel aesthetic ideas and indeterminate concepts of reason. We do not gain an awareness of ideas of reason independently of this aesthetic presentation. Again, Kant's scrupulous separation of judgement of the sublime from any form of knowledge suggests that the presentation of an object *as* aesthetic, as the creation of an autonomous imagination, is a constitutive part of aesthetic experience.

Kant thinks that in aesthetic judgement the imagination produces 'symbols', and uses this notion to describe the indeterminate character of the concept, rule or law which the imagination freely gives itself in aesthetic judgement. 'Schemata contain direct, symbols indirect, presentations of the concept.' He believes that in 'language we have many such indirect presentations modelled upon an analogy enabling the expression in question to contain, not the proper schema for the concept, but merely a symbol for reflection.'[58] This is the language which he must regard the poet as using when he applies 'the mere rule' by which the imagination represents an intuition, 'to quite another object, of which the former intuition is but the symbol.'[59] This has to be the stratagem of the poet dealing with our experience of the sublime. There he is forced to use the expressions we employ in understanding the world; but he uses them to signify a feeling for another order of things altogether. The poet's analogical use of language produces symbols by which we try to grasp in imagination thoughts and feelings which escape the conditions determining knowledge of objects.

Kant's account has therefore fulfilled the requirements for a theory of imagination which could have provided a most relevant introduction to the literary criticism of the second volume of Coleridge's *Biographia*. He has shown that the exercise of imagination is an 'Agent in all human Perception'; and he has shown that imagination can also produce a distinctive language of poetry. The same faculty is active in knowledge and poetry, but its different function in each demands a corresponding difference in language. This implication for language is not the main conclusion of Kant's *Critique of Judgement*.

[58]*Ibid.*, 222–3.
[59]*Ibid.*, 222.

Nevertheless, it is a consequence which Coleridge could have drawn from Kant's theory of imagination when he attempted to justify the existence of a distinctively poetic use of language. Also, a poem which uses the kind of analogical language of symbols described by Kant can for that reason be regarded as a philosophical poem. Its language would give us a feeling and a sense for conditions which philosophy prescribes as necessary for knowledge to be possible. The free play of imagination in poetry allows poetry to reflect upon how our cognitive faculties harmonize in order to become effective. But the philosophical poem can also allow us to figure to ourselves in symbols a sublime sense of being unlimited by the conditions of knowledge.

The post-Kantian philosopher from whom Coleridge was increasingly plagiarizing towards the end of volume I of *Biographia* was Schelling. Schelling did not maintain Kant's strict separation of the aesthetic presentation of ideas of reason and the logical presentation of objects of knowledge. In his *System of Transcendental Idealism* he argued that the artist represents to us a kind of absolute knowledge which the philosopher could not express. Schelling thought that for knowledge of the external world to be possible nature must necessarily function on principles identical with those of the mind. The artist, in giving us a unique insight into and awareness of our mental life, was also revealing to us the necessary constitution of nature. This way of thinking is at the opposite extreme to the view of poetry found in Hume's *Treatise*. Poetry has changed from being an inferior illustration of the workings of human understanding for Hume, to being the most important kind of knowledge there is for Schelling. Poetry has once more collapsed into some sort of science, and has forfeited the autonomy which Kant so carefully created for it. No wonder Coleridge's discussion of imagination in volume I of *Biographia* became more chaotic as its terminology became more like Schelling's. This terminology drove Coleridge towards a conclusion different from the purpose of his Kantian discussion of imagination. He wished to judge poetry as an autonomous order, separate from philosophy, yet capable of being philosophical. But his use of Schelling could only have led him towards a philosophy which once more imprisoned poetry, allowing it everything but its freedom.

SUBLIMITY AND SUBLIMATION

Kant's aesthetic of the sublime contains its own tensions. In his short essay *On The Sublime,* Friedrich Schiller emphasises this, claiming that 'The feeling of the sublime is a mixed feeling . . . a composition of melancholy . . . and of joyousness.'[60] The melancholy arises from the imagination's loss of its empirical employment. In Kant's words, 'it feels the sacrifice or deprivation' this entails.[61] We are no longer at home in the world constituted by our experience when we are enjoying the feeling of being able to think beyond it. This joyful feeling of self-aggrandizement defines itself in relation to an unhappy consciousness of no longer belonging to the phenomenal world.

'Sublime' and 'sublimation' are cognates in English, unlike the corresponding *das Erhabene* and *sublimieren* in German; and the meanings of the words turn out to be mutually enlightening. Freud thought that sublimation was the major force in art and culture. But the losses following from sublimation for the Romantic poet are considerable. Immediacy of perception is sacrificed in the interests of a higher state of mental organization. The poet, expressing this kind of experience, finds that the world he is describing disappears as the mechanism of sublimation goes into action. Wordsworth is a poet who constantly tries to retain a vivid sense of the natural world which has inspired in him experiences which seem to reach beyond it. These experiences demand a personal rhetoric, expressing an egotistical sublime – the language of the expanding self – which menaces the democracy he desired for poetry as 'a selection of the real language of men'. Sublimation also suggests an unstable resting place for the poetic increase in self-awareness. If we now recall the chemical application of the metaphor, there is always the threat that the immaterial state will revert to crude matter. The real world will press through what proves to have been a temporary chimera of questionable value. Returning to psychology, behaviour is usually recognized as sublimating other motives only when the sublimation is wearing thin. Keats, rather

[60] F. Schiller, *Naive and Sentimental Poetry* (1795–6); and *On The Sublime* (1801), trans. Julius A. Elias (New York, 1966), 198.
[61] Kant, *Critique of Judgement,* part I, 120.

than Wordsworth, is the obvious example here. The sublime, seen as a process of sublimation, has an evident economy of gain and loss.[62] In his 'Odes', Keats tries to develop a language capable of accommodating these contradictory impulses and of expressing that mixed feeling of melancholy and joy which they produce. He feels the ambiguity of the responsibility Kant was seen to place on the poet – the onus of producing symbols for an experience which language 'can never get quite on level terms with'.

Kant and Schiller suggest how the poetic use of language can be of philosophical significance without becoming philosophy; but the German tradition, while solving problems which defeated the British tradition, retains its own ambivalences. The aesthetic experience of the sublime is precarious, torn between conflicting loyalties, constituted by opposite feelings. The poet describing this experience, and his reader, are placed under considerable strain. We shall see that Coleridge's appreciation of Wordsworth's poetry in volume II of *Biographia* shows the effects of this tension. The sometimes mutually exclusive 'defects and excellences' he detects in Wordsworth's work, and in particular his ambivalent attitude towards the central symbol of the child-philosopher in the 'Immortality Ode', reflect Coleridge's contradictory feelings of resentment and sympathy for the poet's sublimation. He shows this inconsistency by finding in the same poem both material too literal to be transformed symbolically, and symbols which traduce the logic of the natural world. In his unfairness to Wordsworth, Coleridge involuntarily defines the melancholic side of the aesthetics of sublimity. On the other hand, he quickly forgets the poet's unhappy sacrifice and deprivation when he commends the language of the 'Immortality Ode' as the sole avenue to our 'modes of inmost being'. The flexibility and ambiguity required of poets dealing with so mixed a feeling necessarily produced a language of considerable range, and poetic structures of subtle dialectical complexity. In discursive criticism, though, the fully responsive critic was often driven, like Coleridge, into open contradiction; or else, like Friedrich Schlegel, he was forced to evolve

[62]See T. Weiskel's useful discussion, in *The Romantic Sublime*, 58–63.

a generic description – *der Roman* – so elastic as to be capable of accommodating all contradictions.

Coleridge's difficulty was perhaps prophetic. Even poetry subsequently found intolerable the strain of sustaining so rich a response. Schlegel's notion of *romantische Poesie* leads to a visionary realism, in the belief that the plenitude of phenomena can only be adequately evoked in art.[63] The subsequent replacement of the natural world in much symbolist and modernist poetry by a supreme fiction in which the poet can say 'Let be be finale of seem' resolves the tension in the Romantic aesthetics of sublimity. But it does so by abandoning the effort to render the contradictory claims of the phenomenal self to be present in a poem symbolically describing the noumenal self. Dualism vanishes from the poetry which develops the Romantic tradition, just as it disappeared from a post-Kantian philosopher like Schelling.

[63]For the theory of *der Roman*, see especially F. Schlegel's *Literary Notebooks 1797–1801*, ed. H. Eichner (London, 1957). Eichner refutes Lovejoy, and shows the connections between *der Roman*, *romantische Poesie*, and *Romanpoesie*, in 'Friedrich Schlegel's Theory of Romantic Poetry', *Publications of the Modern Languages Association*, lxxi (December 1956), no. 5, 1018–42.

CHAPTER THREE

The Whole World of Language

COLERIDGE AND THE TWO TRADITIONS

So far we have been discussing the two philosophical traditions which provided the background to Coleridge's interest in the philosophical status of poetry. The first was his native British tradition which had come to regard language in general, and poetry in particular, as being relevant to philosophy. The second was the German tradition. Coleridge's uses of both are far from straightforward. As regards the first, he had scarcely a good word to say about Kames, Reid and Beattie, but he had a lot to say for and against the notion of common sense. More importantly, his statements about common sense betray his habit of treating the phenomenon of language as evidence for a particular kind of philosophy. However, he moves beyond the conservatism of the common-sense philosophers to describe the development of knowledge as being analogous to the growth of a language. He thinks that language grows like an organic body, and that the principle explaining this growth is the progress of the human intellect. And, further, that language exemplifies the identity of the principles of natural growth and intellectual progress, and can be used as the model of this identity. The degree to which we can make sense of his language-model is the subject of this chapter.

As regards the second tradition, it has already been suggested that Kant's theory of imagination would have been an appropriate introduction to the literary criticism of volume II of *Biographia*. In Germany, the thinker who best expounded the implications of Kant's aesthetics in a Kantian spirit was Schiller. In his *Letters on the Aesthetic*

Education of Man, Schiller investigated that area of self-consciousness which Kant's aesthetic had isolated from scientific knowledge, and emphasized its radical implications. He developed Kant's ideas on the consciousness of the free play of our faculties in aesthetic judgement in accordance with his own belief in the primarily educative power of art. Schiller thinks that aesthetic experience gives us a much richer sense of all our powers than does the specialized knowledge of any particular science. Kant had argued in the *Critique of Judgement* that it is not the essence of art to improve because it is not a science; but that aesthetic appreciation nevertheless works in the interests of 'a continually progressive culture'.[1] Schiller developed these ideas, and argued that the fuller sense of our human powers – the sense of beauty and sublimity felt outside knowledge and in aesthetic experience – encourages us to try to realize this potential when we return to the proper realm of science and knowledge. Schelling partially echoes Schiller when he writes that, 'Philosophy, to be sure, reaches the highest level, but it brings only, as it were, a fragment of man to this point. Art brings *the whole man,* as he is, to that point, namely to knowledge of the highest of all, and on this rests the eternal difference and the miracle of art.'[2] Kant and Schiller would have agreed that art has the power of grasping 'the whole man' with a completeness not given in philosophy. But they would have thought that to call this aesthetic insight knowledge, as Schelling does, is just to eliminate 'the eternal difference and the miracle of art'. It is because art is *not* scientific or philosophical knowledge that it can suggest an ideal understanding of man which science ought to strive for. That, in Schiller's opinion, is art's educative function.[3]

Coleridge too, as much as the so-called philosophical radicals –

[1]Kant, *Critique of Judgement,* part I, 170, 183. English radicals like Blake and Hazlitt made the same point against the notion of the arts as progressive. See Blake, *Complete Writings,* 470; W. Hazlitt, *The Complete Works of William Hazlitt,* ed. P. P. Howe (London, 1930–4), 21 Vols, XVIII, 7–8.

[2]F. W. J. Schelling, 'System of Transcendental Idealism', trans. A. Hofstadter, in *Philosophies of Art and Beauty, Selected Readings in Aesthetics from Plato to Heidegger,* ed. A. Hofstadter and R. Kuhns (New York, 1964), 375.

[3]F. Schiller, *On the Aesthetic Education of Man,* trans. E. M. Wilkinson and L. A. Willoughby (Oxford, 1967), 147–9.

Godwin, James Mill, Bentham – believed that we are essentially progressive creatures even if, as in his late political writings *On the Constitution of the Church and State,* he held that such progressiveness must exist in harmony with certain permanent political interests. He thought that we displayed an intellectual resistance to the conceptual captivity which we inherited from past thinkers. Humanity was always trying to make further discoveries, and show improved powers of discrimination in the understanding of the world. Coleridge, like Schiller, thinks that poetry is philosophically important because the poet 'brings the whole soul of man into activity' (*BL* II 12): his self-conscious use of language draws attention to the kind of medium and symbolism required to give a fully adequate account of human nature. The next chapter will try to show how Coleridge's belief in what constitutes the right kind of philosophy, religion and politics stems from his understanding of the human character given in poetry. He thought that the exemplary consciousness of the humanity whose different aspects – epistemological, spiritual and political – those forms of thought describe is found in poetry. In this the Kantian origin, as well as what Marcuse called 'the explosive quality of Schiller's conception', should now be recognizable.[4] Like Schiller, Coleridge thinks that poetry affords us an unequalled sense of our own possibilities and so educates us radically in our potential for progress and improvement. With this fully-fledged concept of poetry in mind we shall at last be able to appreciate Coleridge's criticism of Wordsworth, Milton and Shakespeare.

Before we reach the point at which we can begin to discuss volume II of *Biographia,* Coleridge's idea of the language which he thought poetry could use to such effect must be understood. His conception of language in general, as distinct from poetry, derives partly from his native philosophical tradition – the first of the two traditions discussed above. But he tries to assimilate the idea of the philo-sophical importance of language, which was seen to be a conclusion of the first tradition, to his understanding of the Germans. For Coleridge, the difference between the poetic and the prosaic uses of language corresponds to the difference between aesthetic experience

[4]H. Marcuse, *Eros and Civilization* (London, 1969), 143–58.

and knowledge in Kant's philosophy. In other words, Coleridge describes our prosaic uses of language as though they reveal the conditions under which it is possible to have knowledge. And he describes poetry as giving us a special awareness of these conditions.

Sometimes, however, he writes as if he thinks that language does not merely represent the world according to our manner of understanding it. In *Biographia* he moves on from his admiration of Kant to profess the coincidence of his own thought with Schelling's. Coleridge's language-model confusingly tries to cater for Schelling as well as Kant. If he remained loyal to a Kantian position he would have to say that language refers to the world, but only to the world as we experience it. But sometimes he states that language shows the real identity of the principles explaining growth in nature and progress in knowledge. Then he takes language as evidence for the belief that we can have knowledge of the world because mind and nature are homogeneous. Coleridge's frequent insistence on the living character of words suggests that he does not always regard language as being like a Kantian schema, representing our view of the world and leaving the character of things-in-themselves untouched. His early advice to Godwin in a letter of 1800 is 'to destroy the old antithesis of *Words* and *Things* . . . elevating, as it were, words into Things, & living Things too' (*CL* I 625–6). Words, Coleridge seems to be saying, have a life of their own, in which we not only see our thought represented, but recognize the powers of growth and production in things. This belief anticipates the influence of Schelling on Coleridge rather than Kant, and could have been used by him as evidence for the 'genial coincidence' of their thought. It was Schelling, not Kant, who believed in the absolute identity of the principles of mind and nature. Kant only believed in the harmony the imagination created between different cognitive faculties. This made possible our experience of the world but, unlike Schelling's philosophy, left open to question the character of nature existing outside that experience.

However it is fundamental to understanding Coleridge to realize that he almost always thinks of poetry in the way that Kant thinks of aesthetic experience. Even in his Schellingian moments Coleridge still believes that poetry and the poetic imagination only give us a feeling for how we apprehend things. What we are capable of apprehending, according to Schelling, is far grander than Kant found admissible in his theory of knowledge. But while Schelling thought that the artist was peculiarly possessed of this knowledge, Coleridge always maintains a distance between poetry and knowledge or science. Poetry lets us feel the extent of our resources, but only gives us an ideal, imagined sense of these powers: what Kant describes as an aesthetic idea. In *Biographia* Coleridge states that in poetry 'The *rules* of the IMAGINATION are themselves the very powers of growth and production' (*BL* II 65). By that he does not mean, as Schelling would, that mind and nature, conscious rules and unconscious powers, literally become one in poetry. Coleridge goes on to state that 'the legitimate language of poetic fervour [is] self-impassioned', as the example he immediately quotes from Donne is intended to show. Poetry preserves its own identity, its own self, in its imagined integrity, distinct from nature, science or anything else. And it is only within this self-conscious, autonomous realm of poetry that the integration of mental rules and natural powers takes place. This completeness can provide a symbol for what science is trying to achieve: making our rules of knowledge adequate to describe the powers of nature. But Kant, Schiller and Coleridge all believe that poetry can only imagine symbols for such wholeness, and cannot present it to us as part of our knowledge. Poetry gives us an idea which science has not yet realized; but it is an aesthetic idea, 'self-impassioned'.

DESYNONYMY, COMMON SENSE AND BIOGRAPHIA

Coleridge developed the concept of language employed for philosophical purposes by the British thinkers who opposed Hume. He refined their regard for the relevance of language to philosophy in the light of his reading of Kant and Schelling. He was philosophically opposed to common sense when it was nothing more than a group of unreflective prejudices, but he was equally opposed to a philosophy which, like Hume's, tried to remain sceptical in the face of assumptions which have to be made if there is to be any knowledge at all. In a passage from *Omniana,* published in 1812, he summarizes his objections to philosophical scepticism:

I have noticed two main evils in philosophizing. The first is, the absurdity of demanding proof for the very facts which constitute the nature of him who demands it – a proof for those primary and unceasing revelations of self-consciousness, which every possible proof must pre-suppose . . .

But Coleridge is careful to distinguish 'the very facts which constitute the nature' of the thinker, from unphilosophical prejudices. The passage from *Omniana* proceeds to outline the second evil which Coleridge thinks can beset philosophy:

The second evil is that of mistaking for such facts mere general prejudices, and those opinions that having been habitually taken for granted, are dignified with the name of COMMON SENSE. Of these, the first is more injurious to the *reputation,* the latter more detrimental to the *progress* of philosophy. (*CSC* 394–5)

Common sense, when it is not detrimental to the progress of philosophy, is described by Coleridge as a category which does contain the facts constituting human nature. In a notebook entry of 1804, he expresses the hope that by preserving distinctions 'which all men are conscious of and which all languages express . . . I may combine & harmonize Philosophy and Common Sense' (*NB* II 2382). When worried about the popularity of his periodical *The Friend,* he reiterates his belief in the harmony of philosophy and common sense in a letter to Thomas Poole of 1810. 'For no two things, that are yet different, can be in closer harmony than the deductions of a profound philosophy, and the dictates of plain Common-sense . . .' (*CL* III 281–2). He goes on to illustrate his point with an example he claims to have found in 'Beattie's Immutability'. The reduction of philosophy to common sense was also, it is reported, the 'wonderful' insight of his old age (*TT* II 169).

Common sense is condemned in *Biographia* when it tries to substitute mere prejudice for rational argument, usurping 'the throne of philosophy'. Rather, 'it is the two-fold function of philosophy to reconcile reason with common sense, and to elevate common sense into reason' (*BL* I 182). When this effort to harmonize philosophy and common sense is absent, common sense poses as a self-sufficient body of knowledge, and directly impedes intellectual progress. This is the gist of Coleridge's attack in *Biographia*. 'By the very same argument the supporters of the Ptolemaic system might have rebuffed the Newtonian, and pointing to the sky with self-complacent grin have appealed to *common sense,* whether the sun did not move and the earth stand still' (*BL* I 93).

Nevertheless, Coleridge's objections do not interfere with his sympathy for common sense when it supports the kind of philosophy he favours. At one point in *Biographia* he appeals to common sense as an antidote to philosophical extravagance. It should make us distrust, for example, Leibniz's doctrine of a pre-established harmony of mind and nature because it was 'in its *common* interpretation too strange to survive the inventor – too repugnant to our *common sense*; (which is not indeed entitled to a judicial voice in the courts of scientific philosophy, but whose whispers still exert a strong secret influence)' (*BL* I 89). Coleridge continued to share Kant's objections to the anti-theoretical prejudice inherent in British common-sense philosophy. In his 'Logic', Coleridge cited this prejudice as one of the two 'most notable Stratagems of the present age'. The first is an excessive distrust of language, denying any philosophical importance to a question because it reduces to 'a mere difference of words'. The second was the habit of the 'self-presumed advocate of common sense' who replies whenever he is challenged that 'there is no sense in asking what the thing is: it can have no answer because it is properly speaking no question' (Log II 144, 160–1). But Coleridge's objection to the guillotine engineered by the phrase 'properly speaking' does not stop him opposing the first stratagem of the age with a trust in language, and with a belief in the philosophical importance of its syntactic structure virtually identical with views expressed by common-sense philosophers. Coleridge's chosen philosophy:

has this advantage over the Berkeleian in the very outset that in agreement with common sense and all known languages, it makes, feel and see verbs active with a distinct objective case; while the philosophers who assert that all perceptions are to be resolved into sensations and that sensations are but modifications of the sentient, ought not if they spoke consequentially to say, 'I see a chair', but I see or I see myself in the form of a chair. To see, hear, touch &c being with them verbs reflex and intransitive (Log II 166–7).

Throughout Coleridge's writings we find similar moments at which he discusses common sense, and its expression in language, in a manner reminiscent of the British opponents of Hume. But he differs fundamentally from his conservative predecessors where he links the notion of common sense to a theory of the progressive character of human knowledge. He does this by means of his ideas on desynonymy.

Desynonymy for Coleridge means increasing the vocabulary of a language by showing how words which were thought to be synonymous in fact mean different things. The original thinker adds to the number of meanings in the language we use. He does this by coining new words, and showing that we need them. Or he can desynonymize existing words by showing that we are putting words which we mistakenly think are synonyms to quite different uses.

That is how desynonymy works within our linguistic usage. It has hardly been commented on by Coleridge's critics, and if that were all he had to say about desynonymy then the theory might not merit further comment, and remain a peripheral curiosity. However desynonymy also furnishes Coleridge with a model of the workings of human understanding. He frequently presents it as a model with which to explain how a science progresses and improves. Sometimes it sounds as though he conflates the model with the actual words we use. Then language-model and vernacular merge in a confusing manner. This is particularly so when he is describing improvements in language-related disciplines like philosophy. But he still makes claims for desynonymy which are much more general than this. In his *Philosophical Lectures* he maintains that 'the whole process of human intellect is gradually to desynonymize terms.' The growth of language is a model for intellectual discovery in general: 'in proportion as one and identical becomes several, there will necessarily arise a term striving to represent that distinction' (*PhL* 173). In a late notebook whose entries begin in 1825 Coleridge wrote that 'A man of Genius using a rich and expressive language . . . is an excellent illustration of the ever individualizing process and dynamic Being, of Ideas.' The genius improves knowledge in the particular case by adding to the vocabulary of a language; but he also illustrates how all knowledge progresses through the discrimination of new particulars towards an ideal understanding (*CLL* 138).

But, as we have seen, Coleridge thinks that such philosophical discoveries must be harmonized with common sense. When, in *Biographia*, he advocates desynonymy as a model of progressive research, he describes the public appropriation of the researcher's private distinction as assimilation to the language of common sense:

> When this distinction has been so naturalized and of such general currency that the language itself does as it were *think* for us (like the sliding rule which is the mechanic's safe substitute for arithmetical knowledge) we then say, that it is evident to *common sense*. (*BL* I 63n.)

This moment of assimilation is always related to the forward movement latent in Coleridge's belief that we must try 'to elevate common sense into reason'. He suggests that common sense is not the passive repository of our shared beliefs, but something which grows through the agency of desynonymy to encompass new meanings:

> in all societies there exists an instinct of growth, a certain collective, unconscious good sense working progressively to desynonymize those words originally of the same meaning, which the conflux of dialects has supplied to the more homogeneous languages, as the Greek and German: and which the same cause, joined with accidents of translation from original works of different countries, occasion in mixt languages like our own. (*BL* I 61)

The most famous contribution of Coleridge himself as an individual researcher attempting to discover a distinction which would subsequently play an important role in our language is his separation of fancy from the uses of imagination. This act of desynonymy concludes the earlier part of *Biographia* which was severed from the later practical criticism by Coleridge's insertion of his attempt to produce a formal deduction of the imagination. The distinction reappears, in three parts this time, after the deduction breaks down at the end of volume I. Coleridge belatedly recovers the original purpose of his philosophical excursion: the explanation of the need for an act of desynonymy which would justify the distinction of the language of poetry from that of prose.

The method Coleridge was following before the ill-fated deduction, and the progressive movement of thought to which he believed desynonymy contributed, are supposed to show how within language 'truth soon changes by domestication into power' (*BL* I 62). Coleridge's distinction between the two imaginations and fancy was meant to result in an increase in critical power to be displayed immediately in the discussion of Shakespeare, Milton and Wordsworth in volume II. Before embarking on that Coleridge must have hoped to have established that poetry is the product of a use of imagination which is separate from the primary function of imagination in perception and knowledge. Coleridge defines the secondary imagination strictly in relation to the ideal unity it strives to create: it can only appear in poetry or art. We presumably cannot recognize it without being made aware of its aesthetic status. Fancy, on the other hand, may appear in poetry, but can exist elsewhere. The theory establishing this is missing from *Biographia*; we are only given 'the main result' of which this interpretation is the one that answers Coleridge's purposes in the second volume best of all. But at least we can now understand the distinctions between the two imaginations and fancy in the first volume as a result of desynonymy: a result which is then deployed as part of our common language in the practical criticism of the second volume. Coleridge does, then, provide us with an oblique way of seeing a coherent pattern of philosophical explanation in *Biographia* not dependent on the missing transcendental deduction. *Biographia* fits into a general pattern in which the assimilation of the private individual discovery to the common sense of mankind is explained on the model of how a new word, the product of desynonymy, finds its place within the language.

This provides *Biographia* with, at best, a subliminal unity, and raises the question of whether there are any important reasons for why this striking argument was repressed. In a notebook entry of 1809 Coleridge asked:

What is common sense? – It is when the language has been so determined in its meanings by great men (being in itself mere arbitrary counters, or physical equivalents, as compulsion & obligation &c) that the very words of a language as used in common Life carry with them the confutation of an error or establishment of a Truth, then we call convictions so received common sense, bearing to the original reason the same relations as operations by an Arithmetical Rules to those by universal Arithmetic. (*NB* III 3549)

Language contains in a communal form the individual achievements of outstanding minds; in this way it illustrates the assimilation of philosophical discoveries to common sense which Coleridge thought so important. In *Biographia* language looks towards human progress while preserving a historical record of human achievement. 'For language is the armoury of the human mind; and at once contains the trophies of its past, and the weapons of its future conquests' (*BL* II 22). However Coleridge often suggested that the possible harmony of philosophy and common sense was now much more difficult to realize than before. Isolated from each other, common sense degenerates into bigotry, and philosophy becomes incommunicable. In the *Critique of Pure Reason* Kant had expressed the fear that 'to coin new words is to advance a claim to legislate in language that seldom succeeds.' He called this a 'desperate expedient',[5] yet clearly had recourse to it in creating a specialized philosophical terminology which his successors modified, and from which Coleridge borrowed. Coleridge often writes as if a philosophy which relies on the existing common language risks equally grave dangers. The possible philosophical value of common sense was threatened by a pervasive relativity. 'Common sense . . . differs in different ages' (*BL* I 63n.). 'The science of one age becomes the common sense of a succeeding' (*C&S* 167). A Kantian might argue that there are common factors which remain constant throughout the growth of knowledge because they ensure that it is communicable at any point in its history. But Coleridge's worry was that the present age itself, the particular historical period in which the currency of contemporary knowledge was being minted, was infringing upon the progress of knowledge. Forces other than those of natural growth from within were dissociating the new from the old, suggesting a disruption in knowledge comparable to the political revolution of 1789.

[5]Kant, *Critique of Pure Reason*, B 369.

Coleridge always held that, as he put it in *The Statesman's Manual*, it was the 'modern metaphysics' of empiricism with its 'direful', 'levelling' effects whose 'figures of speech' had informed the language of the Jacobins (*LS* 12). He was convinced that the French Revolution, valuing 'the universals of abstract reason instead of positive institutions', showed the truth of his belief that 'all the *epoch-framing* Revolutions of the Christian world . . . have coincided with the rise and fall of metaphysical systems.'[6] In a letter of 1817 to the Prime Minister, Lord Liverpool, Coleridge explicitly described the philosophical aims of *Biographia* as politically conservative and anti-Jacobin (*CL* IV 758–62). However, the important contradiction in all this is that his own Kantian-derived mode of philosophical speech exhibits a rupture with any common cultural inheritance just as much as empiricist terminology might do. He inadvertently lends support to the claims of Heine and the young Marx that it was Kant who was the theorist of the French Revolution, questioning all established philosophies which were now asked to justify themselves in the light of his critical method.[7] An awareness of this contradiction – that Coleridge used transcendentalist terminology to obfuscate a critical theory whose radicalism it in fact supported – is fundamental to understanding the dilemma of *Biographia*. Either way, as transcendentalist philosopher or practical critic, Coleridge seemed bound to express unconsciously the radical spirit of his age.

Coleridge complained that any attempt to produce original thought in his own day seemed divorced from a common cultural tradition. It was impossible to accommodate the researches of the desynonymizing philosopher within the language he is trying to improve: they obstinately demanded a specialized terminology of their own. But in this case our common language will no longer exhibit in the present the trophies gained in the past by mental

[6]*LS* 63–4, 14–15.
[7]*CL* IV 758–62; H. Heine, 'Zur Geschichte der Religion und Philosophie in Deutschland', *Sämtliche Werke*, Düsseldorfer Ausgabe, ed. M. Windfuhr (Hamburg, 1973), Band 8/1, 90–1; K. Marx, 'Philosophical Manifesto of the Historical School of Law', in *Writings of the Young Marx on Philosophy and Society*, ed. L. Easton and K. Guddat (New York, 1967), 100.

armoury. Common sense is described by Coleridge in a notebook entry about the time of writing *Biographia* as the 'Shells, or the Wampum, or the Minted Coin, or the Bank, or Country, or Town Notes, which happen at *the moment* to be current & in credit, tho' the month after a Bankruptcy shews the hollowness of the Foundation' (*NB* III 4247). In another related entry of 1816 the common element vulgarizes rather than humanizes discovery: 'that every thing clearly perceived may be conveyed in simple common language, without thinking on – to whom? is the disease of the age – an arrogant pusillanimity – a hatred of all information that cannot be obtained without thinking . . .' (*NB* III 4309). Coleridge's attack on those who rely on common language 'without thinking' is inconsistent with his idea of a language embodying common sense which can '*think* for us', a language 'as used in common Life' containing meanings determined 'by great men'. The 'great men' of the present age are now set against any trust in the language of ordinary life, and the values discovered by desynonymy appear detached from any demotic universal.

This is confirmed by that desire which Coleridge occasionally expresses for a philosophical language different from the one in use, devoid of its errors, imprecisions and inadequacies, providing an alternative to rather than a modification of the existing language. 'The first lesson of philosophical discipline is to wean the student's attention from the DEGREES of things, which alone form the vocabulary of common life, and to direct it to the KIND abstracted from *degree*' (*BL* I 108).[8] In this context Coleridge talks of the specialization of intellectual discipines, and common sense slips back into the category of prejudices politically opposed to the realm of sophisticated scientific theory – 'the *sans culotterie* of a contemptuous ignorance'. With this political distrust, Coleridge loses a unified, cultural background to his theory of knowledge. 'The best part of language' becomes a selective thing which does not play an active part in the lives of 'uneducated' people (*BL* II 39–40). A notebook entry

[8]See a letter to Hartley Coleridge of 1820 (*CL* V 99): 'It is this which constitutes the difference between the *proper* Nomenclature of Science and the inevitable language of ordinary life'; see also *SC* I 182–3, 'If our language have any defect, it is in its want of terms expressing *kind,* as distinguished from *degree.*'

for 1815 claims that the motives for using ordinary language are wholly different from those for using philosophical language and scarcely contribute to a common activity.

A philosopher's ordinary Language and Admissions in general Conversation or writings ad populum is his Watch compared with his astronomical Timepiece – He sets the former by the Town Clock, not because he believes it right, but because his Neighbors, & his Cook *go* by it. (*NB* III 4260)

In another entry of 1808 Coleridge notes how Latin was prevented from becoming a 'Lingua Communis' because of the devotion of scholars to its period of 'classical purity'; that is, to its best period:

for in order to write Ciceronianly we must *think* in the age of Cicero. Erasmus fought nobly against this; but the fine gentlemen of Classical Literature, in Italy, were too hard for him. Perhaps if some great Philosopher had arisen, laid down the foundations of philosophical Language, cleansed from Idioms; & made it the sole law of Latin Style, that it should be equally intelligible to a Swede as to a Sicilian, &c., something might have been done – we might have escaped the French. (*NB* III 3365)

The full implications of the fracturing of a common background to philosophy and the language in use now begin to emerge. The philosopher's desire to cleanse language of its idioms places poetic or literary values in conflict with philosophical values. The idea of what constitutes the 'best part of human language' now varies between the two disciplines rather than supplying unified support for the humanities in general. The philosopher who establishes a philosophical language by showing a bold disregard for canons of classical purity is surely at odds with the Coleridge who wrote in a notebook entry of 1805 that:

our Language has made no steps, endured no real alteration since the Time of Elizabeth at least. Every 5 years, has it's affectation; but he who writes simply well, must write now, both words and construction as our ancestors, two or even three hundred years ago. (*NB* II 2645)[9]

In contrast to this literary conservatism, Coleridge, in the role of specialized philosopher, appears as a radical ideologue.

[9]See also *NB* III 3954 (1810).

When Coleridge does believe in the possibility of harmonizing philosophy and common sense, then the workings of language remain his guide, and it is poetry which becomes an incentive to progress. He postulates a linguistic ideal, pursued by desynonymy, where every word has a separate meaning. Poetry, by being untranslatable, symbolizes the completion of this process. Language encapsulates the crudely abstract views which a creative writer can transcend; and discrimination in the use of language is the model of a progressively more astute apprehension of the world. Synonyms are 'defects in Language; but yet such defects as permit a progress in its powers' (NB III 3312). His tendency to doubt that this progress could be achieved within the boundaries of ordinary language furnishes one reason for why the notion of a transcendental deduction of the imagination in a specialized philosophical vocabulary so attracted him, politically disarming radicalism by supporting it with an exclusive, *soi-disant*, professional expertise.

He seems to be drawn to that way of thinking which tries to retrieve a common culture whose sensibility is imagined to have been free of dissociation or fragmentation. But this aim is found in competition with an equally powerful instinct towards progress. The latter demands specialization and a technical, professional devotion which ignores received traditions and shared ways of thinking in the interests of its own improvement. 'All industries, arts, and crafts have gained by the division of labour,' wrote Kant.[10] Poetry bridges the gap between the two attitudes, generating a nostalgia for an exemplary literary past, and supplying a model of the perfection for which knowledge strives. In *Biographia* the attempt to desynonymize words we all use gives way to a new, specialized philosophical terminology – Kant's 'desperate expedient'. However, Coleridge's other writings show the extent to which he had thought about desynonymy, and suggest how it could have provided him with a means of supplementing or replacing the abortive deduction of *Biographia*.

[10] *The Moral Law – Kant's Groundwork of the Metaphysics of Morals*, trans. H. J. Paton (London, 1966), 54.

DESYNONYMY AS COLERIDGE'S
'TRUE SOCRATIC METHOD'

In his *Philosophical Lectures* Coleridge describes philology as 'all the pursuits in which the intellect of man is concerned' (*PhL* 390). This claim makes no sense unless it is interpreted as describing the illustrative power of language as a model of knowledge. In a notebook entry of about 1808 we find Coleridge making a typically ambitious claim for the significance of desynonymy.

By Synonymes I mean words really equivalent, both in material meaning & in the feelings or notions associated with them . . . and by Homoeonymes those words, falsely thought or carelessly used as Synonymes. – To *make* real Synonymes into Homoeonymes, is the privelege of Genius, whether poetic or philosophic. (*NB* III 3312)

The word 'homoeonyme' does not appear in the *Oxford English Dictionary* (the prefix 'homoeo' means 'of the same kind, similar'); Coleridge is therefore describing desynonymy as a process of showing that words which we think have identical meanings in fact only have similar meanings. The insights of original thinkers remedy our lax use of words in the past. Coleridge believes that these particular improvements in language possess the power to model advances in all forms of knowledge. When, however, he writes of philosophy, his ideas of language as instance and illustration of the progress of knowledge merge. Desynonymy produces diversity by increasing the number of particular meanings within a language. Nevertheless, while its whole tendency seems to be productive of individuality, those new individuals can only be identified within a definite frame of reference. This double movement is described in *Biographia* as being the '*process*' and the '*result*' of philosophy.[11] Each newly distinguished meaning takes its place within an already existing scheme of relations

---

[11]'The office of philosophical *disquisition* consists in just *distinction*; while it is the privilege of the philosopher to preserve himself constantly aware, that distinction is not division. In order to obtain adequate notions of any truth, we must intellectually separate its distinguishable parts; and this is the technical *process* of philosophy. But having so done, we must then restore them in our conceptions to the unity, in which they actually co-exist; and this is the *result* of philosophy.' (*BL* II 8)

– a language – and it is only against such a background that it can appear as being 'new', gaining its meaning, as Saussure would say, through its 'difference'. The scientific discoveries of today become the common sense of tomorrow.

According to Coleridge's description so far, desynonymy defines changes in a language from within the structure of that language, as though by a process of self-analysis. The changes envisaged occur in vocabulary, but not in grammar. It is an alternative to inventing an entirely new terminology or scientific paradigm whose differences do not place them within existing schemes, but rather show them breaking irrevocably with the community of knowledge. In desynonymy an analysis within current language reveals a confusion of meanings in accepted usage and each distinct meaning is allocated to a separate word. This is Coleridge's 'analytic', the 'Socratic method' described in another of the undated Egerton MSS.

Whenever I can convince a man that another term would express his meaning far more unexceptionably, the term used was not *appropriate* – but the rule is that the same word should not have heterogeneous or even disparate senses. Thus instead of asking, Was *Schönheit sey?* I would enquire what schön properly meant – i.e. what men mean when they use the word *schön* in preference to any other epithet. . . . And this, if I mistake not, is the true Socratic Method: assuredly that which best suits the Dialogue form, which only the analytic suits at any time, but this piece of analysis, i.e. desynonymization, best of all – it so naturally arises out of conversation. (*IS* 99–100)

Coleridge's Socratic philosopher is asking us to justify our use of a word by showing that we would use that word and no other for a particular purpose. The Platonic comparison is plausible as far as it goes. By exposing the inconsistencies in someone's use of a word – say, 'justice' in *The Republic* – Socrates shows the need for further and more discriminating philosophical distinctions which he then goes on to provide in a common language through dialogue.

Coleridge's 'analytic' was not to be a complete account of how we gain knowledge. Knowledge demands an additional, synthetic activity. His description of the 'synthetic', in the continuation of the passage just quoted, suggests that it was to provide the rationale of Coleridgean projects such as a philosophical dictionary and grammar which would order and arrange the new insights gained by the 'analytic' of desynonymy: 'The Synthetic on the contrary demands the paideutic continuous form. We want a classification of words sadly – into the universals . . . the generals . . . the words appropriate to each particular sense' (IS 100). In this way the differences discovered by desynonymy are placed in meaningful relation to the rest of language. 'Paideutics' is defined as 'the science or art of education'; thus Coleridge thought that a philosophical dictionary or grammar would educate us in recognizing the 'result' which the analytic 'process' of desynonymy was trying to achieve.

If, for Coleridge, language and knowledge share the same pattern of progressive development then, as he states in *Philosophical Lectures*, 'it is the business of the philosopher to desynonymize words originally equivalent, therein following and impelling the natural progress of language in civilized societies' (PhL 152).[12] We have already seen how Coleridge found historical precedents for desynonymy in Plato. He also found the contribution of the scholastic philosophers significant. The desynonymizing activities of the schoolmen was sometimes justified, giving to words 'perfectly just and distinct meanings', and sometimes not; however their distinctions 'whether true or false laid the foundations of our modern languages' (PhL 276). However, as might be expected, the history of desynonymy which Coleridge wishes a philosophical dictionary to record is far more than pure philology. He frequently quotes Hobbes' dictum that men are liable to fall into errors about things from the improprieties about their use of words, although it is often Hobbes he uses as an example. His conflation of obligation and compulsion is one of Coleridge's favourite instances of the need for desynonymy.[13] He thought that Hobbes' false identification of two disparate meanings, his 'moral sophisms' (BL I 64n) far from being mere infelicities in style implied the removal of 'the condition of all moral responsibility' (IS 102–3). In the *Philosophical Lectures* he goes so far as to draw the conclusion that the movement of society depends on the advancement of philosophy through language:

[12]*Ibid.*, II 255.
[13]*Ibid.*, II 22; CL II 691 (to J. Wedgwood, 1801); NB I 911 (1801); A vii, 24–5.

the whole process of society, as far as it is human society, depends upon – it may sound as a paradox but it is still a very serious truth – the progress of desynonymizing, that is, the feeling that there is a necessity for two distinct subjects which have hitherto been comprehended in one. (*PhL* 174)[14]

The development of society can then be measured by the extent to which the language it uses approximates to an ideal theory of meaning where each word has its unique, desynonymized meaning. A philosophical dictionary, therefore, should be able to record a society's progress by recording the tendency to desynonymy within its language. This kind of dictionary would, by its very nature, outline a philosophical programme full of Enlightenment optimism: for 'the duty of a philosopher is to aid and complete this process as his subject demands' (*PhL* 368–9).[15] Past linguistic usage is no longer a static model, but the philosopher's directive for radical change.[16]

Coleridge here is employing various strains of eighteenth-century thought about language. He does not produce a genetic theory of the origin of language, but is preoccupied with language's expression of the formal characteristics of human understanding, and is anticipated in this interest most notably by Herder and Rousseau. Herder, for example, thought a philosophical dictionary 'would be a chart of the

[14]See *SC* II 246; *CSC* 63.

[15]See *BL* I 165n.; *NB* III 4210; *TofL* 25, for Coleridge's repudiation of those 'verbal definitions of lexicography' which dwell only in the past, 'a history, not a definition', unrelated to any forward-looking scientific method which attempts to announce 'the law of action in the particular case, in subordination to the common law of which all the phenomena are modifications or results'. Coleridge later described Voltaire's philosophical dictionary as 'the work of the Devil'. But he would have intended his opposition to Voltaire's atheism to enhance his own radicalism, widening the definition of human nature to include theological possibilities. (Log II 382)

[16]*NB* III 3268: 'Important Hint suggested itself to me, 10th Feb. 1808. The powers of conscious intellect increase by the accession of an organon or new word – try this in that abominable word, Idea/ how have I been struggling to get rid of it, & to find some exact word for each exact meaning – but no! – look into Bacon, Hooker, Milton, and the best Writers before Locke – & then *report.*' See also *A* 235n.: 'the important truth that Language (as the embodied and articulated Spirit of the Race, as the growth and emanation of a People, and not the work of any individual Wit or Will) is often inadequate, sometimes deficient, but never false or delusive. We have only to master the true origin and original import of any native and abiding word, to find in it, if not the *solution* of the facts expressed by it, yet a finger-mark pointing to the road on which this solution is to be sought for.'

human spirit, a history of its development . . . a most remarkable sample of the inventive skill of the human soul.'[17] Herder's rationalism, more than Rousseau's emotivism, provides a source for Coleridge. But Coleridge's idea of a philosophical dictionary differs from Herder's putative dictionary principally because the progress of language which Herder records is towards abstraction not particularity.[18] He therefore, as far as I know, has no theory of desynonymy, although in his attacks on Kant language is presented as philosophical evidence much in the manner of the common-sense philosophers, as is also the case with J. G. Hamann. James Burnett, Lord Monboddo, much admired by Herder, also thinks that language records rational progress, but regards abstraction as being an activity by which we consider things in their particularity. This does result in a covert theory of desynonymy to explain progress in thinking and language:

the great defect of all barbarous languages is, the expressing different things by the same word, without abstracting and separating them one from another: where-ever we see any one thing expressed by a distinct word, it is to be reckoned an improvement of the people in the faculty of thinking, and by consequence of their language; for if they had not first formed a separate idea of the thing, they would never have expressed it by a separate word.[19]

[17]J. G. Herder, *Essay on the Origin of Language* (1772), trans. A. Gode (New York, 1966), 132–3.

[18]*Ibid.*, 133, 155. In her edition of the *Philosophical Lectures* of Coleridge, Kathleen Coburn finds 'no evidence' that Coleridge had read Herder's essay, and writes that 'Coleridge's theories about the relations between a society and its speech are to be seen in the van of contemporary thinking.' But see E. S. Shaffer on British interest in Herder, in *'Kubla Khan' and 'The Fall of Jerusalem'* (Cambridge, 1975), 310–11, 333. Vico's idea of a 'mental dictionary' which will gain us access to the 'common sense' of all nations by identifying a 'common mental language' is an idea which is 'proper' to his 'New Science', *The New Science of Giambattista Vico,* trans. T. G. Bergin and M. H. Fisch (New York, 1948); 'Introduction' D6, I9; §145, 162, 245, 473–82. Vico's influence on anybody is notoriously difficult to substantiate exactly, but it is undeniable that Herder and Coleridge display 'animae naturaliter Vichianae'. See the 'Introduction' to *The Autobiography of Giambattista Vico,* trans. T. G. Bergin and M. H. Fisch (New York, 1944), 83–4. Coleridge probably did not read Vico until 1825, when he wrote, 'I am more and more delighted with G. B. Vico . . . "Pereant qui ante nos nostra dixere".' (*CL* V 454)

[19]Monboddo, *Of the Origin and Progress of Language,* I, 143, 394–5, 397; for Herder's 'laudatory preface' to the German translation of Monboddo, see Aarsleff, *The Study of Language,* 41–2.

Most importantly, Coleridge's ideas on desynonymy arise out of his attempts to explain the development of his own thought. In 1804 he defined his early necessitarianism, 'the pernicious Doctrine of necessity', as something which he had found credible because of a deficiency in his understanding of this particular use of language. In advancing on his former view he grasps the process by which language changes, develops and improves its discriminating power. He claims in a letter to Thomas Poole of 1804 to have convinced Wordsworth and Southey

of the sophistry of the arguments, & wherein the Sophism consists – viz. that all have hitherto, both the Necessitarians & their Antagonists, confounded two essentially different Things under one name – & in consequence of *this* Mistake the Victory has always been hollow in favour of the Necessitarians. (*CL* II 1037)

In a letter to Southey written about a month later he accuses Godwin of using language in a private, eccentric manner as though he could exclude from his argument language's public, social dimension, with all the history of its development. Instead, Godwin inveighs 'mōre Godwiniānō – in language so ridiculously and exclusively appropriate to himself, that it would have made you merry' (*CL* II 1072). Coleridge's escape from the influence of necessitarians like Hartley, Priestley and Godwin is presented here as the insight into the true character of language as an expansive force for change within society as a whole.

Examples of desynonymy abound within Coleridge's thought,[20] and it is Coleridge's habitual practice of interrogating his own and others' uses of language which lies behind his distinction in *Biographia* between fancy and the two imaginations. Critics have taken little account of the fact that the distinction is produced by an act of desynonymy. Yet from the evidence we have considered in his other writings, he himself would have attached considerable significance to this example of his 'true Socratic method'.

---

[20]Most obviously *NB* II 3224 for/because; III 3268 idea; 3311 conceive/comprehend; 4422 Pleasure/gladness/happiness/bliss; *PhL* 184–5 abstraction/generalization; *IS* 102–3 fanaticism/enthusiasm.

Coleridge has been seen to regard language as the embodiment both of common sense and of an 'instinct of growth' working progressively in 'all societies', enabling it to '*think* for us'. 'Truth,' he wrote in chapter 4 of *Biographia,* 'soon changes by domestication into power; and from directing in the discrimination and appraisal of the product, becomes influencive in the production' (*BL* I 62). Discoveries of desynonymy are quickly translated into a common practical ability. In the same chapter he does not give reasons for why he is able to distinguish between examples of fancy and imagination. As Arnold was to do later, he merely quotes his 'touchstones': 'Lutes, lobsters, seas of milk, and ships of amber', and 'What! have his daughters brought him to this pass?' This form of justification certainly lets the language '*think* for us', untouched by any extraneous theory. But at the same time it is not explained, as T. S. Eliot thought it was, by saying that the distinction Coleridge is making is simply between good and bad poetry. The unspoken assumptions which we have been examining behind Coleridge's linguistic innovation show us that it is intended to release an explanatory theory. His analytic success in discrimination leads us to expect illumination from his synthesis of the new discovery with the rest of language. We are confronted with one of those Coleridgean examples in which 'the very words of a language as used in common Life carry with them the confutation of an error or establishment of a Truth' (*NB* III 3549). This is the mode of argument of the second part of *Biographia* once the attempted transcendental deduction of the imagination and the plagiarism from Schelling in volume I peter out. The critical practice in the second volume *is* the assimilation of the desynonymizing of the two imaginations and fancy achieved in the first part. The resulting increase in critical understanding and theoretical power, allowing the new use of language to unburden itself of the new truth it carries, is meant to be displayed in Coleridge's discussion of Shakespeare, Milton and especially Wordsworth.

Viewed as a protracted act of desynonymy, *Biographia* aims to confute Wordsworth's mistaken views of poetic diction by establishing the need for a new distinction in language. This would enable the critic to insist upon the difference between the peculiarly poetic imagination and the imagination as it functions in prose. A change in usage, evolving from the way in which poetry is described, points to the need for a more exact theory of imagination. This is the reverse of Coleridge's declared ambition in *Biographia* of deducing rules of critical discrimination from the nature of imagination. However, this alternative to Coleridge's public failure to produce a transcendental deduction remains subliminal. Coleridge has insufficient political confidence in the adequacy of the common language to which the innovations of desynonymy would have to contribute. On the other hand, he remains blind to the cultural divisiveness of the alternative transcendentalist terminology. The 'very words . . . of common Life' will not suffice, and the conclusions Coleridge draws from his most famous act of desynonymy are scattered throughout all his writings rather than focused definitively in an explanation given in *Biographia*.

Biographia exemplifies Coleridge's reaction when he felt that philosophical originality could no longer be assimilated to common sense; when 'the principal means of improvement in any language in the desynonymizing of words' (Log II 151) becomes irrevocably opposed to ordinary usage. His distrust of the common sense of his own age constitutes social criticism. He doubted if the discoveries of the contemporary philosopher could find a place within a common culture. As will be seen in the next chapter, his complaints about the public reception of *The Friend* epitomize this anxiety. The spirit of the age, the public expectations concerning an original philosophical work, could only be reconciled with the genuine product by distorting and vulgarizing its hard-won distinctions. Political confidence in the possibility of progress within a unified culture at all levels of society – the liberal enthusiasm which had greeted the French Revolution – had been broken in Coleridge's case by the time he came to write *Biographia*. However much the later Coleridge claimed he was never a Jacobin, it remains true that he could never have written in *Biographia* as he did in *The Watchman* that it 'has ever been our opinion, that in England the people are better than the government' (*TW* 212). The contradictions in *Biographia* then express the fissures in Coleridge's radicalism. He wants to govern from the top, an authoritarian author expert in a specialized language. But his real

discoveries come from below, from the popular language, undermining the author's exclusive status by locating his originality in a
common medium – 'collective' and 'unconscious'. Still, *Biographia*
fails to allow precedence to the theory behind the central acts of
desynonymy, although it is unable to relate the prevailing, plagiarized, transcendentalist theory to these important original critical
distinctions made in ordinary language. *Biographia's* radical poetic
theory survives in spite of itself.

DESYNONYMY AND 'LIVING WORDS'

The extent of Coleridge's preoccupation with desynonymy, and so the
full significance of its repression within *Biographia*, is more fully
appreciated when it is realized that he also used desynonymy to
express the 'genial coincidence' of his thought with Schelling's. In a
marginal note to Schelling's *System of Transcendental Idealism*, the work
from which he plagiarized most copiously in *Biographia*, Coleridge
explicitly desires that unity of philosophy and common sense,
transcendentalism and ordinary language, which the two volumes of
Biographia have been seen to fail to achieve. He writes that it 'would
have been well to shew, how much better Schelling's meaning might
have been given in simple common life words.'[21] Coleridge's remarks
on language elsewhere confirm that he did have the means of
expressing the substance of Schelling's philosophy without recourse
to a specialized philosophical terminology. It will be important to
understand how Coleridge's allegiance to Schelling embarrassed his
Kantian theory of poetry. But first it is necessary to recognize
confirmation in this of Coleridge's use of Schelling's own words to
exalt the role of the philosopher to that of a sage condescending to
communicate his insights in a language he does not expect non-
professionals to understand. This purloined, sham authority contrasts
with the popular, collaborative activity of the other Coleridge whose
purpose is to effect philosophical advances through his discriminating, original use of 'simple common life words'.

[21]Reproduced by H. Nidecker in 'Notes marginales de S. T. Coleridge', *Revue de
littérature comparée*, 7 (1927), 740.

Coleridge sometimes describes language as dividing and multiply-
ing its meanings in the way that a basic organism separates and
becomes two distinct organisms. In 1808 he wrote to Southey that he
had 'many a scrap, illustrating the laws by which Language would
polypize ad infinitum – and a compleat History of its original
formation' (*CL* III 58). The history is not extant, but the theory of
desynonymy scattered throughout Coleridge's writings helps substantiate the first claim. One of the most accessible fragments which
explicitly makes the connection between desynonymy and what
might be meant by 'polypize' is the footnote to 'desynonymize' in
chapter 4 of *Biographia.*

There is a sort of *minim immortal* among the animalcula infusiora which has
not naturally either birth, or death, absolute beginning, or absolute end; for
at a certain period a small point appears on its back, which deepens and
lengthens till the creature divides into two, and the same process
recommences in each of the halves now become integral. This may be a
fanciful, but it is by no means a bad emblem of the formation of words, and
may facilitate the conception, how immense a nomenclature may be
organized from a few simple sounds by rational beings in a social state. For
each new application, or excitement, of the same sound, will call forth a
different sensation, which cannot but affect the pronunciation. The after
recollection of the sound, without the same vivid sensation, will modify it
still further; till at length all traces of the original likeness is worn away. (*BL*
I 61n.)[22]

The exact parallel between biological and linguistic development is
certainly 'fanciful'. Coleridge does not distinguish between the
notions of individuation and evolution: the former activity increases
the number of particulars of which we have knowledge; the latter
results in the proliferation of organic life. Coleridge's confusion is to
think that progress and growth are necessarily the same thing. His
own failure to desynonymize here leads him to write around 1815 the
hotch-potch of *Naturphilosophie* published posthumously as *Hints
towards the Formation of a More Comprehensive Theory of Life,* in which his

[22]For the impetus which Coleridge thought a change in pronunciation can lend to
desynonymy, see a marginal note to Milton's poems (*CSC* 561), and *NB* III 3834. I
have found no evidence to suggest that *BL* I 61n. could possibly derive from Horne
Tooke, as Fruman seems to imply, following a marginal note to this passage by John
Thelwall, *Coleridge, The Damaged Archangel,* 98.

mistake draws him away from Kant and towards Schelling. In this work he attempted to define life through 'its tendency to progressive individuation as the law of its direction' (*TofL* 67).[23] He wanted to restore older, animistic theories of life, discredited by empiricism, and to show their further application to mental processes. Mind and nature were to be shown to be operating on the same principles.[24]

Coleridge is engaged in constructing a Schellingian philosophy of identity; and language becomes for him 'by no means a bad emblem' of the converging patterns of mind and nature. This idea appears in its most literal and extravagant form in the notebook entry of around 1808 on desynonymy.

I am persuaded that the chemical technology as far as it was borrowed from Life & Intelligence, half-metaphorically, half-mystically, may be brought back again . . . to the use of psychology in many instances – & above all, in the philosophy of Language – which ought to be experimentative & analytic of the elements of meaning, their double, triple, & quadruple combinations, – of simple aggregation, or of composition by balance of opposition. (*NB* III 3312)[25]

---

[23]See Dorothy Emmet's reservations concerning 'seeing the creative powers of the mind as an extension of the powers of growth', in 'Coleridge on Powers in Mind and Nature', *Coleridge's Variety*, ed. J. Beer (London, 1974), 175. See also *TofL* 41–2, 49–50.

[24]Coleridge contrasts this with Priestley's illusory philosophy of identity: 'Even so did Priestley in his controversy with Price. He stript matter of all its material properties; substituted spiritual powers; and when we expected to find a body, behold! we had nothing but its ghost! the apparition of a defunct substance!', *BL* I 91. He thought that Schelling's philosophy advanced beyond the old empiricist opposition of matter and spirit which had so exercised Priestley.

[25]See M. H. Abrams' helpful summary of the relations between neoplatonic metaphysics and post-Kantian philosophy, in *Natural Supernaturalism* (New York, 1971), 169–72. This book makes no claim to document the influences contributing to the 'living' character of the natural pole of the epistemological relation. What is here described simply as one of the formal requirements of a philosophy of identity was coloured, in Coleridge's thought, by his reading of, amongst others, Plato, the neoplatonists, Bruno, the Cambridge Platonists, Berkeley, Boehme, Cudworth, Swedenborg, the translations of William Law and Thomas Taylor and the *Naturphilosophie* of Schelling, Steffens, Oken, Schubert, Oersted and friends. For commentaries on this vast area, see J. H. Muirhead, *Coleridge as Philosopher* (London, 1939); J. Beer, *Coleridge the Visionary* (London, 1959); P. Deschamps, *La Formation de la pensée de Coleridge (1772–1804)* (Paris, 1964), 372–406; G. Marcel, *Coleridge et Schelling* (Paris, 1971); O. Barfield, *What Coleridge Thought* (Oxford, 1972); and the

Coleridge thinks that the 'analytic' of language which moves it to growth from within is like a polar logic which he calls 'the unceasing polarity of life, as the form of its process' (*TofL* 67). It is this assumed identity which is important for our discussion, rather than the strange details of its possible implementation. In the last-quoted notebook entry about 'the chemical technology' there is a bare sketch of the mechanics of this identity. Distinctions in meaning are assimilated to either negative or positive poles. Change in meaning can be described by evoking the conditions under which a meaning decomposes and reorientates itself once more in relation to the negative and positive poles.[26] The details are again what Coleridge modestly calls 'fanciful', and what is important is the 'emblematic' relation which he thought obtained between life and words. This theorizing grows out of his earlier, better-known intuition that

Nature has her proper interest; & he will know what it is, who believes & feels, that every Thing has a Life of its own, & that we are all *one Life*. A Poet's *Heart* & *Intellect* should be *combined, intimately* combined & *unified*, with the great appearances in Nature – & not merely held in solution & loose mixture with them, in the shape of formal Similes. (*CL* II 864)

The poetic use of language which reveals the 'one Life' is far more intimate with its subject-matter than a medium which needs to preserve its link with life by means of formal notices and declarations of complicity, such as similes. Poetry, as an untranslatable medium, symbolizes an ideal for desynonymy to aim at.[27] Equally, poetry is a

---

most recent and exhaustive treatment of Coleridge's interest in *Naturphilosophie*, T. H. Levere, *Poetry Realized in Nature* (Cambridge, 1981).

[26]*NB* III 3312, 'SYNONOMYSTIC. P. = positive, N. = negative, < = equal to][contradistinguished from > P. Innocent][N. Blameless, guilt[l]ess, of unblemished character. . . . Thus Innocence as distinguished from Virtue, & vice-versa – In both there is a positive, but in each opposite, A Decomposition must take place in the first instance, & then a new Composition, in order for Innocence to become Virtue. It loses a positive – & then the base attracts another different positive, by the higher affinity of the same Base under a different Temperature for the Latter/.' See Levere's discussion of this, *Poetry Realized in Nature*, 98ff.

[27]M. K. Havens, in 'Coleridge on the Evolution of Language', *Studies in Romanticism*, vol. 20, no. 2 (Summer 1981) gives a useful sketch of some of Coleridge's main ideas on desynonymy, but tends to force his poetics into a Schellingian position rather than a Kantian one, seeing poetry as the end result of desynonymy, 169, 182–3.

use of language so adequate to its purpose that it must exemplify that complicity of mind and nature which Coleridge believes all language strives to show.

Coleridge emphasizes the connection between language and life resulting from his philosophy of identity in order to distinguish his philosophy of language from the ideas of eighteenth-century grammarians. Coleridge's early advice to Godwin was 'to destroy the old antithesis of *Words & Things,* elevating, as it were, words into Things, & living Things too' (*CL* I 626). This was to be part of an attempt to 'philosophize' Horne Tooke; and it contains the seeds of the full-blown philosophy which located the principles both of knowledge and of nature within the living structure of language. The Tomalin report of the fifth of Coleridge's lectures on Shakespeare and Milton of 1811–12 records Coleridge's belief that Tooke would have done better to sub-title his *Diversions of Purley* 'Verba Viventia, or "living words"', rather than '*Epea Pteroenta,* "winged words"'. The point of Coleridge insisting on the slogan 'living words' is that 'words are the living products of the living mind and could not be a due medium between the thing and the mind unless they partook of both' (*SC* II 104–5). Coleridge's claim is that we could not use language for the purposes we do if it did not occupy a common ground between mind and nature. The words which express our thoughts are 'living Things' as much as things are 'living words'.[28]

In the letter appended to *On the Constitution of the Church and State,* Coleridge argues that if we understand nature properly we must gain some kind of appreciation of the power which produces material objects – 'what you now call things.' It is this power which gives nature its life and which expresses itself in objects. The 'physiognomic expression' he perceives on the face of things leads Coleridge to believe that nature properly understood must be construed as a language. In some way, things can be the *'ΕΠΕΑ Ζ'ΩΟΝΤΑ* – the living words – of the power which produces them. Through his idea of language Coleridge articulates his philosophy of identity. Language illustrates the progress of knowledge and is also the expression of the powers of growth and production in nature.

[28]See especially, *A* vii–viii.

The reader may now quite justifiably feel that the realm of strict philosophical discussion has been abandoned for an area of 'fanciful' intuitions and correspondences. This is true, and what has happened can perhaps best be described as the replacement of the influence of Kant on Coleridge by that of Schelling. The only kind of philosophy which Kant could approve of would be one which described how the imagination creates a schema in order to bring intuitions to concepts. According to *The Critique of Pure Reason* imagination in this way creates the common ground between the faculties of sensibility and understanding necessary for experience to be possible. This schematism occurs within the limits of our experience, defined by the requirements of the cognitive faculties. By contrast, Schelling believes that the principle producing *nature* outside our experience is the same as the imaginative principle which produces our *experience* of nature. Kant would have thought fundamentally mistaken a philosophy which claimed to establish that we could know anything of things as they exist in themselves outside our experience of them. But many of Coleridge's statements about language are unintelligible without taking Schelling's influence into consideration.

Kant thinks that his critique of judgement is a means of connecting our understanding of nature with our ideas of reason.[29] Nature must be capable of being regarded as conforming to an ideal of unity not given in the understanding, but assumed nevertheless in science. We assume, that is, that the laws of nature conspire to make possible our systematic experience of nature. Schelling dismisses Kant's carefully preserved dualism, and holds that we can *know* that mind and nature function on identical principles. This is no longer a regulative idea of reason producing maxims of reflective judgement which the scientist assumes but does not know: Schelling thinks that mind and nature are different forms of the same activity. This absolute activity is supposed to achieve a consciousness of itself through knowledge of its own objectification in unconscious nature. In Coleridge's paraphrase, it is 'a subject which becomes a subject by the act of constructing itself objectively to itself.' (*BL* I 183 and n.)

Schelling attempts to formulate a system in which epistemology

[29]Kant, *Critique of Judgement,* I 14–18, 36–9.

and ontology are mutually necessary; he tries to identify an absolute necessity underlying both categories. Nevertheless, he still finds it hard to explain how he can know this as a *philosopher*. On his own definition, whatever purposes are working through nature are unconscious and unexpressed. That they are so hidden is a requirement of seeing nature as the objectification of the absolute activity whose consciousness still strives to find a reconstruction of itself in nature. Otherwise, if nature were already conscious, the philosophy of identity would have nothing to identify. Schelling's philosopher, therefore, cannot *show* the identity of nature and mind since he must regard nature as being an unconscious something distinct from his own consciousness, although identical for that absolute activity which is their common principle. It is at this point that art becomes crucial to Schelling's thought. Because art *does* show the objective representation of a conscious purpose, it can therefore show how a philosophy of identity is possible, how 'philosophy must be comprehended' [*aufgefasst*]. Art is a particular case of such an identity, but it gains importance from being the prime example of which *we* have more than a purely intellectual intuition. Art 'reflects for us' the identity intuited by the philosopher. The philosopher's intuition 'becomes objective for the first time through aesthetic production'. Art 'sets forth' what philosophy 'cannot represent outwardly'.[30]

Schelling thinks that it is only through the artist's imagination that we can experience the identity of conscious and unconscious activity – an identity which, for the philosopher, is a postulate necessary to explain how knowledge is possible. But Schelling, unlike Kant, thinks that to say that our experience of this identity is aesthetic does not differentiate art from the purpose of science. Schelling makes the strange claim that 'were science ever to have accomplished its whole task as art has always accomplished its, both would have to converge and become one.'[31] He cannot separate art

---

[30]'System of Transcendental Idealism', in *Philosophies of Art and Beauty*, 356, 367, 372, 373; see R. Wellek, 'The Romantic Age', vol. II, in *A History of Modern Criticism 1750–1950* (London, 1955), 75–6, for a discussion of variations in Schelling's views of the relation between art and philosophy.
[31]Schelling, *Philosophies of Art and Beauty*, 370.

from science other than to say that science is as yet imperfect and unfulfilled. If it were complete it would reveal that nature is an unconscious poem: it would describe an aesthetic experience. This seems to be the consequence of his way of thinking, and is entirely different from the account we have seen Kant give of aesthetic judgement. Kant believes that poetry and poetic imagination have a purpose distinct from the imagination's when it contributes to our knowledge of the world. Poetry gives us a feeling for how we apprehend the world through our understanding; or, where it goes beyond this, it gives us symbols with which alone we can represent ideas of reason just because Kant thinks such ideas can never become for us objects of knowledge.

Coleridge sometimes writes as though he was convinced by Schelling. This is especially true of the essay *On Poesy or Art* which is largely a translation from Schelling's oration *Über das Verhältnis der bildenden Künste zu der Natur*. There Coleridge writes that 'nature itself would give us the impression of a work of art, if we could see the thought which is present at once in the whole and in every part' (*BL* II 255). Since science is presumably endeavouring to understand 'the thought' which explains the design of nature, the scientist must ultimately aim at giving us 'the impression of a work of art'. We shall encounter other statements which seem to support this theory. It contradicts his fundamental opposition of poetry to science in *Biographia* which, on the subject of aesthetics, places him on Kant's rather than Schelling's side of the argument. Coleridge's criticism of Wordsworth, drawing on Kant and Schiller, is quite inconsistent with the Schellingian philosophy of volume I, which his idea of language grew to encompass outside *Biographia*. Again, one is forced to view the use of Schelling's terminology as primarily strategic. The influence of Schelling on Coleridge's later extravagant theological schemes will be dealt with in the last chapter.

THE PHILOSOPHY OF IDENTITY

If Coleridge were solely a Kantian, or exclusively a follower of Schelling, then things would be much simpler for his commentators.

In fact he displays both influences. He thinks it possible to detect in nature the expression of the power which produces natural objects: the 'living words' which describe nature are not only a model of how *we* interpret nature, but express the character of nature as it exists in itself – a view completely unacceptable to Kant. *Biographia* voices Kant's successors' characteristic desire to reinterpret him by showing how they think he should be properly understood.

In spite therefore of his own declarations, I could never believe, that it was possible for him to have meant no more by his *Noumenon,* or THING IN ITSELF, than his mere words express; or that in his own conception he confined the whole *plastic* power to the forms of intellect, leaving for the external cause, for the *materiale* of our sensations, a matter without form, which is doubtless inconceivable. (*BL* I 100)

The reinterpretation of what Kant 'meant' leads Coleridge to plagiarize from Schelling in succeeding chapters. The result is the fragmented sketch of a philosophy of identity in which

even as natural philosophers we must arrive at the same principle from which as transcendental philosophers we set out; that is, in a self-consciousness in which the principium essendi does not stand to the principium cognoscendi in the relation of cause to effect, but both the one and the other are coinherent and identical. (*BL* I 187)

The self-consciousness to which Coleridge and Schelling refer is the absolute activity which tries to know itself in nature. They believe that mind and nature are therefore conceived of as separate for us, although they function as two halves of the same activity. The force of this distinction may now seem illusory, but it was real for Schelling, and for Coleridge when he followed Schelling. It is hard to see how mind and nature can retain their independence within a philosophy of identity: calling them different forms of the same activity seems ambivalent, depending on whether one puts the emphasis on the word 'same' or 'different'. Nor, for that matter, is it easy to see how mind and nature remain distinct from the absolute activity which works through them. But the collapse of this distinction would result in pantheism if, as Coleridge did in *Biographia,* we regard the absolute as God. On the same page as the last passage quoted Coleridge writes that the claim 'that we see all things in God, is a strict philosophical truth.' Schelling denied that his system had pantheistic implications; and pantheism would of course have been unacceptable to a Christian like Coleridge. Coleridge must therefore temporarily have taken Schelling's distinctions seriously. His idea of language does assume the force of Schelling's distinction between mind and nature, while the fact that language expresses the 'living' character of mind and nature is taken to show the identity of principle acting in both.

Coleridge believed that the possibility of a philosophy of identity, which was so prominent a concern of the German philosophy of his own time, was only the contemporary formulation of the perennial philosophical inquiry. He thought that philosophy naturally divided into three traditional approaches to the question. In his *Philosophical Lectures*, philosophers either display an exclusive allegiance to one or other of the poles of the epistemological relation – mind or nature – or else they provide conciliatory arguments for the actual identity of the principles governing these apparent antinomies. Coleridge thinks that philosophy begins by questioning the relation between subject and object, but it only progresses in so far as the answers it arrives at contribute to a philosophy of identity. Furthermore, he thinks that this progress was completed, that 'philosophy had formed its circle and appeared in every possible form' by the time of Epicurus; later philosophers only redescribed the same problem underlying all philosophical debate (*PhL* 116, 263).

For Coleridge, Schelling's 'Dynamic Philosophy' was a particular instance of this recurring structure of philosophical debate. In *Biographia* he described it as 'no other than the system of Pythagoras and of Plato revived and purified from impure mixtures' (*BL* I 180) – a revival in which Schelling had been anticipated by Bruno, and indebted to Kant and Fichte, but had himself completed (*BL* I 103–4).[32] It is this argument which Coleridge adopts as his own

[32]In a MS in the Egerton collection, Coleridge argues that the restoration of a dynamic philosophy had been necessitated by the success of Descartes' philosophy in gaining support for epistemological dualism and for belief in the heterogeneity of mind and nature, *IS* 63–4; see also *BL* I ch. 8. According to Coleridge's interpretation, another early supporter of the philosophy of identity is Bacon. Within

presentation of the perennial philosophical question in the first half of *Biographia*. However, he fails to make clear the connection which he thought such a philosophy forged with his idea of desynonymy. Desynonymy's power to model both the progress of knowledge and growth in nature allows it to measure the proliferation of the Absolute through the languages of the human sciences and the 'living words' of nature. However Coleridge's own characteristic articulation of a philosophy of identity by means of his idea of language is present in *Biographia* only in snatches. The conflict between Schelling's poetics and his own would have become more obvious in ordinary language, and would have ceased being something to be dug out of the obscurities of post-Kantian terminology. Elsewhere, Coleridge does assimilate the near-contemporary form of the perennial philosophical debate, as he understood it, to his ideas on language. The following examples only increase the sense of his repression of a truly original exposition in *Biographia* in the interests of appearing in the charismatic role of the philosopher of transcendental deductions, safely isolated from the political vagaries of 'common life words', and legislating for an ignorant readership.

In *Philosophical Lectures* Coleridge describes how in

the commencement of literature man remained for a time in that unity with nature which gladly concedes to nature the life, thought, and even purposes of man, and on the other hand gives to man himself a disposition to regard himself as part of nature. Soon however he must have begun to detach himself. (*PhL* 343)

In the context of Coleridge's interpretation of the history of philosophy, the present concern must be to repair this detachment and re-establish a philosophy of identity. It has been seen how Coleridge found it hard to believe that Kant could have regarded his critical philosophy as self-sufficient without a complementary philosophy of nature – an opinion in line with the criticism of Kant by Fichte and Schelling. In *Biographia* he caricatures the same deficiency

---

the complementary divisions exmplifying the two possible directions of the philosophical deduction of reality, Plato is more inclined to base himself at the ideal pole of the argument, while Bacon provides a philosophy of nature, *TF* I 490–2.

in the monistic idealism in which Fichte absorbed Kant's problematic realm of things-in-themselves. In the notebooks his sympathy for Fichte's idealism is tempered by what he regards as Fichte's tendency to resolve all experience into the single activity of thinking. According to an entry of 1810, this is the '*thinking* disease' of German idealism which, in its quest for first principles, provides an unnaturally abbreviated description of experience (*NB* III 4012). An earlier entry of 1804 claims that the distinctions which Coleridge thinks Fichte elides are those which 'all languages express'. In keeping his '*Faith* . . . with Fichte', while preserving those distinctions, 'human & of our essence', testified to by language, Coleridge hopes to 'harmonize Philosophy and Common Sense'.[33] More precisely, he thinks that the predominant character of Fichtean idealism, prefigured in Kant, amounts to an exaltation of man's moral state detached from his natural and affective state. Coleridge objects to the exclusive supremacy of 'the rational Will', the practical reason which made possible, in Fichte's opinion, the vocation of man.[34] Drawing on the common-sense tradition of ordinary language philosophy Coleridge argues for a more generous definition of the universal character of humanity in order to enrich Kant's '*stoic* principle' of which Fichte's 'moral system is but a caricature'. For

[33]*NB* II 2382, '1. We *feel*. 2. we perceive or imagine. 3. we *think*. ⁂ These are the three distinct classes of psychological Facts, which all men are conscious of and which all languages express. Hartley, and his followers and the French philosophers endeavour to resolve the latter two into the first/ Leibnitz and Wolff the 1st & 3rd into the second, "der grundkraft (der einzige) ist der Vorstellungskraft" – and (as far as Thought may be considered as self-activity of our Being), = the <Will = the *Ich* or I>/ Stahl and Fichte (and, as I believe, Plotinus, &c to Proclus) resolve the 1st & 2nd into the third. Still however the distinction must remain, alike in all – nor can any one be affirmed hitherto to have succeeded in *explaining* the three into one/. My *Faith* is with Fichte, but never let me lose my reverence for the *three distinctions*, which are as human & of our essence, as those of the 5 senses on which indeed a similar process has been tried.
    So doing I may combine & harmonize Philosophy and Common Sense.'
[34]J. G. Fichte, *Science of Knowledge* (Wissenschaftslehre, 1794–5, 1802), ed. and trans. P. Heath and J. Lachs (New York, 1970), 233, 'reason cannot be theoretical, if it is not practical'; also see *The Vocation of Man* (Die Bestimmung des Menschen, 1800), trans. W. Smith, rev. edn, R. M. Chisholm (New York, 1956), 98–9, 'the practical reason is the root of all reason.'

Coleridge, the stoic principle, unrelieved by any affection, becomes 'false, unnatural, and even immoral'.[35]

Coleridge, then, attacks any philosophy exclusively attached to idealism. Like Schelling, he thinks there must exist a complementary philosophy of nature. His concern to provide a 'real' dimension for idealist philosophy leads him to supplement Fichte's kind of idealism with a philosophy which will show the identity of the principles governing mind and nature, thus closely following Schelling's divergence from Fichte. The 'absolute' identity which Coleridge describes in *The Friend* as his 'ground-work' is indistinguishable from the device with which Schelling undermined Fichte's abandonment of nature in the cause of idealism (*TF* I 520–2). Since Coleridge, as we have seen, thought that language was constructed on the basis of principles shared by mind and nature, individuation and evolution, his remarks about the philosophical grammar of this language indicate the extent of his assimilation of Schelling's position.

In the manuscript 'Logic' Coleridge gives his most detailed account of what he could mean by a philosophical grammar. He emphasizes that he is not speaking of language as a repository of historical and etymological facts, but rather of 'the privilege and high instinct of Language' in enabling us to educate ourselves (Log I 29, 20). He thinks that education through the study of philosophical grammar is a joint product of external nature and the internal faculties of man.[36] All words are the product of a basic linguistic item expressing the identity guaranteeing this correlation. Words are the

production from the Verb Substantive. For all words express either Being or Action, or the predominance of the one over the other. In philosophical Grammar, they are either Substantives, or Verbs, or as Adnouns and Adverbs express the modifications of the one by the other. But the Verb

---

[35] In a letter to J. H. Green of 1817, *CL* IV 791–2; for a description of what Kathleen Coburn calls 'Coleridge's lifelong contention against Kant's ideas of pleasure, duty, happiness', see *NB* III 3558n.; A. J. Harding, *Coleridge and the Idea of Love* (Cambridge, 1974), provides a full-length study.

[36] Log I 12–14, 'What Nature has *educed*, Man educates or trains up. . . . The process of *Educing* from without is correlative to the *evolving* nature from within . . .'; see also *TF* I 500.

Substantive (Am, sum, ειμι) expresses the identity or coinherence of Being and Act. It is the Act of Being. (Log I 27)[37]

This 'formal Science' of grammar is intended to reveal that the fundamental division between parts of speech corresponds to the divisions in philosophy between mind and nature, act and being. The common derivation or production of words from the 'Verb Substantive' means that these divisions are only made on the basis of an underlying unity. The example Coleridge gives to illustrate this is 'the fable of Plato and of the Rabbinical Writers' concerning the derivation of the two sexes from a *homo androgynous*. This myth could, Coleridge speculates, have been originally intended as 'a Grammatical Allegory' (Log I 31). The two poles of verb and substantive can only be understood as different because they share an overall similarity, just in the way that male is opposite to female only because they are both susceptible of the same principle of sexual classification. The picture emerging from Coleridge's grammar is of a community or whole world of language which displays the unified vision of his philosophy of identity.

This community and intersimilitude of the Parts of Speech is a necessary consequence of their common derivation, or rather *production*, from the Verb Substantive. For all words express either Being or Act, or the predominance of the one or the other. We cannot conceive even the merest *Thing*, a Stone for instance, as simply and exclusively *being*, as absolutely passive and

---

[37]See Log II 73; *TT* I 64–5. Compare also Horne Tooke who, as Hazlitt recognized, derived all parts of speech from 'the only two intelligible ones, the Verb and Noun', *Works* XI 54. According to Tooke, where this act of derivation is possible '*there* is the certain source of the whole', although other influencing factors 'forbid the deduction of the *whole* of a language from any one single source', *The Diversions of Purley* (London, 1786–1805), 2 vols, I, 192. Coleridge may well have been influenced by Tooke's conclusion, but he must have thought that his own grammar philosophized Tooke's result, as he had advised Godwin to do in 1800 (*CL* I 625–6). Otherwise Tooke's theory remains a purely genetic one, concerned with 'a mere accident of . . . the formation of words . . . [not] explaining the philosophy of language, which is a very different thing', as Coleridge said of Tooke in 1830 (*TT* I 93). See also J. Fearn, *Anti-Tooke* (London, 1824–1827), 2 vols, who attacked Tooke by insisting on distinguishing etymology from universal grammar, and is usefully discussed in M. C. Yarborough's *John Horne Tooke* (New York, 1926), ch. 5. Fearn produces formalist objections to Tooke's etymological logic similar to the philosophical ambitions in Coleridge's 'Logic', minus the idealism.

actionless. Were it but the act of reflecting the Light by which it is seen, or as the sum of the acts of attraction by which its particles cohere, and the Stone *is* . . . [nor can we imagine an act] as *merely* an act, or without an abiding or continuing Somewhat. (Log I 35)[38]

Coleridge's 'Science of Grammar' provides 'the highest possible external evidence' for 'the perfect identity of Being and Knowing' (Log I 69), and goes beyond the Fichtean formulation of the principle of identity within a monistic idealism.[39] Coleridge's idea of language records the unity of an active universe and a real knowledge, uncovering the principles of their common speech.

If we ask ourselves how we know any thing, that Rose for example or the Nightingale hidden in yonder tree; the reply will be that the rose (rosa subjecta) manifests itself that it renders itself objective, or the object of our perceptions by its colour and its odour and so in the Nightingale by its sound. And what are those but the goings from the subject, its words, its verb, The rose blushes, the Nightingale sings. (Log II 69–70)

Coleridge believes that when the necessity of having a philosophy of identity is admitted, then the use of language can be seen to express its coherence. A passage at the beginning of the tenth of the 'Essays on the Principles of Method' shows the extent to which language lends support to the philosophy of identity.

In a self-conscious and thence reflecting being, no instinct can exist, without engendering the belief of an object corresponding to it, either present or future, real or capable of being realized: much less the instinct, in which humanity itself is grounded: that by which, in every act of conscious perception, we at once identify our being with that of the world without us, and yet place ourselves in contra-distinction to that world. Least of all can this mysterious pre-disposition exist without evolving a belief that the productive power, which is in nature as nature, is essentially one (i.e. of one

[38]See Notebook no. 38, f3 (B. Lib., add. MS 47, 533), 'it has often been objected to Spenser, that his Personifications are now active, and now passive, now the cause inflicting, and now the suffering inflicted. . . . But this is in the very nature of human language & human thought & no error of the Poets!'

[39]Coleridge uses Fichte's formal description of the principles of identity and contradiction from the *Wissenschaftslehre* in Log II 80, but he expresses dissatisfaction with Fichte's exclusive commitment to the idealist pole of mind and reason: 'In short the subject of these boasted principles is a mere assertion of the act of reflection implying the Reason as one universal in all individual reasoners – ', Log II 86.

kind) with the intelligence, which is in the human mind above nature: however disfigured this belief may become, by accidental forms or accompaniments, and though like heat in the thawing of ice, it may appear only in its effects. So universally has this conviction leavened the very substance of all discourse, that there is no language on earth in which a man can abjure it as a prejudice, without employing terms and conjunctions that suppose its reality, with a feeling very different from that which accompanies a figurative or metaphorical use of words. (*TF* I 497–8)

In this passage, the appeal to language characteristic of the British opponents of Hume – Kames, Reid, Beattie, Alison and Jeffrey – feeds into a philosophy taken from the German tradition. The reference to beliefs which have 'leavened the very substance of all discourse' strongly recalls the common-sense trust in language. But 'the instinct, in which humanity itself is grounded' and to which the beliefs embedded in language testify is derived by Coleridge from the absolute activity underpinning Schelling's philosophy of identity – 'evolving a belief that the productive power, which is in nature as nature, is essentially one (i.e. of one kind) with the intelligence, which is in the human mind above nature.' Coleridge's philosophical grammar articulates his characteristic assimilation of the two traditions. In *Biographia,* however, he preferred to ignore the form of argument which his theory of desynonymy had suggested, leaving its presence in that work suggestively subliminal. Instead of drawing philosophical conclusions from distinctions in language, he made a great show of arguing in exactly the opposite direction. The voice which would have been his was only heard intermittently.

CHAPTER FOUR

Coleridge's Radical Argument

LANGUAGE AND THE RADICAL TRADITION

This chapter will try to describe the kind of radicalism resulting from Coleridge's critical response to his own and others' language: the radicalism whose methodological implications were repressed in *Biographia*. Coleridge's views on language have shown that he had available the means to express his most exotic philosophical borrowings in 'simple, common life words'. In disguising this fact in transcendentalist terminology, he hides from himself his radical notion that philosophical discovery springs from the discriminating use of a shared language. But Coleridge often describes man unequivocally as a progressive creature, despite his refusal to draw the appropriate political conclusions. In 1795 he wrote that 'we are progressive and must not rest content with present Blessings. Our Almighty Parent hath therefore given to us Imagination . . .' (*LPR* 339). In his last published work he was still trying to tame this belief within the existing political hierarchy. Mankind is not just intellectually progressive, for in his *Lay Sermons* Coleridge describes the radical impulse as residing in man's 'nature'. The 'Nature of Man' or 'the natural Man' is the character in which humanity is regarded as advancing by Coleridge, morally and politically, as well as scientifically. He made it a matter of philosophical principle to record this progress in all forms of human experience. Poetic language is crucial for his radicalism because he thinks it alone can suggest the progressive potential in human experience which goes beyond all existing definitions. Eventually we shall see that this is Coleridge's way of defining poetic artifice. Poetry, self-consciously ideal, challenges the pretensions to adequacy of any systematic description of human nature.

Coleridge criticizes radical theories which explain progress as though human nature was an easily understood mechanism. In contrast to these closed theories of human nature, he argued for an element in our progress beyond the reach of scientific vocabulary. The point is to find philosophical principles which do justice to the progressive impulse in all forms of human experience. A preoccupation of all his writings is the desire for as wide a definition of human nature as possible. The young Coleridge was greatly attracted to the radical theories of Hartley, Priestley and Godwin. However, there existed a problem for him in the fact that the radical tradition in English thought had always paid scant respect to linguistic usage. These thinkers, who advocated wholesale transcendence of our human limitations, were not interested in how language might express what is characteristic in human nature. But Coleridge sought an idea of language which would express what is natural to human beings in such a way as to encourage their efforts to progress and better their condition. His ideas on desynonymy were intended to illustrate a progress which is measured against a background of common sense.

From Coleridge's earliest writings onward there can be found the habit of criticizing narrow views of human nature by drawing attention to the deficiencies of the language used. As with desynonymy, critical awareness leads to philosophical distinction. Godwin, Tooke, Burke and Pitt are all attacked for their poor understanding, or deliberately partial use of language. Coleridge also blames the critical reception of *The Friend* on the limitations of the contemporary public's understanding of literary and philosophical means of expression. The *Lay Sermons* again show him trying to do justice to the whole of human experience, scientific, political, moral and religious within a literary form. The awareness of the expressive power and range of language – a power represented for Coleridge by poetry – is necessary for understanding his ambitions in these writings. He regards poetry as the exemplary use of a language generous enough to describe human nature when it escapes the definitions of all sciences and forms of thought: poetry becomes the symbol for the catholic understanding which they all desire.

Thinkers in the radical tradition of British thought from Bacon to Bentham view language as hopelessly imprecise, and in need of replacement by a code approximating much more closely to a mathematical or scientific ideal. Although Bacon acknowledged the expressive value of language in matters of religion and poetry, he prepared the way for the exclusively scientific attitude of his followers in the Royal Society.[1] John Wilkins is an example of a Baconian so disillusioned with the humanistic side of language, with its ineradicable complexities and ambiguities, that he wants to construct an entirely new language on a scientific model. In Wilkins' view, a grammar which systematizes already existing and instituted languages will suffer from their unnecessary ambiguities, the grammar being 'adapted to what was already in being, rather than the Rule of making it so.' Instead of grammar being suited to the language, the language must be made to suit the ideal grammar.[2]

Any tendency to value the expressive quality of language was opposed in the eighteenth century by the scientific, materialist school of thinking which parallels the attitude represented by Wilkins in the seventeenth century. Hartley and Priestley both believed in one standard of absolute certainty, mathematical in nature, and not dependent on anything so variable as human nature. In *The Diversions of Purley* Horne Tooke claimed that his own work superseded that of James Harris who had written *Hermes*, a treatise on grammar, in 1751. Harris did value the expressive character of language, believing that 'a SYMBOL or SIGN . . . is wholly in our own power, as depending singly for its existence on our imagination.'[3] But Horne Tooke thought, with the other radicals, that the objectivity of his study depended on a disregard for the imaginative expression of human nature in language. 'In this our inquiry, my dear Sir, we are not poets

[1] F. Bacon, *Works,* ed. Ellis and Spedding (London, 1858), 7 vols, III 382; IV 316–17. See R. F. Jones, *Ancients and Moderns* (Washington, 1961), 91.

[2] J. Wilkins, *An Essay Towards a Real Character and a Philosophical Language* (London, 1668), 19, 21.

[3] J. Harris, *Hermes* (London, 1751, 1765), 337, 333 and n.

nor dancers, but anatomists.'[4] Tooke's etymological anatomy dislocates language entirely from its expressive uses. In Hazlitt's words, he 'saw language stripped of the clothing of habit or sentiment.'[5]

Hartley, Priestley, Godwin and Bentham saw humanity moving inevitably along the road to perfection. But in describing this perfection those necessitarians adopt a closed view of human nature, and declare that it is in this character only that man can advance. Any concern for the variety of human expression is therefore regarded as distracting from this singleminded purpose. Language is an institution in need of drastic reform, deserving the treatment meted out, for example, by Priestley to the idea of an established system of education, or by Godwin to the concept of law.[6] Romantics like Coleridge and Hazlitt objected only to the diminished character in which human nature is supposed to progress.

Ultimate values for Hartley and his followers are abstract and mathematical. In trying to free man from the bondage of inherited institutions they force him to submit to a set of even stricter categories. This was Coleridge's point of disagreement with their tradition. The visual paradigm of knowledge typical of British empiricism eventually combines most strikingly with the necessitarian doctrine of man's inevitable progress in Bentham's *Panopticon*, his plan for a model prison. Here the despotism of the prison inspector's total supervision is supposed to deprive men of the power to do evil, and so to facilitate their moral reformation and general improvement. The despotism of the eye becomes the experimental condition under which the radical tradition may flourish. As Bentham makes frighteningly clear, he regarded his project as embodying a principle which could be applied more generally. Governments would find it 'a very useful instrument' whose application Bentham recommends to 'factories, mad-houses, hospi-

[4] J. Horne Tooke, *The Diversions of Purley,* II 95. Tooke looks back to Bacon at 19, and to Wilkins at I 124–6, and regards common-sense philosophy as 'nonsense', I 281.

[5] Hazlitt, *Works,* XI 54.

[6] J. Priestley, *An Essay on The First Principles of Government* (London, 1768, 1771), 83–98; W. Godwin, *An Enquiry Concerning Political Justice* (London, 1793), 2 vols, II 769–80.

tals, and even to schools'.[7] Bentham's model of effective knowledge thus encourages us to construe society on the analogy of a prison: as closed a system as it is possible to imagine.

Bentham, far from being able to regard linguistic usage as illustrative of human potential, thought 'that the tyranny of language makes its sport of scientific industry.'[8] Hartley wanted to replace our present language with something that he can only describe as a kind of algebra. The mark of progress is to become spiritualized, and those who 'have spiritualized men's understandings . . . taught them to use words in reasoning, as algebraists do symbols.'[9] Priestley's study of language reveals it to be progressing towards a state in which all that is redundant, deficient, and ambiguous in it will be replaced. Literary critics who are devoted to language as it is used, and who do not have the vision of perfection proper to the philosopher, are reactionaries preserving linguistic imperfection, and not to be listened to.[10] Godwin also wants the language of the necessitarian philosopher to prevail over the language in use which at present displays a confused mixture of necessitarian and libertarian assumptions. Like Priestley, he sees the need for language to be known 'as an abstract science'.[11]

It is therefore in complete contrast to the radical tradition in British thought that Coleridge tries to illustrate his belief in man's progressive character by means of the language in use whose undesynonymizable ideal is a poetic usage adequate to express human nature in all its complexity, symbolizing its progressive potential. Since this view is absent from the British thinkers whose radicalism first attracted him, Coleridge's thought on the subject begins in a quandary. Gradually his ambitions for describing human progress

[7]Quoted in Halévy, *The Growth of Philosophical Radicalism*, 82–4.
[8]J. Bentham, *Of Laws in General*, ed. H. L. A. Hart (London, 1970), 277.
[9]D. Hartley, *Observations on Man* (London, 1749), 2 vols, edited by Priestley as *Hartley's Theory of the Human Mind* (London, 1775), 28. Priestley's exclusion of Hartley's theology from his edition makes more obvious the continuity between Hartley and Bentham.
[10]J. Priestley, *A Course of Lectures on The Theory of Language and Universal Grammar* (Warrington, 1762), 180–2; Priestley's approval of 'Figurative expressions' is on the understanding that they 'are scarce considered and attended to as *words*', *A Course of Lectures on Oratory and Criticism* (London, 1777), 77.
[11]Godwin, *Enquiry*, I 317; Priestley, *A Course of Lectures*, 301–2.

become clearer. Eventually it is to the German philosophical tradition – not the British – and to Kant and Schiller in particular, that Coleridge's practical understanding of poetry leads.

THE NOTEBOOKS, GODWIN AND TOOKE

In the 1790s Coleridge's necessitarian dogmatism is undeniable and easily documented. But in the notebooks of that period there was already the suggestion of a more flexible attitude towards constantly increasing apprehension of truth. Later, in 1804, Coleridge was to describe these journals as 'the history of my own mind for my own improvement' (*NB* II 2368), and these personal gains begin, early in his life, to escape any dogmatic net in which his public theorizing might try to trap them. Here, around 1795–96, he advocates his radicalism by quoting Milton, and by asserting an image of truth unconstrained by an overweening sense of conformity or tradition. 'Truth is compared in scripture to a streaming fountain; if her waters flow not in perpetual progression, they stagnate into a muddy pool of conformity & tradition. Milton' (*NB* I 119). Entries like this one are peculiarly appropriate in their setting within the literature of the notebooks, that perpetual, subterranean accompaniment to Coleridge's published writings which was not subject to the same conventional restraints and expectations.

Perhaps we are seeing philosophical implications in what, after all, is a straightforward dichotomy between public argument and private, introspective expression. But when Coleridge is exercised by the problem of definition the medium necessarily becomes philosophically important. The way in which a philosophy of human nature is written is for him a large part of the philosophical issue at stake. This preoccupation lends a detectable pattern to his speculative writings and suggests reasons for the variety in the forms of expression which he uses. In the notebooks, for example, he writes entirely on his own terms. He can always reply to impatience on the part of an imaginary reader by appealing to the rudimentary form of expression appropriate to their experimental character. Essentially, they are an 'exercise', or 'acts of obedience to the apostolic command of Trying all things' (*NB*

II 2406; III 3881). Less obviously, though, they constitute a reasoned alternative to the completeness expected of any public form of communication. Since we can scarcely have any preconceptions about them, their fragmentariness is acceptable even though we know that Coleridge was not averse to the thought of their being published (*NB* III 3881). The private freedom of this form of writing begins to have general implications for the public writings: Coleridge's assiduous note-taking begins to suggest philosophical reservations as regards the sufficiency of the public writings. Coleridge wrote in an early notebook entry of 1799 about this contrast between public and private. 'Man but half an animal without drawing – but yet he is not meant to be able to communicate all the greater part of his Being must [be] solitary – even of his Consciousness' (*NB* I 524). In a later refurbishing of substantially the same entry the meaning of 'meant' and 'must' is made more explicit. Investigating human nature is now linked to questioning the adequacy of the media of communication.

Without Drawing I feel myself but half invested with Language – Music too is wanting to me. – But yet tho' one should unite Poetry, Draftman's-ship & Music – the greater and perhaps nobler parts of one's nature, must be solitary – Man exists herein to himself & to God alone/ – Yea in how much only to God – how much lies below his own Consciousness. (*NB* I 1554)

In this entry of 1803 different media compete with each other in filling out a concept of language which can express 'one's nature'; and these media themselves must retreat before an essential solitude, a private, subconscious existence which eventually God alone can comprehend.

In a letter of March 1796, Coleridge expressed dissatisfaction with Priestley's theology, criticizing his unwillingness to allow for '*Incomprehensibility*' in his theory. This contrasts with the continuing favour shown to Priestley's mentor, Hartley, who remains, in a letter to Thomas Poole of November, a 'great master of *Christian Philosophy*' (*CL* I 192–3). The inconsistency is explained when we remember that Priestley's edition of Hartley's *Observations on Man* limits Hartley to a theory of mind found in the first volume, depriving his theory of the scriptural dimension of the second volume praised in *Biographia* (*BL* I 84). Coleridge was interested by what this chapter will describe as the religious *transposition* of the thought of philosophers who, like Hartley, were apparently bound by a limiting physical or mathematical system. He describes Newton as one of the 'material theists' (*NB* I 203), and was familiar with his religious writings (*NB* I 83, 88 & n.). He read Hartley in the edition of Pistorius – an edition which, unlike Priestley's, pays great attention to Hartley's theology (*NB* I 120 & n.). Coleridge, unlike a modern reader of, say, Newton, seems to have found it quite natural to move from an author's formal theoretical philosophy to its extension in scriptural exegesis. Later he regarded the possible correlates for a theory as even more diverse and in, for example, the *Lay Sermons*, politics, religion and aesthetics combine to enrich an originally abstract theory of human nature. But this dissatisfaction with a single form of definition had been evident from an early age.

Coleridge's criticism of Godwin in a letter to him of 22 September 1800 also takes the form of drawing his attention to the philosophical implications of the medium in which he writes.

I wish you to write a book on the power of words, and the processes by which human feelings form affinities with them – in short, I wish you to *philosophize* Horn Tooke's System, and to solve the great Questions – whether there be reason to hold, that an action bearing all the *semblance* of pre-designing Consciousness may yet be simply organic, & whether a *series* of such actions are possible – and close on the heels of this question would follow the old 'Is Logic the Essence of Thinking?' in other words – Is thinking impossible without arbitrary signs? & – how far is the word 'arbitrary' a misnomer? Are not words &c parts and germinations of the Plant? and what is the Law of their Growth? In something of this order I would endeavor to destroy the old antithesis of *Words & Things,* elevating, as it were, words into Things, & living Things too. (*CL* I 625–6)

It has already been suggested that this passage anticipates Coleridge's later philosophy of identity in which language is taken as evidence for a common ground or principle shared by mind and nature, thought and things. Coleridge thinks that a proper understanding of language, which would replace Tooke's grammar, reconciles these opposites by showing that they are inevitably described in terms of each other. He is intent on turning Godwin's desire at that time to increase his philosophical appeal by writing for the theatre into practical criticism of the medium of his thought. If Godwin could only achieve this linguistic orientation, then his philosophical outlook would change. Instead of trying to gain support for his ideas through a new, dramatic mode of presentation, he could do this by writing a new philosophy which would be a philosophy of language. So, to continue Coleridge's plan for Godwin, he was 'to exhibit before a larger & more respectable Multitude, than a Theatre presents to you, & in a new part – that of a Poet employing his philosophic knowledge practically' (*CL* I 636). If, as Coleridge thought, a proper understanding of language has important philosophical implications, then the poet's sensitivity to language will be a powerful philosophical weapon. With this poetic enrichment of Godwin's philosophical role Coleridge can now return to a favourable discussion of Godwinian radicalism. Transformed into a philosophy of language through a critical consciousness of its own medium, Godwin's theory of 'moral progressiveness' can appeal to a much wider audience. For, concludes Coleridge, 'he who reasons best on the side of that universal Wish will be [the] most popular philosopher' (*CL* I 636).

Coleridge was at least making attempts to procure Horne Tooke's *Diversions of Purley* by September 1798, and he described the man himself in a letter to Thomas Wedgwood of January 1800, in which he qualified criticism of Tooke's personal manner with respect for the linguistic orientation of his thought:

He is a clear-headed old man, as every man needs must be who attends to the real import of words; but there is a sort of charlatannery in his manner that did not please me. He makes such a mystery & difficulty out of plain & palpable Things. (*CL* I 559)

The 'mystery' which Coleridge objects to as indulgence on the part of Tooke is obviously not that open-ended quality prized by Bacon, Hazlitt and Keats. It is more explicable as the kind of mystery condemned in Coleridge's allegory of 1795, 'A Letter from Liberty to Her Dear Friend Famine'. Here 'mystery' is linked with 'Despotism', and this fits the mechanical authoritarianism of Tooke's obscure etymologies. Alternatively, we could remember Coleridge's strictures on Pitt's 'Mystery concealing Meanness' where language, instead of being mechanically predictable, is put to the equally suspect use of being systematically misleading (*LPR* 63). This will be dealt with in more detail in the next section. Tooke, on either interpretation of his 'mystery', represents a false contribution of the study of language to philosophy. His appreciation of the central role of a study of language in any explanation of how we think is salutary; his actual discussion of the problem is misguided, and so in need of philosophizing. The use of Tooke as example was not only tactful in the attempt to reform Godwin, but represented a more profitable synthesis for Coleridge himself.

FLIES IN AMBER – BURKE AND PITT

In Coleridge's early writings there is a recurring argument which tries to reform closed and narrow philosophical views of human nature by showing implications to the contrary in the medium in which these views are expressed. Coleridge's desire for a truly comprehensive understanding of experience leads to the practical criticism of the language of restrictive views. Early notebook entries suggest his growing interest in how language can be adequate to convey the progress of the human mind. His political criticism, primarily of Burke and Pitt, continues this inquiry. In a letter to John Prior Estlin of July 1797, Coleridge shows a Burkean acceptance of the fact that we all 'must necessarily be prejudiced' (*CL* I 337). But, in 1795, he had attacked the baleful influence of prejudice upon Burke's thought. Coleridge uses the idea of an imbalance in evidence being equivalent to a word in a language accruing a disproportionate power.

Susceptibility of Truth depends on the temper of our Hearts more than even on the strength of our Understandings. The mind is predisposed by its situations: and when the prejudices of a man are strong, the most overpowering Evidence becomes weak. He 'meets with darkness in the day-time, and gropes in the noon-day as in night.' Some unmeaning Term generally becomes the Watch-word, and acquires almost a mechanical power over his frame. (*LPR* 52)

That Burke is intended here (although not mentioned) is suggested by the examples Coleridge gives of such watch-words. 'The favourite phrases of the present Day are — "It may be very well in *Theory*" and the "effects of Jacobine Principles"' (*LPR* 52–3).[12] It is hard not to recognize the language in question as Burke's, criticized by Tom Paine.[13] Burke uses the power of language to prejudice theory, rather than broadening and enriching it after the Coleridgean pattern. His language limits rather than extends thought. Coleridge thinks this travesty can be accomplished either in the manner of Burke or in the manner of Pitt. Burke is responsive to the power of human feeling; Pitt exploits it coldly and callously. Burke remains admirable in his excesses; Pitt does not. Burke is the 'Hercules Furens of Oratory' (*LPR* 62–3), his conspicuously creative use of language a dazzling distraction from the truth. Coleridge writes scornfully to Poole in 1796 that Burke's *Letter to A Noble Lord* is 'as contemptible in style as in matter — it is sad stuff' (*CL* I 195). But a month earlier, in the first number of *The Watchman* (1 March 1796), his delight in Burke's language carried the day, as it would in subsequent references in less embattled times. He extols Burke's facility for 'remote analogies', and his ability 'to argue *by* metaphors' (*TW* 31). In a later notebook entry he groups Burke with Jeremy Taylor and Shakespeare as writers most in harmony with the genius of their native language, its 'mono-syllabic, naturalizing, and marvellously metaphorical Spirit' (*NB* II 2431). In 1796, however, Coleridge was deeply suspicious of this facility. Burke's deception is exposed in a comparison with Plato in which Plato is presented as the philosopher of a closed system of ideal

---

[12]Coleridge did not think Pitt capable of manufacturing such watch-words — 'not a sentence of Mr Pitt's has ever been quoted, or formed the favourite phrase of the day — a thing unexampled in any man of equal reputation' *EOT* I 224; Pitt found his watch-words ready-made, see *EOT* I 367. See also his condemnation of 'fanaticism, which masters the feelings more especially by indistinct watch-words' (*BL* II 117).

[13]Paine, *The Rights of Man,* 59–60, 73, 212; Paine attacks Burke's use of language throughout, but he does so from a traditionally empiricist viewpoint, objecting when we cannot 'connect any certain idea with the words.' Burke had already, as early as 1757, argued for the legitimate independence of words and images or ideas in their separate effects, maintaining that words themselves can affect us 'as strongly as things in nature do, and sometimes much more strongly', *A Philosophical Enquiry into the Origin of Our Ideas of the Sublime and Beautiful,* V, especially 174–5, 184.

worlds opposed to any experimental theory. But this disingenuous view is then dismissed by Coleridge's ironic recollection that Plato's thought unfolded into a programmatic theory of human nature and the projection of an ideal human community. His thought was progressive and utopian, and therefore inimical to Burke, whose prejudices now appear disablingly limited in comparison, and whose view of human nature seems as stunted as that of any 'speculators' he condemns. The 'flies and weeds' of Burke were preserved in 'the purest amber', but in 1796 Coleridge still thought they were flies and weeds.[14]

The other exploiter of language is Pitt: the 'mystery' in Pitt's use of language stops his words from having any clear meaning at all. The political opposition to Pitt, led by Fox, thought him contrary on principle: he spoke in order to be misunderstood (*LPR* 63n). Coleridge's main critique was expressed in *The Watchman* and in the columns of *The Morning Post* — articles and reports later reprinted by his daughter in her edition of *Essays on His Own Times*. In *The Watchman*, Coleridge indulges in a laboured joke of a hand-bill advertising a reward for the recovery of the meaning lost by Pitt in a speech of the previous Monday night (*TW* 47–8). The humour may be heavy but the point is clear, and its political relevance momentous. Pitt's linguistic virtuosity enables him to trade in perpetual equivocation; and this abdication of any responsibility for telling the truth or expressing a consistent meaning allows a bloody war with France to continue unabated. Pitt breaches the barrier between word and thing all right; but his language is a mystifying thing which obscures rather than informs us of the structure of reality. Pitt is able to equivocate on war and peace because of his isolation of what should be a relational medium. He is as self-conscious of his medium as Coleridge advised Godwin to be, but for the opposite reasons. As will be seen, it was just this isolation of language — treating it as monistic, intransitive, sequestered from the world of human actions — which it was Coleridge's and Wordsworth's 'motives, poetical & political' to

[14]*W* 34; *TF* II 22 (1809): 'the very Flies and Weeds of BURKE shine to us through the purest amber, imperishably enshrined, and valuable from the precious material of their embalmment.'

oppose by means of the idea of language embodied in the *Lyrical Ballads* (*CL* II 665–6).

Almost exactly four years later, in 1800, Coleridge produced an exhaustive analysis of Pitt. His character of Pitt is a forerunner of the kind of study in depth which found its most rounded expression in Hazlitt's gallery of *The Spirit of the Age,* where individual biography lends a focus for historical explanation. When Hazlitt himself first writes on Burke and Pitt in 1806, he reiterates many of the points Coleridge had already made.[15] Coleridge in 1800 was prepared to grant Burke the '*prescience*' of a 'great man'. This need not suggest political sympathy. Hazlitt, a militant radical, was still prepared to allow Burke in 1806 'profound legislative wisdom' – one of a series of compliments. Later, looking back on this and to his character of Burke of 1807, he wryly disowned his belief that he 'could do justice or more than justice, to an enemy, without betraying a cause.'[16] In Coleridge's view it is the parasitical nature of the political relationship of Pitt to Burke, and of Pitt's language to Burke's language, which renders Burke's definitions 'philosophical' in comparison with the derivative reasoning and eloquence of the younger man. Burke, at his best, explores the humanity of language, its expressive metaphorical life, while at the same time distracting us from the real nature of the evidence with which his argument purports to deal. Pitt uses words at a still further remove from the truth by employing Burke's phraseology without understanding it, simply for the effect which it

---

[15]See, for instance, the way Pitt is presented by Hazlitt as a living example of the limitations of an empirical philosophy with no place for the imagination, agent of our future self and of our knowledge of other minds. Pitt suffers from exactly the same epistemological disqualification as the kind of empiricism criticized in Hazlitt's *An Essay on The Principles of Human Action* a year earlier. 'Having no insight into human nature, no sympathy with the passions of men, or apprehension of their real designs, he seemed perfectly insensible to the consequences of things, and would believe nothing until it actually happened . . . he never seemed to consider . . . that future events were in our own power' (*Works* I 109). It was the language deriving from this empiricism which Burke, in Coleridge's opinion, 'beat him [Pitt] out of' (*EOT* I 223).

[16]*EOT* I 223. In *Biographia* Burke is accorded the vatic status of a true scientist with genuine insight into the principles of life (*BL* I 125). Hazlitt, *Works,* I 111; VII 301n.

produces. Pitt does not only talk in abstractions, but at a departure from abstractions themselves:

Call upon him to particularize a crime, and he exclaims – JACOBINISM! Abstractions defined by abstractions! Generalities defined by generalities! As a Minister of Finance, he is still, as ever, the man of words, and abstractions! . . . One character pervades his whole being. Words on words, finely arranged, and so dexterously consequent, that the whole bears the semblance of argument, and still keeps awake a sense of surprise – but when all is done, nothing rememberable has been said. . . . (*EOT* I 223–4)

Burke's genius is the origin of Pitt's talent.[17] The difference between the two men's use of language instructs the observant philosopher, thinks Coleridge, in the political force of words:

the philosopher neither admires nor condemns, but listens to him with a deep and solemn interest, tracing in the effects of his eloquence the power of words and phrases, and that peculiar constitution of human affairs in their present state, which so eminently favours this power. (*EOT* I 225)

Pitt's pernicious use of language to obfuscate knowledge is explained by Coleridge as being the result of an extraordinary education, as emotionally crippling as anything James Mill and Bentham might have devised. The public performances Pitt was encouraged to give as a child-orator set in motion a psychological mechanism which conditioned his future employment of language. Language ceased to be informative, and functioned instead on a basis of stimulus and response: 'Not the *thing* on which he was speaking, but the praises to be gained by the speech, were present to his intuition; hence he associated all the operations of his faculties with words, and all his pleasures with the surprise excited by them' (*EOT* I 219–20).

That is why Pitt could treat the value-laden rhetoric of Burke as though it were morally neutral. Burke, with admirable art, used the power of language to establish his prejudices; but Pitt treated Burke's language as though it just happened to elicit a public response useful for his own political purposes. To regard Coleridge's criticism of Pitt's language as extravagant is to ignore its point. It is just such a contemporary undervaluing of the moral role of language that he is

[17]*EOT* I 223; and see J. Colmer, *Coleridge, Critic of Society* (London, 1959), 59, 62, 64.

attacking. Practical criticism of Pitt's language is not the contingent accompaniment of Coleridge's dismay that it was 'so denaturalised . . . [a] spirit, on whose wisdom and philanthropy the lives and living enjoyments of so many millions of human beings were made unavoidably dependent' (*EOT* I 221). The travesty of language enables the political immorality, as he argued in January of the same year, 1800, in his critical notice of *Lord Grenville's Note*. In this short polemic he argues, as he advised Godwin to do in the same year, as 'a Poet employing his philosophic knowledge practically'.

We think *in* words, and reason *by* words. – The man who, while he is speaking or writing his native language, uses words inaccurately, and combines them inconsequentially, may be fairly presumed to be a lax and slovenly reasoner. False reasoning is perhaps never wholly harmless; but it becomes an enormous evil, when the reasoning, and the passions which accompany it, are to be followed by the sacrifice of tens of thousands. If this be a true statement, even a merely verbal criticism on an important State-paper merits the attention of the public; and believing that it is a true statement, we shall proceed to consider Lord Grenville's Note, relatively to the language and stile. (*EOT* I 114)[18]

And this he does to considerable effect, exposing 'ministerial *duplicity*' in stylistic ambiguities: how Windham's writings 'will die of a *plethora* of meaning'; how ministers will confound 'a metaphor and a reality' when this is politically convenient (*EOT* I 114–16, 198). Above all, there is present in the practical criticism of political jargon Coleridge's own respect for his language as a basic tool of philo-sophical discrimination. It is the same philosophical and political

[18]Later Cobbett was to use his own *Grammar* as an instrument of political criticism for the same reason. 'Confusedness in words can proceed from nothing but confusedness in the thoughts which give rise to them. These things may be of trifling importance when the actors move in private life; but, when the happiness of millions of men is at stake, they are of importance not easily to be described', *A Grammar of the English Language* . . . (London, 1819, 1823), 185. Coleridge and Cobbett were at the polite end of a growing awareness of the ideological interests served by apparently impartial uses of language, an awareness focused by Burke's brilliant rhetoric. Working-class polemicists tried to turn the independent power Burke attributed to words against him, exposing his tendentiousness sometimes by gleefully adopting the implications of his language, sometimes by showing that public virtues are best defined as private vices – a tactic which achieved its literary apotheosis in Blake. See especially *A Political Dictionary, by the late Charles Piggot* (London, 1795).

sensitivity to language which created Coleridge's own difficulties with ideologically competing terminologies, transcendentalist and 'common life', in *Biographia*.

PRINCIPLES AND THE FRIEND

The 'Friend' is a secret which I have entrusted to the public; and, unlike most secrets, it hath been well kept.[19]

During the gap in Coleridge's published theoretical and polemical writings, between the last articles in *The Morning Post* of 1802 (mostly reiterating points made in 1800) and the first issues of *The Friend* ('Prospectus' 1808; no. 1, 1809), the pattern of radical argument continues within his private writings. In a letter of 1801 he told Humphrey Davy of his philosophical interest in language and again reaffirmed his belief in the poet's philosophical importance: 'the affinities of the Feelings with Words & Ideas' are best discovered through an investigation of the nature of poetry. Such an investigation 'would supersede all the Books of Metaphysics hitherto written and all the Books of Morals too' (*CL* II 671). The previous October he had told Davy of his ambition to write an 'Essay on the Elements of Poetry' which 'would in reality be a *disguised* System of Morals & Politics' (*CL* I 632). This otherwise alarming conceptual leap or transposition from poetry to metaphysics, morals and politics will, I hope, be more easily understood now. It does not signify the reduction of poetry to something else. Instead, Coleridge's transposition registers the idea of a philosophy which, because it deals with human nature, does not define its subject-matter within a single, closed system. It resists artificial uniformity by being critically conscious of its own medium, prepared to change its form of expression if it becomes dogmatic or restrictive. Poetry, representing language at its most self-conscious, becomes illustrative for Coleridge of a correct philosophical attitude. In its generous awareness of the capability and variety of human expression it symbolizes an ideal for morals and metaphysics. Poetry is not tailored to fit Coleridge's

[19]T. Allsop, *Letters, Conversations and Recollections of S. T. Coleridge* (London, 1836), 2 vols, I, 233.

theoretical beliefs and doctrines: it itself has theoretical implications concerning the form such doctrines ought to take. The alternative argument of *Biographia,* the reverse of its declared aim of deducing the nature of poetry from philosophy, is beginning to take shape.

By 1808, back in England after travelling in Malta and Italy, Coleridge was lecturing at the Royal Institution on 'Poetry and Principles of Taste'; and in the same year he issued the first Prospectus of *The Friend* which was published from June 1809. Early on in *The Friend* he opposed '*verbal* truth' to '*moral* truth', and noted that in the second category language is necessarily involved in a richer capacity than in the first. Language is expressive as well as extensional: words correspond to thoughts as much as to things; and this expressive logic of language preserves the personal character of an utterance, while submitting it to a disciplined order which ensures the communication of its meaning to others. 'In *moral* truth, we moreover involve the intention of the speaker, that his words should correspond to his thoughts in the sense in which he expects them to be understood by others . . .' (*TF* II 42). Coleridge thinks this constitutes the meaning of a word. Later, discussing the untranslatability of poetry in chapter 22 of *Biographia,* he writes:

I include in the *meaning* of a word not only its correspondent object, but likewise all the associations which it recalls. For language is framed to convey not the object alone, but likewise the character, mood and intentions of the person who is representing it. (*BL* II 115–16)

It is only when we include the intentional aspect that we can lay claim to have considered 'the total impression left by such words': and this is to accept that language is not a thing of 'moral indifference', but something which describes things from a moral or immoral point of view. It is to realize 'that we may relate a fact accurately and nevertheless deceive grossly and wickedly' (*TF* II 47). Language is made up of 'moral Acts' and is the vehicle of practical reason, obedient to its command to convey an '*adequate* notion' or, if that is impossible, at least a '*right* notion' of whatever is under discussion. The criterion of 'adequacy' comes from Spinoza's *Ethics*; but Coleridge's unspoken standard of adequacy and rightness is poetry which no translation can enhance (*TF* II 59, 43).

The Friend is a huge essay in communication of this kind: it tries to make public and common currency of difficult philosophical ideas. Charles Lamb, writing about *The Watchman*, had tried to suggest to Coleridge which strategy would best realize his talents within the form of a periodical; but his formula for success ends up as an appeal to Coleridge to indulge his range of intellectual interests. What Lamb suggested for *The Watchman* describes *The Friend*: 'change the name, leave out all the articles of News . . . and confine yourself to Ethics, verse, criticism, or, rather do not confine yourself. Let your plan be as diffuse as the Spectator, and I'll answer for it the work prospers.'[20] Only the reference to *The Spectator* makes one doubt that Lamb knew exactly what he was doing by encouraging Coleridge's catholicity. Referring to a Prospectus in a letter to George Coleridge of December 1808 Coleridge wrote, 'I play off my whole mind in this work' (*CL* III 133).

He regarded playing off his whole mind in this way as a philosophical task because it could only be done by means of 'principles' which make the larger claims of the human vocation heard within specific forms of thought. Coleridge never describes principles as a particular set of rules, and this makes him appear deceptively vague. His appeal to principles is an appeal for different forms of thought — religion, politics, science — to remain open to considerations of the 'whole mind': an area beyond the scope of their expert, systematic legislation, and an area which Coleridge thought was most fully expressed in poetry. Principles are intended to unite philosophy and common sense, or to place the specialized discoveries of modern thought within a humane culture.

Coleridge had recommended principles from an early stage in his writings. In *A Moral and Political Lecture* of 1795 he proclaimed 'the necessity of *bottoming* on fixed Principles' (*LPR* 5). But a reviewer noted the concurrent problem of how to express these guidelines, and pointed out the conflict of traditionally opposed ways of thinking, imaginative and scientific, in Coleridge's writing.

---

[20]*The Letters of Charles Lamb to which are added those of his sister Mary Lamb,* ed. E. V. Lucas (London, 1935), 3 vols, I, 10.

This little composition is the production of a man who possesses a poetical imagination. . . . he has not stated in a form sufficiently scientific and determinate, those principles to which . . . he now proceeds as the most important point.[21]

In the first issue of *The Friend* it was Coleridge's purpose 'to refer man to PRINCIPLES in all things; in Literature, in the Fine Arts, in Morals, in Legislation, in Religion' (*TF* II 13). In the sixth issue he announced his intention of correcting the erroneous principles of taste, morals, religion and politics 'which are taught in the commonest Books of recent composition' (*TF* II 87). The sub-title of the 1818 'rifacciamento' of *The Friend* records the same desire of aiding 'in the formation of fixed principles in politics, morals, and religion' (*TF* I 1); while in the introduction to the second *Lay Sermon* Coleridge described the function of principles as being the 'chapter of contents' of his writings at any time (*LS* 126).

The programmatic character of principles raises the problem for Coleridge of how they are to be adequately expressed; or rather they raise the problem of the adequate expression of the subject of which they are the principles. They eschew conclusive definitions, and instead reveal a law in accordance with which future definitions of the same thing will have to conform. In *Biographia* Burke is praised as a principled thinker because he

possessed and sedulously sharpened that eye, which sees all things, actions, and events, in relation to the *laws* that determine their existence and circumscribe their possibility. He referred habitually to *principles*. He was a *scientific* statesman; and therefore a *seer*. For every principle contains in itself the germs of a prophecy. . . . (*BL* I 125)

This prophetic understanding which language has to be adequate to deal with is described in *The Friend* as demanded by the progressive character of human experience.

I have indeed considered the disproportion of human passions to their ordinary objects among the strongest internal evidences of our future destination, and the attempt to restore them to their rightful claimants, the most imperious duty and noblest task of genius. The verbal enunciation of this Master Truth could scarcely be new to me at any period of my life since

[21]*Coleridge, The Critical Heritage,* ed. J. R. de J. Jackson (London, 1970), 24.

earliest youth; but I well remember the particular time, when the words first became more than words to me, when they incorporated with a living conviction and took their place among the realities of my Being. (*TF* II 31)[22]

In this passage the loss of adequate correlates for the progressive elements of our being results in the need for a more exalted concept of language: the idea of a medium 'incorporated with a living conviction', not merely verbal but having an existential dimension of 'Being'. The strains which critics, following W. J. Bate, have argued were put on the Romantic language of poetry by the burden of the past were also imposed by the promise of the future. The 'disproportion' felt by Coleridge, the dissatisfaction with those 'ordinary' correspondences by which we are assumed to publicize our inner life and communicate our most essential experiences, leave him at first without a language. The need for a language capable of expressing the dynamic growth fostered by principles becomes the philosophical preoccupation of *The Friend,* and is an attempt to convey an adequate notion of principles in a literary form.

When writing to friends about the aim of the periodical Coleridge emphasized his desire to establish principles holding true generally, through subjects ranging from legislation to the fine arts. Experience can be described scientifically, religiously, politically and poetically. To regard one of these descriptions as excluding another is to rest in an inadequate understanding of the experience. Intrinsic to this plea for generality is the idea that principles do justice to human growth, 'the nobler Germ'.[23] Coleridge believed that to recognize the potential integrity in someone's actions is to understand his behaviour as constituting a language. In a letter to Thomas Smith in 1809 he

[22]Wordsworth, writing *The Convention of Cintra* in 1808–9, expresses the same thought: 'the passions of men (I mean, the soul of sensibility in the heart of man) – in all quarrels, in all contests, in all quests, in all delights, in all employments which are either sought by men or thrust upon them – do immeasurably transcend their objects. The true sorrow of humanity consists in this; – not that the mind of man fails; but that the course and demands of action, and of life so rarely correspond with the dignity and intensity of human desires.' (*W* I 339)

[23]In letters of December 1808 to Thomas Poole, Daniel Stuart and Sir George Beaumont (*CL* III 131, 141, 146); and of April 1809 to George Coleridge and Thomas Longman (*CL* III 197, 202–3).

described language as the expression of practical reason, the responsible structure of our lives, the principle of growth, and writes of *The Friend:*

I . . . shall deem myself amply remunerated if in consequence of my exertions a Few only of those, who had formed their moral creed on Hume, Paley, and their Imitators, with or without a belief in the facts of mere historical Christianity, shall have learnt to value actions primarily as the language & natural effect of the state of the agent; if they shall consider what they *are* instead of *merely* what they *do*; so that the fig tree may bring forth it's own fruit from its own living principle, and not have the figs tied on to it's barren sprays by the hand of outward Prudence & Respect of Character. (*CL* III 216)[24]

He believed he was not so rewarded partly because of the inadequacy of his language to realize clearly his intentions for the journal. This led him to write the revisions for the 1812 edition and the 'rifacciamento' of 1818. But he also thought there were failings in the quality of the public reception of his efforts, founded on inadequacies in the public concept of language and common expectations as to the form literary communication should take. Coleridge is well aware of the infelicities in his attempts to do justice to the complexity of his ideas of October 1809. In letters to Poole and George Coleridge he describes the '*entortillage* in the sentences', the taxing protraction of a subject in the 'stately piling up of *Story* on *Story* in one architectural period, which is not suited to a periodical Essay' (*CL* III 234, 237). Such difficulties perhaps inevitably accompanied a work which, Coleridge tells Poole, with a few exceptions is 'both the Reservoir & the living Fountain of all my mind' (*CL* III 235). The burden is quite unmanageable. Nevertheless, he also felt himself defeated, and often said so, by the spirit of his times. He described *The Friend* to Poole as 'least of all suited to the present illogical age, which has in imitation of the French rejected all the *cements* of language; so that a popular Book is now a mere bag of marbles, i.e. aphorisms and epigrams on

---

[24]See *NB* II 2495 (March 1805), 'for if mind acts on body, the purest Impulse can introduce itself to our consciousness no otherwise than by *speaking to us* in some bodily feeling.'

one subject' (*CL* III 234).[25] The problem of the inadequacy of publicly accepted literary forms is one to which Coleridge returned throughout his life, perhaps most famously in *Biographia*. According to his critical remarks on contemporary language in chapter 2, again associating the politically disruptive French with linguistic fragmentation, the increase in size of the reading public with 'the present Anglo–Gallican fashion of unconnected epigrammatic periods' conspire to render all literary 'trades' devoid of talent: 'now, partly by the labours of successive poets, and in part by the more artificial state of society and social intercourse, language, mechanized as it were into a barrel-organ, supplies at once both instrument and tune' (*BL* I 25). This mechanical fixity obstructs any creative use of language which attempts to become adequate to new discoveries. Language in Coleridge's time has become 'a press-room of larger and smaller stereotype pieces'; and the intellectual and creative indolence of the act of turning the handle of the barrel-organ is matched by the mechanical task of composing periods by varying the order of fixed, unchangeable pieces of type. The poet employing a stereotyped poetic diction finds that his poem has been written 'without his previous consciousness'.[26] Within such restricted boundaries there is certainly no 'danger of an intellectual plethora' (*BL* I 26) – a danger which the most sympathetic critics of Coleridge must recognize as oppressing his work. But if an author is to be one of 'the *constructors*' of language, eliciting a variable music rather than a repetitive tune from his medium, then, Coleridge implies, he must take a risk. When his criticism of the contemporary idea of language is taken into consideration the apparently irresponsible promiscuity of Coleridge's aesthetic, political and religious ideas takes on the character of a methodical hazard, a consiously accepted danger of the philosophical

[25]Coleridge repeats this criticism in letters of 1809 to George Coleridge, Richard Sharp, Samuel Purkis and Southey (*CL* III 237, 242, 245–6, 254). For a discussion of Coleridge versus epigrams and aphorisms, see J. R. de J. Jackson, *Method and Imagination in Coleridge's Criticism* (London, 1969), 28–9; and contrast Coleridge's own rationale of aphorisms, *A* 18–19 and n., 20.

[26]See Coleridge's remarks in a letter to Thomas Curnick of April 1814 (*CL* III 468–70); see also *NB* III 4313; *TT* II 24 (21 April 1832).

manner he thought was forced upon him by the deficiencies in current forms of philosophical expression.

Owing to the closed quality Coleridge attributed to his native philosophical tradition, he was always trying to incorporate within his own philosophy other forms of thought which would allow him a more flexible and open-ended definition of experience. These forms, however, sometimes obstinately retained their original shape and resisted assimilation. Instead of expanding the range of his thought from within, they often imposed on it from without, producing ragged contradictions and lumpish, half-digested plagiarisms. The unacknowledged quotation of Schelling in *Biographia* is the most obvious example. Or else Coleridge wrote in forms which escaped the responsibilities of the public writings. The perpetual accompaniment of the notebooks continued to provide an alternative genre in which the rudimentary and the experimental were the norm. In a passage near the start of *The Friend* Coleridge wrote:

I was still tempted onward by an increasing Sense of the Imperfection of my Knowledge, and by the Conviction, that, in Order fully to comprehend and develope any one Subject, it was necessary that I should make myself Master of some other, which again as regularly involved a third, and so on, with an ever-widening Horizon. Yet one Habit, formed during long absences from those, with whom I could converse with full Sympathy, has been of Advantage to me – that of daily noting down, in my Memorandum or Common-place Books, both Incidents and Observations, whatever had occurred to me from without, and all the Flux and Reflux of my Mind within itself. (*TF* II 16–17)

Coleridge's grasp of the principle behind one subject is improved by the act of transposing to another. The notebooks represent an ideal literary form, read by a perfectly sympathetic reader, in which Coleridge's 'whole mind', the exchange between inner and outer, private and public, can be recorded without loss. But they only achieve this by refusing to take the decisions which would render a public work coherent and free from contradiction. Their public remains private – the figure of Coleridge himself, cut off from his audience, his own reader.

This is only the other side of Coleridge's conviction that his problem was aggravated by the spirit of an age unsympathetic to and often intolerant of the stylistic latitude his principles required for their full expression. Contemporary discussions of principles dwindled into talk about personalities; principles succumbed to 'Men'.[27] Coleridge railed at 'that sad sad stain of the present very *anti-gallican* but woefully *gallicizing* Age, the rage for personality . . . names, names, always names! The alliterations, 'Names & Novelties', would go far in characterising the *bad* parts of the present generation . . .' (*CL* III 84). The reference to France again suggests the political overtones of Coleridge's loss of intellectual confidence in the communal language. In a letter of October 1809 he solicited from Southey, in view of *The Friend*'s lack of public success, a letter which would plead for some public sympathy for his own style, contrasting it

with the cementless periods of the modern Anglo–Gallican style, which not only are understood *beforehand,* but, being free from all connections of logic, all the hooks and eyes of intellectual memory, never oppress the mind by after recollections, but, like civil visitors, stay a few moments, and leave the room quite free and open for the next comers. (*CL* III 254)

This recourse to a letter, anticipating the pseudonymous one which brings transcendental matters to a halt in *Biographia,* is a desperate remedy. But Coleridge does not retreat just yet from the problem of communication into a solitary world of purely private justification. When he comes to criticize literature of the present Coleridge insists that his critical principles should not be deduced from philosophy but should emerge from his practical engagement with the texts.

Principles of criticism drawn from philosophy, are best employed to illustrate the works of those whose fame is already a *fatum* among mankind, and to confirm, augment, and enlighten our admiration of the same. The living, on the other hand, ought always to be appreciated *comparatively* – their works with those of their contemporaries, each in its kind, and in proportion to the kind. (*CL* IV 967)

Again, in this letter of 1819, we find that it is a critical awareness which generates the distinctions between different kinds of writing to be subsequently rationalized by philosophy. In *Biographia* this critical

[27]In letters to George Coleridge and Thomas Longman of April 1809 (*CL* III 197, 198, 202–3).

astuteness leads Coleridge to an act of desynonymy which he fails to explain systematically. Here he calls for a theory of genres based on contemporary literary practice. His aim must be belatedly to revise the public's literary expectations and preconceptions which he thought had helped scuttle *The Friend*.

TRANSPOSITIONS AND THE LAY SERMONS

The Friend was Coleridge's attempt to convey an adequate notion of principles in a literary form. For Coleridge, principles inspire a progressive, open-ended view of human nature in different forms of thought. In the *Lay Sermons* principles are exemplified by transpositions. In portraying 'the natural Man' in his two main tracts for the times, Coleridge transposes rapidly through philosophical, religious, aesthetic and political descriptions of human nature, criticizing their individual claims to self-sufficiency in comparison with a poetic ideal.

In the introduction to his edition of *Lay Sermons* R. J. White remarked that 'perhaps the "key" to Coleridge's lay preaching is his remark that religion is "a total act of the soul". For first and last and all the time he was a poet, even when he wrote in prose. Poetry, as he said, brings the whole soul of man into activity' (*LS* xliii). His suggestion contains a rather vague conviction that something poetic underlies Coleridge's intellectual commitments. White himself makes his point by transposing between two related phrases of Coleridge, bridging two distinct areas of discourse, religion and poetry, by means of their common principle, their openness to the 'whole mind'. Coleridge's mature philosophy of human nature substantiates White's vague conviction. His apparently negligent comparisons of different areas of thought can be found to display conceptual connections which themselves constitute a methodology. Religion for Coleridge may have been, as Basil Willey says, 'the *raison d'être* of everything else'.[28] But the reasons Coleridge gives for such a view *are* the practical connections of his thought, mapping the totality of the soul, criticizing the restraints which specialized disciplines impose on its description.

[28]B. Willey, *Samuel Taylor Coleridge* (London, 1972), 69.

The response Coleridge desired from his readers is written in a marginal note to James Gillman's copy: 'it professes to be nothing more than a maniple or handful of loose flowers, a string of Hints and Materials for Reflection/ The Object was to rouse and stimulate the mind – to set the reader a thinking . . .' (LS 114n). But contemporary reaction to the Lay Sermons was notoriously scornful, both in published attention and private neglect. Hazlitt's reviews anticipated and then found The Statesman's Manual to be virtually unreadable, and took many pages in The Examiner and The Edinburgh Review to say so. He either thought Coleridge's transpositions incoherent, or suspected the 'senseless jargon' to be a philosophical mask for political reaction and legitimacy.[29] Southey and Wordsworth probably did not even read the Lay Sermons; and Dorothy Wordsworth found The Statesman's Manual 'ten times more obscure than the darkest parts of the Friend.'[30] Crabb Robinson tries hard to find something nice to say: he described the German, alien character of The Statesman's Manual, but also connected this with Coleridge's critique of contemporary language:

What he has to say cannot be rendered intelligible in merely popular language; and if he uses only the language of the schools, nobody will understand it. Under such circumstances the temptation is scarcely to be resisted, of endeavouring to blend in one mass heterogeneous materials, and adorn the abstractions of a scholastic system by a popular rhetorick.[31]

He thus pinpoints the problem of expression, and sees that the Coleridgean 'blend' is a mixture which must be separated out if the Lay Sermons are to be understood. But he feared they were incorrigibly unsystematic, a hopeless mélange of different kinds of discourse, the presentation distorted by the author's awareness of the hostility of his potential audience. The 'abstractions' of philosophy and the 'popular

---

[29]Hazlitt, Works, XVII 100–16.
[30] LS xxx and n., 240; all copies mentioned by White in the libraries of Wordsworth and Southey were uncut when the libraries were sold. The Letters of William and Dorothy Wordsworth, III, The Middle Years, 1812–1820, ed. E. de Selincourt, 2nd edn, rev. M. Moorman and A. G. Hill (Oxford, 1970), 373 (to Catherine Clarkson, March [1817]).
[31]Jackson (ed.), Coleridge, The Critical Heritage, 280.

rhetorick' of common sense are once more in competition, rather than in harmony. Coleridge too is aware of the problem: in his epigraph he encourages the reader to try to 'discover the rational principles behind his . . . madness', and so appreciate the methodological significance of the practical continuities of his thought.

These methodological transpositions appear definitively in Appendix C to the *Manual* where he describes a radical philosophy in which human progress is inspired by the 'resistance' of reason to the conceptual 'captivity' of different forms of thought. As in Kant's philosophy, reason supplies us with an idea of totality, 'the comprehension of all as one'. The passage then seems to suggest, again in keeping with Kant, that while such an idea of reason may inspire progress, it can never become knowledge. When we grasp things as a whole, as a 'ONE' in understanding, we lose the 'INFINITE' dimension of reason. But, equally, we can only be aware of the infinite dimension of reason as an idea which resists any conceptual scheme, any 'ONE', whose captivity we need to describe our knowledge of the world. Coleridge has to define our natural state as one either of resistance or of captivity:

the Reason first manifests itself in man by the *tendency* to the comprehension of all as one. We can neither rest in an infinite that is not at the same time a whole, nor in a whole that is not infinite. Hence the natural Man is always in a state either of resistance or of captivity to the understanding and the fancy, which cannot represent totality without limit: and he either loses the ONE in the striving after the INFINITE (i.e. Atheism with or without polytheism) or the INFINITE in the striving after the ONE (i.e. anthropomorphic monotheism). (*LS* 60)

Coleridge expresses a Kantian distrust both of the claims of pure reason to supply knowledge, and of the claims of the understanding to supply complete knowledge. Our natural state is the tension existing between the two sets of claims. Reason undermines the understanding's claims to sufficiency, and the understanding sets a standard of conceptual coherence to which pure reason cannot submit.

In this passage we should note the suggestive parenthesis on the religious implications of Coleridge's description of an epistemological problem. The succeeding pages provide more and more varied elaborations of the original thesis, variations which imaginatively extend the basic theme through different contexts. Coleridge goes on to argue that an incontinent resistance on the part of reason to human limitations produces an imbalance in our natural constitution, explaining the concept of the Fall. The resisting reason in pursuit of the infinite becomes abstracted from its proper sphere, and so constitutes pride, the desire to 'be as gods!'. It also abandons the rest of human nature to a captivity of the lowest kind – 'the lusts of the flesh, the eye, and the understanding' (*LS* 61). The fact that we have a natural tendency towards this constitutional imbalance does not alter our responsibility for it when it occurs. Religion is the proper regulator of our natural tendency to re-enact the Fall, and in this capacity it is the firm supporter of the fine arts. He argues that the perfection of the fine arts is in achieving the union of the finite and the infinite in exemplary harmony. The poetic symbol can express the infinite character of reason because it does not try to define it within a closed, scientific system. Yet its particularity avoids abstraction, and does not allow reason to become 'mere visionariness'.

Finally, the harmony expressed in art reflects the political unity of a perfect state. Coleridge claims that the balance of resistance and captivity illuminates the ideal of Plato's *Republic,* and opposes Jacobinism, which he analyses into a political illustration of the temptation and tendency towards a self-disruptive way of thinking.[32]

In these pages we move from a critique of pure reason to an interpretation of the Fall, a Romantic theory of art and symbol, and a political theory referring both to Plato and to near-contemporary history. Coleridge tries to do justice to traditional categories of human thought, but avoids dogmatic captivity within any one by insisting on the infinite range of reason. Just as in his attempt to balance the claims of common sense and desynonymy, the drive towards holism and unity exists in tension with the analytic power of reason to see beyond established cultural categories to an as yet unmediated variety. Reason has to constrain itself temporarily to some orthodox procedure in order to become articulate; but it leaves that procedure enriched by its passage.

[32]*LS* 61–4; and see I. A. Richards, *Coleridge on Imagination* (London, 1962), xv.

Coleridge's transpositional argument can be followed in more detail in his other writings. Belief in the progressive character of our own nature, a sure hope, is both our greatest ornament and the common condition of our lives. Reflections on *Macbeth* make him realize that hope is 'the master element of a commanding genius' (*SC* I 81).[33] But in his later political thought hope is also 'an instinct' distinguishing us from the beasts, 'an indispensable condition of [man's] moral and intellectual progression' (*C&S* 73). The ordeal of King Lear is the temporary suspension of this most human part of his nature, so that in his ravings 'there is only the brooding of the one anguish, an eddy without progression' (*SC* I 65). In marginalia to Swift, Coleridge argues that the Houyhnhnms' rationality is defective because they are not progressive. This, for Coleridge, is an 'inconsistency' in any attempt to define reason (*MC* 129). Definitions of human nature are inherently problematic: they must have built into them a clause ensuring their own open-endedness and so, strictly speaking, their own failure as definitions: 'for man is destined to be guided by higher principles, by universal views, which can never be fulfilled in this state of existence, – by a spirit of progressiveness which can never be accomplished, for then it would cease to be' (*SC* I 152). Human nature is defined by a critique through transposition of the claims to self-sufficiency of any description of it. Coleridge thought this unsusceptibility of definition to be the defining essence of the life shared in various degrees – one of which is human – throughout the universe. This paradox is extended in the *Theory of Life* (1816; published posthumously) into Coleridge's exposition of Schelling: there is a tension in the natural world corresponding to the epistemological problem. Thus 'the full applicability of an abstract science ceases, the moment reality begins' (*TofL* 51). Our ambitious attempt to capture that resistant element in life refutes itself. In his *Treatise on Method* Coleridge reiterates that 'Every Physical Theory is in some measure imperfect, because it is of necessity progressive' (*TM* 58).

In the domain of theology faith enriches and augments the part so far attributed to reason in epistemology. It is faith which must resist

[33]See the eleventh of the 1818 lectures (*MC* 195); *LS* 18.

'the mechanical understanding' (*LS* 30; *BL* I 84, 135–6). Religion, the human institution of this faith, is the proper framework for the creative resistance of reason: it does not allow resistance to become the rebellion of pride and anarchic freedom. Coleridge thinks that without religion 'all the pursuits and desires of man must either exceed or fall short of their just measure.' Under a religious dispensation the whole of human nature can be fulfilled, for 'never yet did there exist a full faith in the divine WORD . . . which did not expand the intellect while it purified the heart; which did not multiply the aims and objects of the mind, while it fixed and simplified those of the desires and passions' (*LS* 175). In the *Lay Sermons* and *Biographia* it is religion which is the progressive agent of this fulfilled unity.[34] This is obviously carried on to the much later work on the idea of a National Church whose 'paramount end' would be 'the progressive civilization of the community', and which would be active throughout every parish in the land to this effect (*C&S* 81, 75–6).

The later work, *On the Constitution of the Church and State*, is an attempt to describe an established institution that will implement the demands of religion – demands which, according to earlier arguments in the *Lay Sermons*, are 'the EXECUTIVE of our nature' (*LS* 64). The description of such an institution, though, is only found in the later work. It is as though the volatile forces of man's progressive nature in the earlier writings still undermine any comprehensive definition. What remains is the unsurpassed example of the Bible which Coleridge described in the *Lay Sermons*. In the mixture of tenses involved in its proper interpretation, the Bible accommodates both history and prophecy, captivity and resistance. The unity of biblical history is 'continuous as life'. Its comprehensiveness lets it participate in something necessarily beyond all definition. It is 'a symbol of Eternity', symbolic in its openness to the progressive possibilities to be found in every apparently fixed stage in human history: 'According therefore to our relative position on its banks the Sacred History

---

[34] A 'total act of the whole moral being', *BL* I 84, 135–6; II 215–16; *LS* 196; and see J. D. Boulger, *Coleridge as Religious Thinker* (New Haven, 1961), 96–7; J. R. Barth, *Coleridge and Christian Doctrine* (Cambridge, Mass., 1969), 28, 32–3.

becomes prophetic, the Sacred Prophecies historical, while the power and substance of both inhere in its Laws, its Promises, and its Comminations.' (*LS* 29–30)

The transposition into theology implies that an aesthetic mode of expression is more appropriate to its subject than scientific description. 'In the Scriptures therefore both Facts and Persons must of necessity have a two-fold significance, a past and a future, a temporary and a perpetual, a particular and a universal application. They must be at once both Portraits and Ideals' (*LS* 30). Coleridge makes the connection with aesthetics quite explicit:

in all the ages and countries of civilization Religion has been the parent and fosterer of the Fine Arts, as of Poetry, Music, Painting, &c. the common essence of which consists in a similar union of the Universal and the Individual. In this union, moreover, is contained the true sense of the IDEAL. (*LS* 62)

It is the peculiar character of the fine arts as a form of expression which Coleridge regards as particularly relevant. They contrast with the closed definitions, the wholes, the 'ONE' of temporary intellectual captivity, displaying an ideal openness to the intellectual resistance to such categories, bringing the infinite into play. In the *Shakespearean Criticism* it is the activity of the poet which approximates most closely to this freedom, resisting temporal closures in the way Scripture does in the *Lay Sermons*:

It is a mistake to say that any of Shakespeare's characters strike us as portraits: they have the union of reason perceiving, of judgement recording, and of imagination diffusing over all a magic glory. While the poet registers what is past, he projects the future in a wonderful degree, and makes us feel, however slightly, and see, however dimly, that state of being in which there is neither past nor future, but all is permanent in the very energy of nature. (*SC* II 168)[35]

The histories retold by Scripture are, for Coleridge, different from the histories of his own age and of the preceding century primarily

---

[35]See also Coleridge's description of the poetical character of Shakespeare's historical drama: how its organic unity replaces a purely temporal order of succession, *SC* I 138–9; see also *SC* II 160–2 for Shakespeare's 'power over space and time'.

because of their mode of expression.[36] The symbolic advantages which religion reveals in poetry also enrich Coleridge's notion of a political individual and all those associated metaphors for social cohesion. Coleridge's concept of political individuality is fundamental to his political theory:[37] 'The perfect frame of a man is the perfect frame of a state' (LS 62). Plato's *Republic* and Bunyan's 'Town of Man-Soul', while illustrating this fact, misleadingly present elements of their subject as separate and distinct rather than combined in each political individual: Plato's 'guardians', thinks Coleridge, could never be wholly rational, but the Bible is the true manual of the statesman, containing models of political economy as it does of history because it suggests an adequate language of the self. Bentham condemned the concept of a 'body-politic' as an example of how 'poetry has invaded the domain of reason.'[38] Poetry remains perpetually important to Coleridge's thought because reason needs the support of poetry in order to be able to figure to itself its own infinite resources. What was later in *On the Constitution of the Church and State* to become the description of possible political institutions, involving compromises with Coleridge's conservative political interests, here remains at the level of the kind of symbolism necessary for the political accommodation of human integrity. Coleridge's objection to the political reification of men by the spirit of commerce and trade (LS 206, 219–20) is based on the larger view of experience which religion points to in poetry.

[36]See MC 425–6 (*Table Talk*, 15 August 1833) for Coleridge's criticism of Gibbon's lack of a philosophy of historical explanation, and a letter of 1826 to John Hookham Frere (CL VI 853) for the limitations of the histories of Gibbon, Robertson and Hume in comparison with 'Herodotus, and the Hebrew Records' which alone are adequate to 'The Historic *Idea*'; this criticism of these historians, without the biblical example, is perpetuated by Leslie Stephen: 'The fault, briefly stated, seems to be an incapacity to recognize the great forces by which history is moulded, and the continuity which gives to it a real unity', *History of English Thought in the Eighteenth Century* (London, 1876), 2 vols, I, 57–8.
[37]See D. P. Calleo, *Coleridge and the Idea of the Modern State* (New Haven and London, 1966), 9, 17; William P. Kennedy, *Humanist Versus Economist* (University of California, 1958), 21.
[38]See R. Preyer, *Bentham, Coleridge and the Science of History* (Verlag Heinrich Pöppinghaus, 1958), 52–3.

Poetry now seems to have been allocated the responsibility for showing how wide-ranging and comprehensive his idea of a philosophical description of human nature could be. It is its approximation to a poetic symbol which guarantees that a religious, political or scientific description of experience is sufficiently catholic, and does not restrict or distort its subject-matter. There is a danger here that Coleridge may collapse separate ways of thinking into poetry. This would lead to Schelling's idea that science literally tries to achieve the condition of poetry. In the *Lay Sermons* Coleridge sometimes sounds as though he agrees with Schelling: he forgets the important opposition he preserves between poetry and science on other occasions, and writes that 'natural philosophy is comprized in the study of the science and language of *symbols*' (*LS* 79). A slightly earlier passage suggests that he thought this language is understood when we consider nature as 'the natural symbol of that higher life of reason'. This is a language of Schellingian grandiosity which 'inchases the vast unfolded volume of the earth with the hieroglyphics of her history' (*LS* 72–3), and leads to the Schellingian conclusion that the 'genuine naturalist is a dramatic poet in his own line.'[39] Poetry is useful to science because the two are really the same thing; at least, this seems to be Coleridge's conclusion in the 'Essays on the Principles of Method' from the 'rifacciamento' of *The Friend*. There he argues that in a poet like Shakespeare 'we find nature idealized into poetry', and in the observations of true science 'we find poetry, as it were, substantiated and realized in nature: yea, nature itself disclosed to us . . . as at once the poet and the poem.' (*TF* I 471)

Despite this clear use of Schelling, it is only if we assume a Kantian rationale that we can explain many of Coleridge's cryptic remarks about poetry and its relation to science and religion. Coleridge claims in the *Lay Sermons* that poetry is figurative: 'it is the poetry of all human nature, to read it [the great book of nature] likewise in a figurative sense, and to find therein correspondences and symbols of

[39]See *CL* V 19, 'all true science is contained in the Lore of Symbols & Correspondences', and, vice-versa, 'the *Doctrine* of Symbols & Correspondences should first be proved or at least exhibited as a Science', *ibid.*, 325; see also C. Miller, 'Coleridge's Concept of Nature', in *Journal of the History of Ideas*, xxv (1964), 91; and Levere, *Poetry Realized in Nature, passim.*

the spiritual world' (*LS* 70). It is the figurative reading of nature which distinguishes poetry here. Coleridge does not think that poetry gains us access to a world which science will eventually possess. We are always aware of its ideal or self-consciously poetic presentation as an element constituting that world. He thinks that unlike a literal copy of nature, poetic imitation can involve a universal dimension within a particular image because it professes its own artifice and does not pose as a piece of knowledge (*BL* II 33 and n.).[40] Poetry tries to win our willing suspension of disbelief, not our positive belief that something is the case (*BL* II 6). To free the poet from the duty of recording historical fact is to give this art a 'most catholic' dimension (*BL* II 101). For both Kant and Coleridge poetry does not exist on the same continuum as science. In the extraordinary event of a scientific millenium in which we know everything, the artifice of poetry would survive, redundant for science, but obvious to imagination, ensuring the persistence of aesthetic experience. We can always follow Shelley's advice 'to imagine that which we know', to consider the harmonious pattern or order poetry invites us to find in objects for its own sake, and not for the sake of any knowledge it makes possible. Poetry can always remain distinct from science.

Coleridge believes that when religion can 'finitely express the *unity* of the infinite Spirit by being a total act of the soul' it does so through poetry (*LS* 90). But he does not want to suggest that religion *is* poetry any more than he thinks that science is. By means of symbols poetry 'brings the whole soul of man into activity' (*BL* II 12). However, religion uses this sense of personal unity and integrity to express in addition 'the *unity* of the infinite Spirit'. It is different from poetry because it uses the poetic symbol to reflect unity in a different direction, as 'the image or symbol of its great object' (*LS* 90), a divine object separate from the object of poetry. The symbol needs to be 'bi-focal', as Stephen Prickett puts it, in order to preserve a distinction between poetry and religion.[41]

[40]Among many examples see especially *SC* I 200 and n., 204, 222 (lecture notes and fragments), *SC* II 80, 160–1 (reports of 1811–12 lectures on Shakespeare and Milton); *MC* 49 (marginalia on Jonson).
[41]S. Prickett, *Romanticism and Religion* (Cambridge, 1976), ch. 1.

Perhaps developing a thought of Friedrich Schlegel's, Coleridge writes in the second *Lay Sermon* that 'Religion is the Poetry and Philosophy of all mankind' (*LS* 197).[42] For Coleridge, religion is seriously concerned with *knowing* the end of all things, and to that extent it is like science or philosophy. But the truths it wishes to know lie beyond their grasp and so can only be expressed poetically. The scheme which Coleridge seems to be envisaging can be described as follows. If we imagine human experience as a moral and intellectual journey, then religious preoccupations are eschatological: they are concerned with the final destination, and claim to be in possession of the reason for why we are travelling there. Poetry – the form to which religious expression is temporarily confined – feels delight in the imagined visions of the final goal as part of 'the attractions of the journey itself'.[43] Science remembers the journey so far, and tries to learn inductively from that what to expect ahead. It is religion which 'unites in itself what is most excellent' in poetry and philosophy, and 'supplies with the noblest materials both the imaginative and intellective faculties . . . the poetic vision and the philosophic idea' (*LS* 197). As Willey saw, Coleridge's religious understanding provides the *raison d'être* for both. Religion explains why science has a direction, why it progresses, and what it is we can see poetically beyond the present scientific moment. Poetic awareness becomes a sense of religious vocation. But this scheme only retains its illustrative power if we can sympathize or have faith in the original analogy of progress in human experience as a religious pilgrimage. The argument for the necessity of the religious point of view is circular as Coleridge well knew: we must believe before we can understand (*LS* 17; *PhL* 168). In his planned *Opus Maximum* Coleridge's theology was to have been presented as *The Assertion of*

[42]Schlegel, 'Ideen', 46, *Kritische Ausgabe*, II 260–1: 'Depending on the point of view, poetry and philosophy are different spheres, different forms, or the factors of religion; for if you really attempt to combine the two, you will get nothing but religion.'

[43]See *BL* II 11, on reading a poem: 'The reader should be carried forward, not merely or chiefly by the mechanical impulse of curiosity, or by a restless desire to arrive at the final solution; but by the pleasurable activity of mind excited by the pleasures of the journey itself. Like the motion of a serpent, which the Egyptians made the emblem of intellectual power . . .'

Religion. It is only if religion is asserted that the rest follows. My last chapter will analyse the implications of this for Coleridge's idea of language.

The *Lay Sermons*, then, show that poetry is relevant to Coleridge's transpositions between different branches of human thought because it provides a symbolic expression of the ideal understanding of 'the natural Man' which science, political theory and religion all desire. It expresses the common ideal which makes Coleridge's transpositions between separate discourses a necessary, practical critique of their pretensions to systematic adequacy. The argument is very close to Schiller's in his letters *On the Aesthetic Education of Man*. Shawcross thought that Schiller came closest of all the Germans to supplying 'a true parallel' to Coleridge; their aesthetics shared the same Kantian base, and both were devoted to establishing the universal character of poetry (*BL* I lxxxix). Schiller's description of the specialization resulting from the determination of human variety to any one discipline reflects his concern over the effects such a 'captivity' has on human nature. The aesthetic state is presented as the permanent background to transpositions between particular sciences. Aesthetic products document the 'humanity' which we possess '*in potentia* before every determinate condition into which [we] can conceivably enter.'[44] In the seventh of his 1811–12 lectures on Shakespeare and Milton Coleridge also describes

a middle state of mind more strictly appropriate to the imagination than any other, when it is, as it were, hovering between images. As soon as it is fixed on one image, it becomes understanding; but while it is unfixed and wavering between them, attaching itself permanently to none, it is imagination. (*SC* II 138)

Imagination creates a place of reorientation where we repair the distortions imposed upon our nature by a period of exclusive concentration; and it is a place of renewal, where we regain a sense of the extent and harmony of our own powers still to be realized in the world.

Coleridge's affinities with Schiller help explain further the unique

[44]Schiller, *On the Aesthetic Education of Man*, 147; and see 141 and n., 149, 151.

position of poetry within his thought. We can now say that poetry is untranslatable because it is the condition of all translation. It contains within it, 'in potentia', the possibility of all knowledge through its expression of 'the totality of our various functions' without being itself a particular form of knowledge. Its universality means that there is nothing into which it could be translated, and that its boundaries outline the scheme of all possible translations.

Schiller makes the idea of human progress a consequence of aesthetic experience. Coleridge's pattern of transpositions appears as 'the ladder of Nature' by which we try to establish the ideal society and make 'a reality' out of the richer self encountered in aesthetic experience.[45] Poetry, writes Coleridge, has 'boundless power': it 'rejects all control, all confinement' (SC II 139). However, this advantage is its own creation, its representations are ideal. Nevertheless it is just this artifice, this self-consciousness, this autonomy, which give it the licence to figure a harmony replacing the present opposition of 'resistance' to 'captivity'. This explains Coleridge's extravagant enthusiasm for poetry reported in the 1811–12 lectures.

What Hooker so eloquently claims for law I say of poetry. – 'Her seat is the bosom of God, her voice the harmony of the world; all things in heaven and on earth do her homage'. It is the language of heaven, and in the exquisite delight we derive from poetry we have, as it were, a foretaste, and a prophecy of the joys of heaven. (SC II 59)

According to a passage from The Friend, which he reprinted in Biographia, the ancients who considered comedy and tragedy 'as kinds of poetry' wished 'to transport the mind to a sense of it's possible greatness, and to implant the germs of that greatness during the temporary oblivion of the worthless "thing we are" . . .' (BL II 33; TF II 217–18). And in another of the 1811–12 lectures we find that in poetry we

take the purest parts and combine them with our own minds, with our own hopes, with our own inward yearnings after perfection, and, being frail and imperfect, we wish to have a shadow, a sort of prophetic existence present to us, which tells us what we are not, but yet, blending in us much that we are,

[45]Ibid., 147, 149, 167.

promises great things of what we may be. It is the truth (and poetry results from that instinct – the effort of perfecting ourselves), the conceiving that which is imperfect to be perfect and blending the nobler mind with the meaner objects. (*SC* II 80–1)

In his *Treatise on Method* Coleridge notes how the fine arts 'shot up to perfection' in ancient times while natural history and philosophy remained 'rude and imperfect' (*TM* 49). Poetry and the arts are not progressive: we do not chart a gradual improvement in them culminating in the superior productions of our own day. The artificial perfection of poetry and art releases them from the need for progress and allows them to symbolize the methodical success for which imperfect and progressive sciences strive.

But, like Schiller in his essay *On The Sublime,* Coleridge makes the high esteem for poetry's normative qualities inseparable from that Romantic unhappiness arising from its necessarily unliveable, potentially alienating character. Its 'oblivion' is 'temporary'; it exists merely as 'foretaste', 'prophecy' and 'shadow' of 'what we are not.' Its strengths and limitations are described in terms of each other; its self-consciousness is a perpetual defence. With this mature view of poetry's self-defining power to orientate itself in relation to other kinds of experience, both celebratory and defensive, Coleridge approaches his critical task in *Biographia.*

CHAPTER FIVE

The Necessity of Poetry

POETRY AS POETRY

The philosophical principles inspiring the transpositions in the *Lay Sermons* and elsewhere are grounded in Coleridge's appreciation of the independent significance of poetry in relation to other forms of thought. In volume II of *Biographia,* after the failure to complete the transcendental deduction, Coleridge has to allow his practical understanding of different uses of language, 'the principles of writing', to generate his critical and philosophical insights rather than have them prescribe 'rules' of critical discrimination. 'The ultimate end of criticism is much more to establish the principles of writing, than to furnish *rules* how to pass judgement on what has been written by others; if indeed it were possible that the two could be separated' (*BL* II 63). Coleridge's poet is therefore critical, or self-conscious, and writes from 'a knowledge of the facts, material and spiritual, that most appertain to his art' (*BL* II 64), and Coleridge wants to show why this art cannot be replaced by anything else; thus he was able to describe Milton as writing a passage in *Paradise Lost* which contradicted his own religious beliefs, but was nevertheless demanded by 'the necessity of poetry'.

In the preceding chapters some insight has been gained into the philosophical background to Coleridge's belief in 'the necessity of poetry'. In this chapter we shall see how this belief is specified by his literary-critical practice. His dispute with Wordsworth in *Biographia* comes from his feeling that the significance of poetry as poetry had been threatened by a widely-held interpretation of Wordsworth's own poetic theory. This interpretation was partial, and ignored Wordsworth's own profound grasp of the symbolic possibilities of poetry expressed in the 'Advertisement' and 'Prefaces' to *Lyrical Ballads*. Coleridge agreed entirely with Wordsworth's view of the symbolic power of poetry, but he objected to a contradictory strain of literalism which had been generally seized on as the essence of Wordsworth's theory. This literalist interpretation understood him to be dispensing with poetic diction, assimilating the language of poetry to that of prose, and defining poetry as a selection of 'the real language of men'. Coleridge feared that the symbolic dimension necessary for the autonomy of poetry would be completely obscured by this interpretation.

In the controversy with Wordsworth, which Coleridge intended to resolve in *Biographia,* he argues for the autonomous character of poetry by specifying a correspondingly self-conscious use of poetic language. He thinks poetic diction is necessitated by the artificial character of poetic imitation. However poetry should enhance what is literally the case, not deny it. As he told Thomas Curnick in 1814, it 'must be *more* than good sense, or it is not poetry; but it dare not be less or discrepant' (*CL* III 470). According to a notebook entry of 1804, the artistic passion contributes to the 'phantom of complete wholeness in an object'. This integrity is not an aberration from the real, 'for all Passion unifies as it were by natural Fusion' (*NB* II 2012). [1] Poetry should be like Wordsworth's 'Echo' in *To Joanna,* as Coleridge described it to Sara Hutchinson in 1802, 'tho' purposely beyond Nature . . . yet only an *exaggeration* of what really would happen' (*CL* II 827).

[1]See also Coleridge's view of the Shakespearian device of 'doubling the natural connection or order of logical consequence in the thoughts by the introduction of an artificial and sought for resemblance in the words', *SC* I 96. While Schlegel is a partial source for this thought his emphasis is more on the genesis of wordplay – its attempt to 'restore the lost resemblance between the word and the thing' which had been characteristic 'of original nature' – than on the 'artificial' and aesthetic implications of the poet's language stressed by Coleridge. A. W. Schlegel, *A Course of Lectures on Dramatic Art and Literature,* trans. J. Black, rev. edn, A. J. W. Morrison (London, 1846), 366. See also *SC* I 78; II 102–3 on punning 'in a philosophical sense'; and II 190 'in unison with the tone of passion'. *NB* III 3762 refers to the 'intended Essay in defence of Punning'.

In opposing Wordsworth's literalism, Coleridge concentrates on the autonomous, artificial role of the mimetic relation. He wants to show that the peculiarly poetic devices of diction and metre are employed consciously to articulate the significant difference between poetic imitation and reality. This allows poetry to enhance reality, or present it under ideal conditions by defining itself in contrast with other forms of understanding the world. This mature argument was anticipated in the letter of 1802 to William Sotheby where the 'radical' disagreement with Wordsworth first begins to emerge in detail.

In my opinion every phrase, every metaphor, every personification, should have it's justifying cause in some *passion* either of the Poet's mind, or of the Characters described by the poet – But *metre itself* implies a *passion,* i.e. a state of excitement, both in the Poet's mind, & is expected in that of the Reader – and tho' I stated this to Wordsworth, & he has in some sort stated it in his preface, yet he has [not] done justice to it, nor has he in my opinion sufficiently answered it. In my opinion, Poetry justifies, as *Poetry* independent of any other Passion, some new combination of Language, & *commands* the omission of many others allowable in other compositions / Now Wordsworth, me saltem judice, has in his system not sufficiently admitted the former, & in his practice has too frequently sinned against the latter. – Indeed, we have had lately some little controversy on this subject – & we begin to suspect, that there is, somewhere or other, a *radical* Difference [in our] opinions. (*CL* II 812)

In this letter Coleridge has already transformed the concept of passion in poetry from being the contingent accompaniment of figurative language, perhaps explicable along the lines of one of the many eighteenth-century arguments about the origin of language, to being the strict and necessary indication of the independent status of the language of poetry. Poetic passion becomes comparable to the 'feeling' of Kant's aesthetics, and the most significant part of Coleridge's Miltonic definition of poetry as 'simple, sensuous, passionate'. The predominant, passionate category modifies the other two in the interests of what Kant would call the 'subjective' character of the poetic imitation: 'passion, provides that neither thought nor imagery shall be simply objective, but that the *passio vera* of humanity shall warm and animate both'. (*SC* I 166)

'Language,' wrote Coleridge to John Murray in 1814, 'is the sacred Fire in the Temple of Humanity; and the Muses are it's especial & Vestal Priestesses' (*CL* III 522). In this hieratic capacity poetry celebrates the expressive power within the rest of language; it attains sacramental importance by revealing the integrity aimed at by other uses of language. It was seen how in the *Lay Sermons* the unity desired by political, moral and scientific systems was inextricably enmeshed in a religious, eschatological view of life which only poetry was adequate to express. Similarly, in *Biographia* Coleridge describes how the poet should 'understand and command what Bacon calls the *vestigia communia* of the senses, the latency of all in each' (*BL* II 103). This can be glossed by another quotation from *Biographia,* and a marginal note written after 1819, where he suggests that poetry figuratively anticipates the fruition of other forms of thinking.

No man was ever yet a great poet, without being at the same time a profound philosopher. For poetry is the blossom and the fragrancy of all human knowledge, human thoughts, human passions, emotions, language. (*BL* II 19)

as poetry is the *identity* of all other knowledge, so a poet cannot be a *great* poet but as being likewise and inclusively an historian and naturalist in the light as well as the life of philosophy. All other men's worlds (κοσμοι) are *his* chaos. (*MC* 343)[2]

As early as 1804 he had envisaged the poet creating this 'identity' and shaping a world out of the disparate and apparently unrelated forms of human apprehension through the power of love. 'Idly talk they who speak of Poets as mere Indulgers of Fancy, Imagination, Superstition, &c – They are the Bridlers by Delight, the Purifiers, they that combine them with *reason* & order, the true Protoplasts, Gods of Love who tame the Chaos.' (*NB* II 2355)

Another entry of 1807 suggests that it is 'the horror vacui, which is still the law of Hearts preattuned to Love' (*NB* II 3093). He therefore

[2]See the derivative remarks in Shelley's 'A Defence of Poetry', *Shelley's Prose, or The Trumpet of a Prophecy,* ed. D. L. Clark (Albuquerque, 1954, 1966), 293: 'Poetry is the root and blossom of all other systems of thought'; and 'poetry . . . makes us inhabitants of a world to which the familiar world is a chaos. It reproduces the common Universe of which we are portions and participants', 295.

agrees with Wordsworth's description of the poet as one 'who looks at the world in the spirit of love' – a love prized as the medium and carrier of 'relationship' (*WLC* 79, 81). The involution of love within the creative process returns us once more to the concept of a passion indicative of a symbolic and harmonious order. But the poetic order is ideal, or rather, in the words of a lecture on Milton of 1818, 'the translation of reality into the ideal under the predicament of succession of time only. The poet is an historian, upon condition of moral power being the only force in the universe' (*MC* 162). He is referring here to *Paradise Lost*. Paradoxically, the poetic vision approaches the authority of historical fact only given certain ideal conditions not obtaining in the real world. *Paradise Lost* is a particularly good example of this for a Christian like Coleridge:

The connexion of the sentences and the position of the words are exquisitely artificial; but the position is rather according to the logic of passion or universal logic, than to the logic of grammar. Milton attempted to make the English language obey the logic of passion as perfectly as the Greek and Latin. Hence the occasional harshness in the construction. (*MC* 163–4)

Coleridge is arguing that Milton modifies the grammar of language in order to enable the poetic presentation of religious truth. The 'universal' category to which his artificial construction gains him access is the premature fulfilment of the Christian prophecy. In surrendering himself to the logic of 'passion' rather than of 'grammar', Milton forces language to construct an ideally unified vision. His poetry bears the same relation to ordinary language and its growing, living principle as his religious vision bears to the ordinary life where God is the regulative principle, still working his purpose out from year to year. The two poles are distinct – poetry and grammar, prophetic vision and the practical decisions of everyday life – but neither can be properly understood in isolation. Coleridge sees the same dialectic behind Milton's own poetic motives for providing an ideal version of his worldly aspirations:

Milton . . . was, as every truly great poet has ever been, a good man; but finding it impossible to realize his own aspirations, either in religion or politics, or society, he gave up his heart to the living spirit and light within him, and avenged himself on the world by enriching it with this record of his own transcendent ideal. (*MC* 165)

Milton, however, is obliged to use his poetic guile 'by stealth' to show how his ideal transcription enriches its mundane original. The risk is now to the purity of the religious truth, and not to the grammar of ordinary language. He concedes to grammar what is necessary for his total vision to be communicable, and for the logic of passion to be expressed. The dispute between Wordsworth and Coleridge centres on this question of what compromise it is practicable for the poet to make between the poles of the ideal and real.

Milton's successful pragmatism is more fully described in the *Table Talk* entry of 4 September 1833.

Pope satirises Milton for making God the Father talk like a school divine. Pope was hardly the man to criticise Milton. The truth is, the judgement of Milton in the conduct of the celestial part of his story is very exquisite. Wherever God is represented as directly acting as Creator, without any exhibition of his own essence, Milton adopts the simplest and sternest language of the Scriptures. He ventures upon no poetic diction, no amplification, no pathos, no affection. It is truly the Voice of the Word of the Lord coming to, and acting on, the subject Chaos. But, as some personal interest was demanded for the purposes of poetry, Milton takes advantage of the dramatic representation of God's addresses to the Son, the Filial Alterity, and in *those addresses* slips in, as it were by stealth, language of affection, or thought, or sentiment. Indeed, although Milton was undoubtedly a high Arian in his mature life, he does in the necessity of poetry give a greater objectivity to the Father and the Son than he would have justified in argument. (*MC* 429–30)

The Miltonic example begins to fill out Coleridge's concept of the ideal in poetry, and adds substance to the Kantian skeleton of his aesthetic. Milton shows the range of implications in a peculiarly poetic use of language: what is lost in detail through the ideal transcription is offset through its catholicity; and what is lost in spirituality is made up for in expressive power. It was this exalted dialectic of poetry, the economy of imitation, its gains and losses, which Coleridge feared Wordsworth's arguments about diction and metre might be used to obscure. The criticisms he makes of Wordsworth are part of the larger debate in his thought between what may be justified from 'the necessity of poetry', and what may be 'justified in argument': a debate concerned to establish the status of poetry as poetry, to show how the great poet necessarily makes us aware of the symbolic necessity of his vision.

WORDSWORTHIAN ALTERNATIVES:
SYMBOLISM OR LITERALISM

Wordsworth's intention in *Lyrical Ballads* is to provide a language so responsive and flexible that it will be able to describe the human qualities which had eluded the closed systems of those contemporary philosophers with whom (like Coleridge) he had become disillusioned. However, Wordsworth parts company from Coleridge where he can be interpreted as believing the language of a particular class of people in a particular emotional state to be most expressive of human nature, for then all that is left for the poet to do is transcribe most faithfully and literally this specific use of language. Any self-advertisement on the part of poetry could only distract from this task: the literary component should be kept to a minimum; poetic writing should aspire, in Barthes' words, to a 'degré zéro'. There seems no room left for a poetic imitation different from ordinary language. Coleridge worries that such poetic *literalism* denies to poetry the art of providing *symbols* adequate to express human nature.

In the 'Advertisement' to *Lyrical Ballads* of 1798 Wordsworth defined the subject-matter of poetry as whatever it is that can 'interest' the human mind.[3] His reading of Rousseau, Paine, Paley, Mackintosh and, most significantly, Godwin, among others, had led him to a fiercely impartial concept of reason which he adopted even at the expense of this human 'interest'. However after the *Letter to the Bishop of Llandaff* Godwin's influence wanes; and by the time of writing the 'Preface' to *The Borderers* Wordsworth was keen to stress the dangerous uses of pure reason. In an *Essay on Morals* of 1798 he criticized the philosophy of Paley and Godwin for 'an undue value set upon that faculty which we call reason' (*W* I 103). He thinks this imbalance deprives both philosophers of an intelligible philosophy of action. He moves from a Humean dissatisfaction with the notion of purely rational motives to action towards a modified common sense or Burkean alternative. No proposition can move us to action which has

[3]See *The Letters of William and Dorothy Wordsworth, II, The Middle Years, Part I, 1806–11*, 2nd edn revised by Mary Moorman (Oxford, 1969), 147; in 1809 Wordsworth plans the arrangement of a future edition of his poems on 'a scale of imagination or interest', *ibid.*, 335–6.

no connection through 'image' or 'feeling' with 'the supposed archetype or fountain of the proposition existing in human life'. Wordsworth explains this connection by arguing for the necessity of what Burke had called a 'wardrobe of the moral imagination': reasons only present themselves as motives to action when suitably clad. 'These moralists attempt to strip the mind of all its old clothing when their object ought to be to furnish it with new' (W I 103); they deprive the mind of the category of 'interest'. Wordsworth now goes on to claim that Paley and Godwin can only argue as they do by distorting the accepted function of language. Like a common-sense philosopher he attacks them because their philosophical descriptions do not attach to anything:

The whole secret of this juggler's trick [?s] lies (not in fitting words to things (which would be a noble employment) [but] in fitting things to words – I have said that these bald and naked reasonings are impotent over our habits, they cannot form them; from the same cause they are equally powerless in regulating our judgements concerning the value of men & things. They contain no picture of human life; they *describe* nothing. (W I 103)

Wordsworth's condemnation of a certain kind of philosophy on the grounds of its failure as description lends philosophical weight to the task he then saw himself as performing in *Lyrical Ballads*. Poetry remedies a deficient philosophy of action by showing how human actions, whose motives are never purely rational, are significant.[4] Properly described, they become intelligible. Remembering Coleridge's advice to Godwin two years later in 1800 to become more self-conscious about the language he employed, and so to adopt the role of 'a Poet employing his philosophic knowledge practically' (CL I 636), we can now appreciate the extent of the harmony between the two men's thinking at this time, which permitted Coleridge to write the letter Wordsworth sent to William Wilberforce in January 1801. In the general polemic against the language of 'our modern writers in

[4]See P. D. Sheats, *The Making of Wordsworth's Poetry 1785–1798* (Cambridge, Mass., 1973), for a detailed study of the development of Wordsworth's poetic practice from a confrontation with 'a divided culture', separating reason and passion, to the possession of a 'language that, in Bacon's terms, buckles the mind to empirical fact and yet simultaneously acknowledges the power and the authority of the "desires of the mind"', 7, 93 – a language of practical reason.

verse and prose' it is easy to miss the precise philosophical orientation of the opening statement: 'I composed the accompanying poems under the persuasion that all which is usually included under the name of action bears the same pro[por]tion (in respect of worth) to the affections as a language to the thing sign[ified]' (*CL* II 666). Wordsworth's efforts in *Lyrical Ballads* are devoted to making human actions intelligible by showing how they can speak to us, how they can be construed as the language of human 'interest'. However, in addition to this, he thought that a particular class of actions was more interesting than others, and so more readily definitive of human character, passions and incidents. Coleridge always agreed with the former claim for poetry as the most adequate interpretation of human action; but he thought that Wordsworth's choice of subject-matter was bound to work against these grandiose pretensions.

In the 1802 'Preface', Wordsworth suggests that poetry takes delight in the *way* we understand the world. Poetry does not assert scientific propositions, but catches the 'breath', 'finer spirit' and 'expression' characteristic of human apprehension. This is in agreement with the theory of poetry which Coleridge later found confirmed in Kantian aesthetics. The poet uniquely owes allegiance to the expression of human nature and not to any specific scientific knowledge. In Wordsworth's words, he is 'the rock of human nature', and this means that the poet 'writes under one restriction only, namely, that of the necessity of giving immediate pleasure to a human Being possessed of that information which may be expected from him, not as a lawyer, a physician, a mariner, an astronomer or a natural philosopher, but as a Man' (*WLC* 79). In this attempt to give expression to the human nature residing behind all specialized vocabularies, the poet has to use his own symbolic language which consciously escapes the truth-conditions of all the others. Wordsworth's poet fits Coleridge's aesthetic theory examined in chapter 4: he is uniquely equipped to review science in the light of human interest through his power to deliver the most complete expression of human nature possible.

Now in explicit contrast to this interpretation we must find a way of seeing how Wordsworth could have been regarded as having a literalist rather than a symbolic view of poetry. In the 1802 'Preface' he wrote that the discrepancy which poetry might create in imitating the ordinary language of passion could only be in the interest of 'amusement and idle pleasure', a frivolous substitute for the real thing (*WLC* 79). The corollary of this distrust of any claims for the existence of a poetic language different from people's actual articulation of their feelings is the literalism of part of Wordsworth's defence of *Lyrical Ballads*. Poetry is a transcription and not an interpretation. The only difference between the poetic response and certain common human responses is that the poet requires fewer external stimuli: 'How, then, can his language differ in any material degree from that of all other men who feel vividly and see clearly?' (*WLC* 82). And he adds: 'Our feelings are the same with respect to metre.'

Coleridge's criticism of Wordsworth on the basis of this literalism remains as vulnerable as it is partial. There is always present in Wordsworth's thought the alternative theory of poetry as symbol; and Coleridge frequently calls literal what he is ideologically unwilling to accept as symbolic. The problem, then, is not to find a means of defending Wordsworth – he does that well enough in his own writings and Coleridge's theory supports him – but to explain in more detail the persistent attacks of an otherwise staunch defender.

Wordsworth's reluctance to consider the poet as anything other than a faithful transcriber partly arises from the eighteenth-century cast of his thought. Passages in the 1802 'Preface' are reminiscent of Kames' idea that the excellence of a poetic representation is measured by its success in placing the reader in the position of spectator. For this to be possible the poet himself must sympathize completely with his subject-matter. He must not be a spectator of the characters represented, but should 'slip into an entire delusion, and even confound and identify his own feelings with theirs' (*WLC* 78). The opposite of this is when the poet 'describes and imitates passions' and is reduced, in Kames' words, to the 'imperfection' of 'a cold description in the language of a bystander'.[5] Then, thinks Wordsworth, the poet's effort is 'slavish and mechanical'. Wordsworth

[5] *WLC* 79; *Elements of Criticism*, I 456; Kames' argument is also used by Coleridge in *SC* I 214; II 131–3.

seems to lose all confidence in the independent importance of poetic description except as it can efface itself within an exact transcription of the infinitely more flexible and informative responses of real life. The genetic bias of Wordsworth's theory – the importance he attaches to a particular use of language on account of its origin – combines with his view of the sympathetic imagination to conspire against poetry. Modifications of real responses should only be to enable more pleasure by removing 'what would otherwise be painful or disgusting in the passion', and not in order to articulate a more significant view of things. This gives the appearance of a 'revolt' against literature.[6] Poetry cannot claim anything for itself: at best it is an accurate and easily available documentary of what happens; at worst it has become redundant.

Coleridge's unfair concentration on the strain of literalism in the 'Prefaces' is his way of emphasizing the artifice defining poetry – the significant difference of imitation from original, and the aesthetic purpose of the self-advertising features of diction and metre which Wordsworth had pronounced superfluous. Similarly, Hazlitt's objections to the 'literary Jacobinism', as he described Wordsworth's programme for poetry, show his response to what he takes to be Wordsworth's covert admission of professional bankruptcy.[7] Hazlitt resented Wordsworth's presentation of an apparent abdication of poetic responsibility as if it were a radical, democratic extension of the subject-matter of poetry – a radicalism which Wordsworth's own political behaviour belied. Wordsworth purported to give new clothing to human apprehension, to make poetry the instrument of a radical reassessment of the nature of essential human responses, while in fact he was not writing as a poet at all. He may, according to Hazlitt's diagnosis, have been working 'on a principle of sheer humanity', but one which was 'void of art'.[8] It is only if we can grasp the possibly fraudulent character of Wordsworth's aims on this interpretation that we can appreciate the reasons for Hazlitt's

[6]See H. Darbishire, *The Poet Wordsworth* (London, 1950), 35; R. Sharrock, 'Wordsworth's Revolt Against Literature', *Essays in Criticism*, 3 (1953), 396–412.
[7]Hazlitt, *Works*, VII 143–4.
[8]*Ibid.*, V 162.

bitterness, and Coleridge's unfairness. Nevertheless, these attitudes finally reflect more on the critics themselves. Hazlitt, the radical, was infuriated by the way such democratic subject-matter remained, to his sensibility, refractory, and resistant to the art of poetry. He was forced to the conclusion that poetry was an inherently anti-democratic art which put 'might before right'.[9] Coleridge, radical in theory but increasingly conservative in practice, was worried by Wordsworth's attempt to effect a real change in conventional attitudes, and to let us hear symbolic resonances in persons and subjects hitherto regarded as literally insignificant. The border between literal and symbolical, the possibility of Wordsworthian alternatives, was sometimes genuinely problematic for Coleridge, an area whose uncertainty was even proposed by the aesthetics of sublimity. But at other times it was a division which, as we shall see, he found it in his ideological interests to preserve and maintain under strict critical control.

PASSION, DICTION AND METRE

In *Biographia* Coleridge described Wordsworth's 'Preface' to *Lyrical Ballads* as the origin of 'the unexampled opposition' (*BL* I 51) encountered by Wordsworth's own writings. By concentrating on one particular strain in Wordsworth's critical theory Coleridge believed he could investigate the predominant preoccupation of contemporary criticism of Wordsworth. His own work had been included in the same critical reception (unfairly, as he thought) and he was far more concerned to justify the poetry than to salvage the theory. As he wrote to Southey in 1813: 'but if it had not been for *the Preface* to W's Lyrical Ballads they would themselves have never dreamt of affected Simplicity & Meanness of Thought & Diction –. This Slang has gone on for 14 or 15 years, against us – & really deserves to be exposed' (*CL* III 433). The 'Prefaces' do contain outright contradictions and competing arguments; and the literalist emphasis frequently chosen by the critics to represent Wordsworth's thought was one which Coleridge thought '*would* exclude, two-thirds at least of the marked

[9]*Ibid.*, IV 214–15.

beauties of his poetry' (*BL* II 84). Coleridge uses the partial, literalist interpretation of the 'Prefaces' as the device for making clear his own critical priorities and principles.

Coleridge believed that while the metaphysical poets sacrificed passion in poetry to intellect and wit, the moderns sacrifice both to a false diction, 'to point and drapery' (*BL* I 15). The main source of 'our pseudo-poetic diction' is Pope's translation of Homer, not Pope's original compositions, which Coleridge values as 'almost faultless' in their choice and positioning of words (*BL* I 26n.).[10] Modern poetry – an otherwise vague category – seems to be restricted in Coleridge's thought to poetry whose diction can be derived from this model. It betrays a characteristically modern 'ANXIETY to be always *striking*', pursued to the detriment of 'the *inventive* passion' (*NB* II 2728, 2723). This passion is the fundamental category in Coleridge's definition of poetry. It justifies poetic diction, and is implied by the use of metre. He considers passion generally to be productive of the dramatic character of the English language (*NB* III 3970; *SC* II 103); but it is his belief that poetry has its *own* passion, pointing to its own 'necessity', which is relevant here. Diction and metre are devices which ensure poetry's independence from other uses of language by directing the reader's attention towards the expression of an autonomous poetic passion.

Wordsworth describes poetic diction as 'arbitrary and subject to infinite caprices', leaving the reader 'utterly at the mercy of the poet respecting what imagery or diction he may choose to connect with the passion' (*W* I 144). But when he offers a genuine language of poetry, and not a spurious, inherited poetic diction, he describes a feeling similarly wedded to its poetic expression. The 'feeling' in his famous statement that in the *Lyrical Ballads* 'the feeling therein developed gives importance to the action and situation, and not the action and situation to the feeling', is explicitly contrasted with the whimsical emotion he thought was expresssed in 'the popular Poetry of the day'. Wordsworth's poetic feeling is indicative of his art. The 'purpose'

[10]See the letter to Thomas Curnick of 1814 (*CL* III 469–70); *NB* II 2826; *SC* II 220–1.

which he claims each of his poems to embody is 'developed' out of the 'feeling'; and his symbolic 'purpose' is to transform otherwise unfeeling appearances into an intelligible and significant language. He reaffirms for us, through his distinctive poetic vision, an identifiable human 'interest' in situations where we had not felt it before. His expression of feeling is only personal as it imaginatively reveals actions to be legible: it is only Wordsworth's as it adds to our language.[11]

Coleridge's argument for the necessity of a poetic diction distinguishing poetry from prose is not an argument for a separate vocabulary, or 'that a poet ever uses a word as poetical – that is, formally – which he, in the same mood and thought, would not use in prose or conversation.' The difference rather is one of organization, of poetry's stricter conformity to a unified pattern. In a notebook entry of 1809 Coleridge writes that the 'sole difference *in style* is that poetry demands a *severer keeping* – it admits nothing that Prose may not often admit, but it *oftener* rejects. In other words, it presupposes a more continuous state of Passion' (*NB* III 3611). For Coleridge, the stylistic artifice and the passion peculiar to poetry define each other. The poetic passion is different from ordinary passion in the way that poetic language engineers an artificially finished unity, 'a severer keeping', within the open-ended and still growing medium of language.

Coleridge recognizes the important truth that the feelings expressed in art are as different from those felt in real life as the thoughts and events described in art are different from their real counterparts. The fictional distance is the same in each case. This links Coleridge's thought with Aristotle's classical discussion of expressiveness in art by means of the notion of catharsis. In *Biographia* Coleridge tells us that our response to a poem is not 'a separate excitement', but 'a continuous *undercurrent* of feeling' which 'is everywhere present' (*BL* I 15). Aristotle thinks that the emotions which a work of art evokes in us (pity and fear) arise from 'the very structure and incidents' of the

---

[11]Contrast John Casey's criticism of Wordsworth on 'feeling', in *The Language of Criticism* (London, 1966), 88.

work itself. If the passion underlying the 'keeping' of a poem is similarly inseparable from it, then the catharsis of the passion is achieved by reading the poem. The poem is complete, and so, therefore, is the passion of which the poem is the expression. In the continuous experience of real life, as opposed to the artificial foreshortening of it in aesthetic experience, passions can proceed unabated. But while we might do something through feelings aroused in us by art, as a result of its aesthetic education, it would not make sense to say, for example, 'I am helping him because I feel pity for Lear.' Helping him will not help Lear.

For Coleridge, then, the nature of poetic passion distinguishes poetry from expressions of feeling in real life and demands a correspondingly different use of language. Poetry is untranslatable: it cannot be paraphrased in ordinary language and remain poetry. Coleridge often presents this conclusion in an extreme form:

it would be scarcely more difficult to push a stone out from the pyramids with the bare hand, than to alter a word, or the position of a word, in Milton, or Shakespeare (in their most important works at least) without making the author say something else, or something worse, than he does say. (BL I 15)

In chapter 23 of *Biographia* he is bitter about critics who repeat the 'old blunder . . . concerning the irregularity and wildness of Shakespeare', quoting him 'as authority for the most anti-Shakespearean drama' (BL II 184). What Shakespeare (or Milton) says in a particular instance depends on our reading of the whole. It is the pressure of that consideration, making every word which contributes to an image fully intelligible only within a larger pattern, which locks each word in its place. Our understanding of the meanings of a word at any specific moment in, say, *Paradise Lost,* is controlled by what we have read and by our resulting expectations of what is to come. We ought not to be able to substitute one important word in a poem without necessarily altering the context or poetically created register which allows it to mean as it does. Coleridge believes that poetry is untranslatable not because poetic diction is made up of a fixed vocabulary, but because it is the range of meaning set by the artificial limits which each poem imposes upon language. Coleridge's extravagant organicism turns out to anticipate the assumptions behind some of the best modern practical criticism. William Empson knew that it was a 'complex' not a simple truth that 'fool' in *Lear,* 'honest' in *Othello,* and 'sense' in *The Prelude* could not mean in the same way outside these works.

Coleridge's point about having 'the *best* words in the best order' in poetry is to draw attention to the medium, not as an absolute value independent of any individual poem's unity, but something whose 'propriety' is 'relative' to a particular poetic end. In prose, the medium must be unobtrusive because it is not part of the information which it is the purpose of any piece of prose to communicate. In poetry the medium is noteworthy because it is 'beautiful', and so a constitutive part of the aesthetic dimension, the 'purpose', as Wordsworth called it in the 'Preface', the expected end for which we read the poem (*TT* I 76, II 110–11).

Coleridge approves of Wordsworth's repudiation of a poetic diction whose figures and metaphors have been 'stripped of their justifying reasons'; but he objects to reasons adduced by Wordsworth to justify his alternative to the discredited poetic diction. Wordsworth moves from the 'merely comparative' to the 'exclusive' and 'direct partiality' of certain passages in the 'Prefaces' (*BL* II 70). If he succeeded in isolating 'a selection of the REAL language of men' the result would still be irrelevant to poetry. The definition of poetry, in Coleridge's view, is inseparable from the self-defining quality of a poem. It is the 'order' in which a phraseology or vocabulary is arranged which grants poetry its aesthetic importance. Wordsworth's discussion, in Coleridge's opinion, is not only partial, but about the wrong kind of thing; his literal realism is not only 'impracticable', but also 'useless' (*BL* II 43–4).

Coleridge had his own account of the crisis which provoked Wordsworth's experimental attitude. We noted Coleridge's belief that Milton's diction in *Paradise Lost* betrayed occasionally a harshness of construction in its attempt to 'obey the logic of passion as perfectly as the Greek and Latin'. But even these classical ideals are surpassed in Coleridge's esteem for his native language. In a note comparing the virtues of many languages he declares that the English by its <monosyllabic, naturalizing, and> marvellously meta-phorical Spirit (for the excellence wholly out of the Question What language can exhibit a style that resembles that of Shakespeare, Jeremy Taylor, or Burke?) can express more meaning, image, and passion *tri-unely* in a given number of articulate sounds than any other in the world, not excepting even the ancient Greek/ . . . & that the English not by accidental Production of Genius, but by its natural constitution stands unequalled for all kinds of Poetry, in which the more complex and profounder Passions are united with deep Thought. . . . (*NB* II 2431)

However Coleridge found that the rich history of his native language had provoked a crisis in the modern poet's confidence in his own medium. Certainly in retrospect, and perhaps even at the time of composition, he considered the poetry he and Wordsworth wanted to write to require a division of labour. In the modern age, the poetic range mastered so easily by the language of the past must now be recovered through specialization; poets must co-operate, and pool their stylistic resources. The *Lyrical Ballads* were intended to constitute one poem.[12] The individual poems, according to a later notebook entry, were to be the active but partial constituents of a dramatic whole: each was to be understood as existing 'by way of counterbalance to another Truth falsified by having been carried into excess' (*NB* III 3573). The two poets needed to co-operate because the language each used was no longer the uniform expression of a common culture. Poetry was becoming as specialized a discipline as any branch of knowledge, raising awkward problems for those who, like Wordsworth and Coleridge, valued poetry as the universal expression of a unified sensibility. Wordsworth's attempt to combine the personal, accomplished voice of the lyric with the objective, plain narrative of the ballad shows his desire to find a single use of language adequate to extremes of human experience. Coleridge worries that subject and object contradict each other in some of Wordsworth's

[12]See the letter to Joseph Cottle of 28 May 1798 (*CL* I 411–12), 'We deem that the volumes offered to you are to a certain degree *one work,* in *kind tho' not in degree,* as an Ode is one work – & that our different poems are as stanzas'; interestingly, when Coleridge goes on to consider one of the poems in the separate status of its 'degree' – as an extract from his tragedy *Osorio* – he quickly finds it wanting in comparison with Shakespeare. Similarly, he describes Wordsworth as thinking that his own contributions would be unable to stand on their own because 'they would want variety &c &c – if this apply in his case, it applies with tenfold force to mine.'

poems, and his stylistic and political anxieties merge in a complicated critical response, as will be seen in the next section.

This search for a sufficient language reaches into the second generation of English Romantics, and helps explain their modifications of existing literary forms. Wordsworth's visionary revisions of Miltonic epic are matched by the mythopoeia of Keats and Shelley; and Byron's irony exhausts the Romantic sensibility in quest of the more capable language of a new maturity, confidently combining high and low styles without political anxiety. The unlikely mixture of genres — comic, serious, Quixotic and visionary — which sustains the argument of a poem like 'The Idiot Boy' is developed in the work of the later poets who lived at sufficient distance from 1789 for the recovery of a radical enthusiasm to be plausible.

In Coleridge's theory the aesthetic status indicated by the diction of poetry is reiterated by metre. Whatever the difficulties and innovations demanded in devising a competent poetic diction, metre remains a constant ally of poetry. Like diction it shows that poetry can be '*essentially* different' by means of a peculiar '*construction*, and an *order* of sentences' (*BL* II 48–9). Coleridge's arguments for the indispensability of metre to the definition of poetry once more rely on his belief in the need for poetry to place itself as poetry. He emphasizes the artificial, deliberate character of metre. Its initial connection with 'the natural language of excitement' should be enriched by the artistic 'purpose' of the poet, so that what are 'originally the offspring of passion' become 'the adopted children of power' (*BL* II 50). The poetic transformation uses natural excitement in the service of its own power, changing the original into the unifying passion of poetry itself:

where there exists that degree of genius and talent which entitles a writer to aim at the honours of a poet, the very *act* of poetic composition *itself* is, and is *allowed* to imply and to produce, an unusual state of excitement, which of course justifies and demands a correspondent difference of language, as truly, though not perhaps in as marked a degree, as the excitement of love, fear, rage, or jealousy. (*BL* II 56)[13]

[13]See *SC* I 163–4; II 68, 79; this is Shelley's point in 'A Defence of Poetry' when he writes of a 'uniform and harmonious recurrence of sound' which 'is scarcely less indispensable to the communication of poetry's . . . influence than the words themselves, without reference to that peculiar order', 280.

In the third of the 1811–12 lectures, metre generates excitement in a manner constituting 'an analogy of the language of strong passion' (*SC* II 78). The 'analogy' maintains that conceptual distance between poetry and the ordinary, affective language it appropriates necessary to the independent existence of both.

In his marginalia to Selden's *Table Talk* Coleridge describes how metrical language distinguishes poetry as poetry: 'Verse is in itself a music, and the natural symbol of that union of Passion with Thought and Pleasure, which constitutes the *Essence* of all *Poetry,* as contra-distinguished from Science, and distinguished from History, civil or natural' (*MC* 277). Metre maintains a symbolic distance between poetic unity and logical coherence: 'True; they (*i.e.,* verses) are not logic: but they are, or ought to be, the envoys or representatives of that vital passion which is the practical cement of logic, and without which logic must remain inert' (*MC* 277). Coleridge thinks that in the course of the history of English literature a change takes place in the use of metre. After Dryden the effect of metre becomes 'mechanical', and the artistic priorities of the poet are reversed. The poetic transformation becomes something other than the artificially completed development of the meaning of the words. Coleridge tries to rectify this, subordinating once more the classical ideal to the genius of English. He remarks in a marginal note to Beaumont and Fletcher on the subject of 'the philosophy of metre' that it is:

true that *quantity,* an almost iron law with the Greek, is in our language rather a subject for a peculiarly fine ear, than any law or even rule; but then we, instead of it, have, first, accent; secondly, emphasis; and lastly, retardation and acceleration of the times of syllables according to the meaning of the words, the passion that accompanies them, and even the character of the person that uses them. . . . Since Dryden, the metre of our poets leads to the sense: in our elder and more genuine poets, the sense, including the passion, leads to the metre. Read even Donne's satires as he meant them to be read and as the sense and passion demand, and you will find in the lines a manly harmony. (*MC* 66–7)

Coleridge's praise of Donne and his criticism of, for example, Scott (*NB* III 3970), are based on the belief that we should not deduce the metrical character of English verse from a set of classically established precepts. Again we find him arguing that the practical understanding of the language should generate the critical principle. In this he was followed by perhaps the most brilliant metrical innovator between his time and ours. Gerard Manley Hopkins' advocacy of sprung rhythm repeats Coleridge's wish that spoken accent and emphasis replace scansion on fixed classical models. Sprung rhythm helps Hopkins stress the inscape of objects: that quiddity, or inner integrity, which escapes empirical scrutiny. But he also thinks poetry has its own inscape, and, like Coleridge, attributes an independent value to the artificial unity of a poem.[14] Hopkins' reader, as much as Coleridge's, prepares himself to receive a language which will 'produce the effect of a *whole*. Where this is not achieved in a poem, the metre merely reminds the reader of his claims in order to disappoint them . . .' (*BL* II 98). It is 'the *effect* of metre and the *art* of poetry' to produce what Coleridge called in marginalia to Milton's poems, 'the organized version' of their original material (*CSC* 566–7). And this 'organized version' allows Shakespeare, for example, to achieve a power of expression beyond the natural range of human passion:

he always by metaphors and figures involves in the thing considered a universe of past and possible experiences; he mingles earth, sea, and air, gives a soul to everything, and at the same time that he inspires human feelings, adds a dignity in his images to human nature itself. . . . (*MC* 96; lecture of 1818)

His poetry creates an ideal by universalizing, literally, the feelings out of which it is made; and he creates a linguistic world just by allowing feelings that dignity of complete expression so rare in real life.

Wordsworth falls into contradictory positions in his 'Preface' when he tries to allow metre a place in his definition of poetry, while still claiming that there is no such thing as a poetic use of language different from 'the language of men' or 'the language of prose'.[15] The trouble arises at that point where he tries to describe the contribution of metre to poetry as if this is something different from a distinctively

---

[14]*The Notebooks and Papers of Gerard Manley Hopkins,* ed. H. House (London and New York, 1937), 249–50.
[15]W. J. B. Owen, *Wordsworth as Critic* (Toronto and London, 1969), 30–2, tries to make sense of Wordsworth's separation, in the 'Prefaces', of metre and poetic diction.

poetic use of language. He seems to think that language remains constitutionally unchanged even if it conforms to a metrical pattern, and even if the configuration and measured quality has the consequence of producing new feelings in the reader or auditor (*WLC* 83). However, since in the 'Preface' he has already defined 'languages' genetically and affectively, either in terms of the feelings which produce them or the feelings aroused by them, he ought to describe the effect of metre as a substantial modification in the language involved. In Wordsworth's explanation, metre introduces three important considerations on its own account. First, its connotations of the regularity of unimpassioned life introduce 'ordinary feeling' to the language of passion; secondly, metre introduces a feeling (Wordsworth does not make it clear that this feeling is different from the 'ordinary feeling') which is 'not strictly and necessarily connected with the passion'. Finally, this is shown to be 'true' from 'the tendency of metre to divest language in a certain degree of its reality' (*WLC* 84). We now encounter the possibility of an artfully contrived language of poetry.

That this is a conclusion which Wordsworth sometimes reached, and which Coleridge's partial criticism of him ignores, is confirmed by advice which Wordsworth gave to John Thelwall in a letter of 1804. Wordsworth wishes to prescribe 'limitations' to the 'rule' which Thelwall had proposed, and which demands that 'the art of verse should not compel you to read in some [tone some] emphasis etc. that violates the nature of Prose.' Wordsworth thought that Thelwall was forgetting a characteristic of some words in poetry. This has the consequence that 'it will be Physically impossible . . . not to give them an intonation of one kind or another, or to follow them with a pause, not called out for by the passion of the subject, but by the passion of metre merely.'[16] To an ear as sensitive, as 'peculiarly fine' as Wordsworth's the necessity of poetry, indicated by the 'passion' arising out of the 'metre merely', is so powerful that it physically compels a consciously poetic reading.

Finally, we can now try to make sense of Coleridge's puzzling but important statement, arising from another act of desynonymy in

[16]*The Letters of William and Dorothy Wordsworth, I, The Early Years, 1787–1805*, ed. E. de Selincourt, rev. edn C. L. Shaver (Oxford, 1967), 434.

chapter 14 of *Biographia* between poems and poetry, that 'a poem of any length neither can be, nor ought to be, all poetry.' Why not? Coleridge thinks that both poem and poetry are defined in opposition to science, but that poetry can exist without 'the contradistinguishing objects of a poem': diction and metre (*BL* II 8–12). Poetry is not defined by the professed aim of any work in which it appears. The poetry is in the kind of attention it excites, and that, as this section has been suggesting, is defined by the reading appropriate to a poem. We attend to poetry in a manner independent of the truths which its language may be used to communicate. If we find a piece of Isaiah or Plato poetic we read it *as if* it were part of a poem and not part of a religious prophecy or a philosophy. We read it as if it were surrounded by conventions, such as diction and metre, which ask us to find it poetic by being, as Coleridge puts it, '*in keeping* with the poetry'. But if a poem were all poetry these devices would be redundant. There would be nothing else for the poem's 'contradistinguishing objects', diction and metre, to coerce into keeping with the poetry. The poem would therefore cease to be distinguishable as a poem.

We can see this distinction as fitting into Coleridge's view that poems are reflective or 'sentimental' in Schiller's sense, while poetry need not be. Consciousness of its aesthetic status is part of the subject-matter of a poem; hence these defining characteristics of diction and metre by which a poem invites an appropriately poetic reading. We therefore need poems to help us define what poetry is. But couldn't we enjoy poetry without defining it? If the young Wordsworth had based his attack on poetic diction, his revolt against the literary, his desire for a 'writing degree zero' on that challenge, it is hard to see how Coleridge could have answered him. But this would have demanded a degree of professional disinterestedness or scepticism beyond even Wordsworth. Nevertheless, Coleridge like Schiller, assumes that the modern aesthetic consciousness is irretrievably sentimental and literary. Yet if Schiller found Goethe an exception to this rule, why should Wordsworth not have surprised Coleridge?[17]

[17]Schiller, *Naive and Sentimental Poetry*, 137–8; contrast Emerson Marks' discussion of the problem, following T. S. Eliot, in terms of 'intensity', *Coleridge on the Language of Verse* (Princeton, New Jersey, 1981), 72–82.

DEFECTS AND EXCELLENCES

Coleridge assumes the reader's approval of his censure of Wordsworth's literalism when he comes to the task of criticizing his friend's poetry in the long chapter 22 of *Biographia*. This is a premiss of the ensuing argument: 'Let it be observed that I am here supposing the imagined judge, to whom I appeal, to have already decided against the poet's theory, as far as it is different from the principles of the art, generally acknowledged' (*BL* II 97). Throughout volume II Coleridge had been consistently emphasizing the ideal, willed, artificial quality of poetry hinted at by his desynonymizing of secondary imagination at the end of volume I. This was a necessary stage in the process of bringing to consciousness 'the principles of the art, generally acknowledged'. He had already praised Wordsworth's poetry in chapter 4 for

above all the original gift of spreading the tone, the *atmosphere,* and with it the depth and height of the *ideal* world around forms, incidents and situations, of which, for the common view, custom had bedimmed all the lustre, had dried up the sparkle and the dew drops. (*BL* I 59)

This defamiliarization of the real by the ideal once more makes the heuristic, educative quality of poetry inseparable from an awareness of its art, the awareness that it *is* poetry. Defamiliarization assumes Coleridge's arguments for the inspirational significance poetry achieves by separating itself consciously from other, literal orders of thought. Coleridge's review of the defects and excellences of Wordsworth's poetry expounds in detail the practical implications of this poetic self-consciousness.

But first of all Coleridge works Shakespeare into this critical plan. At the end of chapter 15 it is Milton who is distinguished for attracting 'all forms and things to himself, into the unity of his own IDEAL'. But throughout that chapter Shakespeare is Coleridge's example of the poet who exhibits most immediately the advantages of a consciously poetic perspective on the real. Coleridge writes of the youthful poet, the author of *Venus and Adonis* and *The Rape of Lucrece,* that his powers in these poems exist 'even to excess'. Their virtues draw attention to, and foreground the poetical character of, his language perhaps too much, but nevertheless most usefully for Coleridge's attack on Wordsworth's literalism.

According to Coleridge, Shakespeare wrote *Venus and Adonis* in a language of extraordinary self-sufficiency, demanding 'the perpetual activity of attention' on the part of the reader. Coleridge's description of this language sounds surprisingly visual at first. It seems to contradict his remarks elsewhere on the 'despotism of the eye', and his criticism in chapter 16 of poets of the present age who propose 'new and striking images' as their main objects 'even to a degree of portraiture' and to the neglect of 'diction and metre' (*BL* II 21). Shakespeare's achievement is

by the highest effort of the picturesque in words of which words are capable, higher perhaps than was ever realized by any other poet, even Dante not excepted; to provide a substitute for that visual language, that constant intervention and running commentary by tone, look and gesture, which in his dramatic works he was entitled to expect from the players.

However on closer examination it emerges that the poem is praised not because it mirrors life, but because of the unique kind of attention to the experience described which it excites in the reader. *Venus and Adonis* is not pornography because of the more complicated activity forced on the reader by the poetic expression of the experience. 'The reader is forced into too much action to sympathize with the merely passive of our nature' – in other words, to be aroused by the sexuality. The aesthetic dimension, the 'picturesque' organization of the original, enables the reader to see more of the experience than might be the case if he were enjoying it and not sharing the poet's 'aloofness'.

In chapters 16 and 17 Coleridge emphasizes that 'the essence of poetry [is] in the *art*', and that 'poetry as poetry is essentially *ideal*' (*BL* II 23, 33). But the power of defamiliarization which he has attributed to poetry connects it in his thought and in the thought of much subsequent literary theory with the definition of the real. T. S. Eliot was resuming Coleridge as well as Arnold when he claimed that the 'end of the enjoyment of poetry is a pure contemplation from which all the accidents of personal emotion are removed; thus we aim to see the object as it really is.'[18] What is obscured by this tone of high disinterestedness is that the notion that poetry contributes to the definition of the real has its origin in an ideological controversy – Coleridge's objection to 'an equivocation in the use of the word "real"' in Wordsworth's description of the language of poetry as a selection of the 'real' language of men. Ideological disputes generate aesthetic disputes. Defamiliarization implies that poetry views objects with an exemplary generosity and detachment which encourage us to a knowledge of them superior to customary familiarity – a knowledge of them as they really are. However, the ideal views produced by poetry are not timelessly Platonic, but related to the needs of ways of knowing and acting in the world during particular historical periods. And this is what emerges from Coleridge's criticism of Wordsworth's poetry: Coleridge's political and religious bias are just what establish his conception of what constitutes poetic imagination. His feeling that Wordsworth should have foregrounded his poetic art, not hidden it in prose, is not distinct from his desire to see the images of mind and nature possessed by his view of society written large, or set in the round through the adequate idea of them given in imagination. When he did not encounter these images he was inclined to dismiss the poetry as inadequate.

We shall return to the ideological content of the political dispute later on. For the moment it should be noticed how this way of thinking draws an acknowledgement from Coleridge that his theory of imagination is emerging from his practical criticism and not vice versa.

Could a rule be given from *without,* poetry would cease to be poetry, and sink into a mechanical art. . . . The *rules* of the IMAGINATION are themselves the very powers of growth and production. The words to which they are reducible, present only the outlines and external appearance of the fruit. (*BL* II 65)

This means that the rules of imagination can only be described fully through an appreciation of the perspectives poetry gives on experience. In explaining what poems mean, what they amount to, we draw

[18]T. S. Eliot, 'The Perfect Critic', in *The Sacred Wood* (London, 1920, 1976), 14–15.

the shape of imagination: the theory emerges from the practical understanding. Poetic imagination isn't anything other than the increased power of attention released by poetry's defamiliarization of its historically relative object. In just the same way, the ideal Coleridge sought for different forms of thought, through principle and transposition, was still only identifiable as the adequate expression of their object within poetic imagination.

Coleridge's adverse criticism of Wordsworth suggests that his poetry conspires against the nature of poetry itself; chapter 22 of *Biographia* painstakingly elaborates this paradox. When Wordsworth's poetry is defective it is founded on a contradiction. Each of the defects which Coleridge describes is not generically distinct from the others, but contributes to their cumulative effect. When Coleridge finally brings all his critical points to bear on the 'Immortality Ode' he tries to show how Wordsworth's alternatives of literalism and symbolism exclude each other.

Coleridge lists the characteristics of Wordsworth's literalism: incongruities of diction result from 'unprepared' transitions from a recognizably poetic style to a prosaic one (*BL* II 97–8); his 'matter-of-factness' and 'accidentality' offend against the exemplary, Aristotelian aesthetic of Davenant which distinguishes 'the requisites of a poem' from 'the shackles of a historian'; Wordsworth, thinks Coleridge, is inclined to show 'a *biographical* attention to probability, and an *anxiety* of explanation and retrospect' (*BL* II 101–3). In *The Excursion* we are asked to accept the conflation of poet, philosopher and pedlar in the central character on grounds not of poetic probability but of historical possibility. A divisive paradox arises from this category confusion.

Spite of all attempts, the fiction *will* appear, and unfortunately not as *fictitious* but as *false*. The reader not only *knows*, that the sentiments and language are the poet's own, and his own too in his artificial character, as poet; but by the fruitless endeavours to make him think the contrary, he is not even suffered to *forget* it. (*BL* II 107)

This is related to Coleridge's criticism of Wordsworth's 'undue predilection for the *dramatic* form in certain poems' which can only create 'a species of ventriloquism, where two are represented as talking, while in truth one man only speaks' (*BL* II 109). Wordsworth's egotism and his inability to produce a convincing poetic transmutation of his literal content make his choice of material unimportant. Coleridge asks: 'need the rank have been at all particularized, where nothing follows which the knowledge of that rank is to explain or illustrate?' (*BL* II 108). Also, the manner in which his content retains its literal status weakens Wordsworth's poetic ambition, denying it the breadth attributed to poetry in much of the 'Preface' to *Lyrical Ballads*.

In the last chapter we saw that Coleridge regarded poetry as an anticipation, a pleasurable premonition of our perfected state. He thought that Wordsworth's literalism did not permit him to *imagine* such fulfilment, and that the literal reality with which he dealt is far too intractable to be shown in so ameliorating a light. The low remains low when untransfigured by a progressive fiction:

Not till the blessed time shall come, when truth itself shall be pleasure, and both shall be so united, as to be distinguishable in words only, not in feeling, it will remain the poet's office to proceed upon that state of association, which actually exists as *general*; instead of attempting first to *make* it what it ought to be, and then to let the pleasure follow. (*BL* II 104–5)

Wordsworth's wilful attempt to make things different independently of any mimetic or fictional convention flies in the face of nature. Crabb Robinson reports Coleridge criticizing Wordsworth in 1810 for having 'unreasonably attached himself to the low.' He 'fixed "with malice prepense" upon objects of reflection which do not naturally excite reflection' (*MC* 386). This produces 'an intensity of feeling disproportionate to *such* knowledge and value of the objects described, as can be fairly anticipated of men in general . . .' (*BL* II 109). His egotism, which insists on an eccentric response, combines with his poetic literalism, which submits to things as they are, to strand Wordsworth in a hopelessly paradoxical position. Coleridge will not allow Wordsworthian eccentricity to constitute a defamiliarization of the real.

Coleridge believes that the final defect of Wordsworth's poetry

shows all these contradictions converging in the 'mental bombast' of
the 'Immortality Ode' — 'a disproportion of thought to the circumstance and occasion' (*BL* II 109). Here Wordsworth's 'daring spirit of
metaphor' is systematically defeated by the species of pantheistic
philosophy which Coleridge believed he adopted. The basic paradox
is lodged in the conception of a child as a 'philosopher', a 'mighty
prophet', and a 'blessed seer'. To say that the child is conscious of such
abilities is patently absurd. For Coleridge, the only remaining
explanation lies in the existence of a 'thinking Spirit' within the child
which 'may be *substantially* one with the principle of life' (*BL* II
111–12). [19] The 'thinking Spirit' can then act in vatic and philosophic
character through the living virtue of the child. But in that case, there
seems to be no reason why the child should be chosen by the poet as a
revelation of philosophy rather than any other thing participating in
'the principle of life'. Wordsworth's pantheism causes him to lose
hold of his subject; his mental bombast dissolves rather than enhances
the subject of his Ode.

Again, the quarrel with literalism is at the heart of Coleridge's
argument. He objects to a kind of literal pantheism, a genuine
confusion of 'the *part, as* a part, with the Whole, *as* the whole' (*BL* II
112). The relation between the particular and the general in this case
is not a symbolic one: there is no figurative distance between the two
which would allow the individual to represent the workings of a
process larger than itself. It is literally part of the whole, and its
individuality neither comments on, nor offers any interpretation of,
the larger process. A poetic imitation has it in its power to 'do one's
heart good' although we may not have 'the fullest faith in the *truth* of
the observation' (*BL* II 105). Wordsworth's literalism, however, does
not allow the imagination room to produce symbols; and, lacking this
symbolic dimension, his concept of a child-philosopher reveals the
familiar pattern of paradox.

---

[19]*BL* II 113: 'In what sense can the magnificent attributes, above quoted, be
appropriated to a *child,* which would not make them equally suitable to a *bee,* or a *dog,*
or a *field of corn*: or even to a ship, or to the winds and waves that propel it? The
omnipresent Spirit works equally in them, as in the child; and the child is equally
unconscious of it as they.'

Thus it is with splendid paradoxes in general. If the words are taken in the common sense, they convey an absurdity; and if, in contempt of dictionaries and custom, they are so interpreted as to avoid the absurdity, the meaning dwindles into some bald truism. Thus you must at once understand the words *contrary* to their common import, in order to arrive at any *sense,* and *according* to their common import, if you are to receive from them any feeling of *sublimity* or *admiration.* (*BL* II 114)

Coleridge tries to treat Wordsworth's poetry to a *reductio ad absurdum.* He criticizes it for failing to have a meaning; or if it has a meaning, for abandoning its poetic character. The alternatives presented by Wordsworth's 'splendid paradox' invite us to sacrifice either the poetry to the sense or the sense to the poetry: we cannot accommodate both at the same time. In view of the severity of this censure there does not seem any place left in Wordsworth's poetry for 'excellence'. It is surprising, therefore, that Coleridge thinks his strictures only apply to 'instances' in Wordsworth's poetry; and it is confusing that the excellences display nothing less than conformity to the concept of poetry which Wordsworth had apparently disregarded.

This volte-face on Coleridge's part cries out for explanation. The excellences which he lists are just the reverse of the defects and nothing more. It is with some blandness that Coleridge tells us of the last, culminating defect that it 'is a fault of which none but a man of genius is capable' (*BL* II 109). He does not feel threatened or puzzled by this surfacing antinomy, and fails to sense the paradoxes and tensions in his own thought. The result is an undeniable cramping of his critical approach, and a revealing distrust of experiment and originality. The Coleridgean poetic is broadminded in general, but narrow in the particular case. As the symbolic expression of all human apprehension, poetry is allotted immense general significance; it encourages every branch of thought. However, in the particular example, Coleridge often claims this general significance for poetry at the expense of the persuasive powers which the individual poet may exert in an attempt to redefine the universal from a particular point of view. As his criticism of Wordsworth shows, Coleridge is immediately inclined to regard this kind of effort as being misguided, and the aim it sets itself conceptually impossible.

But in his letters to friends, Wordsworth insisted that his critics should be open to persuasion by his particular vision. In writing about an 'Idiot Boy' he is communicating something which he claims to 'know', and creating out of such knowledge fairer 'representatives of the vast mass of human existence'.[20] In doing this he would fulfil his poetic vocation 'to rectify men's feelings, to give them new compositions of feelings'.[21] Ironically, it was Coleridge he cited as his source when he argued in 1807 that the great original writer 'must himself create the taste by which he is to be relished; he must teach the art by which he is to be seen.'[21] He thought that 'every great Poet is a Teacher', and he wished 'either to be considered as a Teacher, or as nothing'. Coleridge often refuses to acknowledge Wordsworth's creative efforts to effect a real change in our attitudes by means of an aesthetic education. The literal remains literal because Coleridge as critic won't allow Wordsworth to redraw the border it shares with the symbolical. This obduracy seems to place him in the position Wordsworth elsewhere allots to Francis Jeffrey:

he says, that, whether from affectation or other causes, I have connected my lofty or tender feelings with objects such as a Sparrow's Nest, a Spade, a Leech gatherer, etc. which to the generality of mankind appear, and will continue to appear, ridiculous. Now Mr. Jeffrey takes this for granted, which was the thing to be proved; and then proceeds to revile the poems accordingly.[22]

Coleridge certainly does not 'revile' Wordsworth's poems, but he does show a similar conservatism in taking for granted 'the thing to be proved'.

There are three main reasons, so far only mentioned in passing, which now explain the contradiction between defects and excellences in Coleridge's criticism of Wordsworth. The first is the difficulty, acknowledged by Coleridge, of preserving a common culture and language capable of containing the increasingly specialized discoveries of modern knowledge, as well as the comparable quest for originality on the part of the modern poet. A culture may be unable to

[20]*The Letters of William and Dorothy Wordsworth*, I 355.
[21]*Ibid.*, II 150.
[22]*Ibid.*, II 195, 162.

recognize the latest poetic manifestation of the awareness of human potential towards whose realization culture is supposed to be guiding us. On the other hand, a poetry which flouts cultural recognition denies itself the power of effective social commentary. Yet equally there ought to exist the possibility of some conflict if the poet is to be able to present his vision as a criticism of life. It is a very fine point as to which side ought to give way: the forces of tradition and convention, or the poet's drive towards originality and change. It is debatable whether there ever is such a thing as a purely aesthetic dispute. The quarrel is usually resolved by other considerations, apparently non-aesthetic, which have been an intrinsic part of the discussion all along.

This leads to the second reason, which is political or ideological. If poetry by presenting an ideal encourages improvement, then it has an obvious political investment in radical causes. It may be in a critic's best political interests not to recognize as poetry writing which represents ideals threatening the *status quo*. The critic then makes a political choice when he finds that a figure of speech posing as a poetic symbol remains literal to his sensibility. The apparent lack of communication between poet and critic is in fact a political disagreement resulting from all too successful communication. Hazlitt was convinced of the Jacobinism of Wordsworth's early poetry; and the Coleridge of *Biographia* would certainly have been quite happy to forget his own politically radical past as he found it preserved in the amber of *Lyrical Ballads*. However, his new political sympathies compete with the radical power we have seen him attribute to poetry. His criticism is torn between contradictory allegiances.

The contemporary theoretical expression of the Romantic poet's dilemma was the aesthetics of the sublime. Its nice balance of gain and loss is the third factor to remember when considering the ambiguities in Coleridge's criticism of Wordsworth's poetry, especially the 'Immortality Ode'. The power of poetry to escape scientific limitations in its expression of human nature is offset by the unhappiness of the imagination at this loss of its empirical employment. The Romantic poets often describe the failure of poetic vision as a necessary part of the definition of the vision itself. The point is not that such visions are delusions, but that they are artificial. We need this sense of their unreality to appreciate their license, the exhilarating increase in range of expression which they incorporate. But along with this new perspective comes vertigo, a feeling of homelessness, of losing touch with one's natural element. This unhappy consciousness can produce a feeling of desolate alienation which vitiates whatever went before. Or it can be transcended within the larger context of a total 'system' of a poet like Blake, or in the capable generosity of a Keats, or in a Wordsworthian rhetoric of spiritual growth. These mature stances allow us to accept the merely symbolic status of the self in its imagined fulfilment: we become reconciled to the fact that the sublime is not our natural state but its sublimation. However the threat of disintegration hovers over the self which identifies too fully with its aesthetic counterpart. Once more we find the Romantic consciousness insisting upon the awareness of artifice as a constitutive component of aesthetic experience, forcing us to feel the coldness of the pastoral. The paradox which Coleridge isolates in his criticism of Wordsworth's poetry is therefore inherent in the Romantic sublime. The literal must be kept in the reader's mind in order to admire the height of the sublime transport of poetic language. Yet this appreciation of aesthetic distance easily turns into a feeling of how far from ordinary life the sublime experience is; how its words, understood according to their 'common' import, only become sublime by losing their sense. The central contradiction in Coleridge's criticism of Wordsworth in *Biographia* – discerning defects and excellences in apparently identical material, at least expresses both the melancholic and the joyful sides of the Romantic aesthetics of sublimity. However, connecting this reason with the last one, it can be seen that, for Coleridge, Wordsworth's imagined poetic fulfilments have to become sublimated to lose their political sting; but this sublimation, like Coleridge's use of transcendentalist terminology, achieves its purpose at the expense of coherence and comprehensibility. The 'splendid paradox' is then also inherent in the structure we have been describing for Coleridge's critical thought.

The excellences which Coleridge now finds in Wordsworth's poetry predictably exhibit the necessity of poetry. His diction, after Shakespeare and Milton, appears to Coleridge 'the most *individualized* and characteristic' (*BL* II 77). This is not due to egotism but a prerequisite of the first in Coleridge's list of excellences, the 'appropriateness of the words to the meaning' ensuring their '*untranslatableness* in words of the same language without injury to the meaning' (*BL* II 115). Returning to the 'Immortality Ode', Coleridge now distinguishes the elements of philosophy from the significance of Wordsworth's poetic language:

the ode was intended for such readers only as had been accustomed to watch the flux and reflux of their inmost nature, to venture at times into the twilight realms of consciousness, and to feel a deep interest in modes of inmost being, to which they know that the attributes of time and space are inapplicable and alien, but which yet cannot be conveyed save in symbols of time and space. For such readers the sense is sufficiently plain, and they will be as little disposed to charge Mr. Wordsworth with believing the Platonic pre-existence in the ordinary interpretation of the words, as I am to believe, that Plato himself ever meant or taught it. (*BL* II 120–1)

Within the ruling, poetic convention the literal failure of language is changed into a symbolic power. The poetic fiction transforms the temporal and spatial categories employed from distortions into symbols valuable as the sole means of access we have to the experience described. The linguistic exigencies to which the poet is driven in fact reveal the untranslatability and necessity of his art.

Coleridge now discovers in the 'Ode' a symbolism untainted by the political originality which he had dissociated from poetry by calling it literalism. But the figure of the child-philosopher remains as potentially subversive of traditional forms of authority as it definitely is in Blake's *Songs*. The ambiguity of Coleridge's position is preserved in Crabb Robinson's report of his remarks in 1810 on the 'Ode', 'which he had formerly referred to as his masterpiece, and spoke highly of it. Now he said it contained bombastic thoughts, which he had wished W. would omit; but he still spoke of it as a grand production' (*MC* 388). In the terminology of Schiller's famous essay, which he had read,[23] Coleridge alternates between the modern

[23]*NB* I 488n.

idealist's sentimental appreciation of Wordsworth's 'childlike' symbol of the child, sophisticated and artificial; and a feeling that
Wordsworth must be making himself ridiculous by using a 'childish'
figure in a paradoxical attempt to write a 'naive' poetry which, in a
modern sentimental age, cannot free itself from an overriding sense of
absurdity. Once Coleridge is prepared to acknowledge that Wordsworth is as 'sentimental' as himself then he finds that he is, in
Schiller's words, 'obliged to respect the object at which [he] . . .
formerly smiled.'[24] In a letter to Thomas Allsop of 1820 he writes of
'the skill to remove the *childish*, yet leave the *childlike* untouched' (*CL*
V 36). Lamb had already made this point in his review of *The Excursion*
in 1814. Again, we can either regard Lamb's enthusiasm for
childhood as paradoxically 'naive', or else, more plausibly, understand him as summarizing the symbolic possibilities possessed by
childhood within the context of poetic remembrance. Wordsworth's

> verses shall be censured as infantile by critics who confound poetry 'having
> children for its subject' with poetry that is 'childish', and who, having
> themselves perhaps never been *children*, never having possessed the tender-
> ness and docility of that age, know not what the soul of a child is — how
> apprehensive! how imaginative! how religious![25]

   Wordsworth himself lends support to the symbolic interpretation
of his poem in his commentary on it recorded in the Fenwick notes.
He does not extol 'the simple creed/ Of Childhood'. He denies any
deliberate attempt 'to inculcate' a belief in Platonic doctrine, and
instead describes his use of it as a poetic stratagem to gain a poetically
privileged view of what he thinks is an essentially human response.
His fiction is justified as poetic pragmatism:

> Archimedes said that he could move the world if he had a point whereon to
> rest his machine. Who has not felt the same aspirations as regards the world
> of his own mind? Having to wield some of its elements when I was impelled
> to write this Poem on the 'Immortality of the Soul', I took hold of the notion
> of pre-existence as having sufficient foundation in humanity for authorizing
> me to make for my purposes the best use of it I could as a Poet.[26]

[24]Schiller, *Naive and Sentimental Poetry*, 87–8.
[25]*The Works of Charles and Mary Lamb*, ed. E. V. Lucas (London, 1903–5, 1912), 6
vols, I, 199.
[26]*The Poetical Works of William Wordsworth*, ed. E. de Selincourt and H. Darbishire
(Oxford, 1940–9), 5 vols., IV, 463–4.

The poetic art of the 'Ode', as this note makes clear, does not desert reality for an 'abyss of idealism', but is rather the result of a considered and mature understanding of a revealing characteristic of the poet's childhood psychology.[27] The child's doubt concerning the reality of the external world worried him; the poet, for whom years have brought 'the philosophic mind', draws analogies with 'the fall of Man', detects enlightening parallels in 'the popular creeds of many nations', or in 'Platonic philosophy', and, with that reflective hindsight, shapes his feeling for the general significance of the childish fright into a poetic symbol. Archimedes' hypothesis and Wordworth's poetic device are equally unsupported by observable facts; but just as the former can be justified in terms of the principles of mechanics, so the latter is founded on poetic principles and becomes the expression through the poet's art of something otherwise indefinable – a lost potential, an ideal integrity of perception, 'worlds not realized'.

When Wordsworth and Coleridge agree about the symbolic status of the 'Ode' they both draw attention to the conspicuously untranslatable quality of the work. Coleridge's list of Wordsworth's remaining excellences reiterates this. He praises the individual strengths of 'single lines and paragraphs', and the 'curiosa felicitas' of Wordsworthian diction. Wordsworth's excellence in particular descriptions proves his 'long and genial intimacy with the very spirit which gives the physiognomic expression to all the works of nature' (BL II 121). Coleridge sees no problem in distinguishing this success from the earlier recorded failure of the symbol of the child-philosopher to be more than a cipher for the 'thinking Spirit' or 'principle of life'. He refers to Wordsworth's 'sympathy with man as man' as an ability to give a poetic reading of the laws defining human nature and its expressive physiognomy:

the superscription and the image of the Creator still remain legible to *him* under the dark lines, with which guilt or calamity had cancelled or cross-barred it. Here the man and the poet lose and find themselves in each other, the one as glorified, the latter as substantiated. (BL II 123)

[27]Compare one of Coleridge's descriptions of the same trait in his own childhood psychology, shaping a similar feeling of identity with nature, in a letter of 1819 to an unknown correspondent (CL IV 974–5).

The religious implications of this perhaps help more to preserve individuality. But again there is a levelling principle at work in the activity of reducing people to a common religious denominator, even if this is grandly called 'the human face divine'. Coleridge admits that distinctions of rank, climate, employment and knowledge dissolve under the religious dispensation; but if he accepts this democracy his militant attitude to Wordsworth's other attempts to extend the poetic franchise outside an apolitical theodicy become less convincing.

The final glory of the Wordsworthian genius, according to Coleridge, is 'the gift of IMAGINATION in the highest and strictest sense of the word' (*BL* II 124). In this Wordsworth approaches nearest of all the moderns to Shakespeare and Milton. The poetic or secondary imagination produces its miracles of rare device by a series of conscious efforts which identify themselves in the structure of the poems. The secondary imagination 'dissolves, diffuses, dissipates, in order to recreate'; and Coleridge's practical experience as a critic qualifies his formula when he continues, 'or where this process is rendered impossible, yet still at all events it struggles to idealize and unify' (*BL* I 202). Understanding a poem involves judging its success; and this decision brings into play our assumptions about just what it is we think would be available to human perception under ideal conditions.

At this point, however, Coleridge remembers the original direction of the argument he had intended for *Biographia*: the deduction of critical rules from an analysis of imagination:

but if I should ever be fortunate enough to render my analysis of imagination, its origin and character, thoroughly intelligible to the reader, he will scarcely open on a page of this poet's works without recognizing, more or less, the presence and the influence of this faculty. (*BL* II 124)

In the absence of the 'analysis' or deduction he has to rely on the evidence of the poetry. But the force of Coleridge's practical criticism has been to develop the power to recognize those moments when the presence or absence of poetic imagination is at issue. We encounter Coleridge's desynonymizing of the poetic imagination in action, and find that questioning the plausibility of poetic symbols leads to as wide a philosophical discussion as he could have desired. In the last section we saw that Coleridge's preoccupation with the poetic passion raised by diction and metre was to show that a poem's own artifice is part of its subject-matter. The definitive experience we derive from a poem is an excited feeling generated by its presentation of itself as poetry. Coleridge's praise and criticism of Wordsworth's work tirelessly – sometimes tiresomely – reiterates this. The central paradox of his opposite reactions to the same poem articulates the ambiguous aesthetics of the sublime and places Coleridge's poetics in relation to his political and religious beliefs. The philosophical consciousness raised by Coleridge's practical criticism returns to interrogate that provisional definition of the secondary imagination's struggle 'to idealize and unify', but now with the authority to dictate rather than have dictated to it the course such an analysis should take.

THE PHILOSOPHICAL POEM

Coleridge concludes his criticism of Wordsworth in *Biographia* with the hope that the poet will write 'the FIRST GENUINE PHILOSOPHIC POEM' (*BL* II 129). Since *The Excursion* had been published, and *The Prelude* had been read to Coleridge in 1806, there seems to be no reason why he could not have given us detailed criticism of work in progress. Perhaps his growing belief that Wordsworth had failed in his attempt to write a philosophical poem made the prospect of such a task too painful. Certainly, from his private criticism the relevance of Wordsworth's attempt to the critical arguments of *Biographia* is obvious. A notebook entry of 1803 describes Wordsworth's concentration upon 'his great work' both as a recovery of the true subject of poetry, 'great Objects & elevated Conceptions', and a proper exploitation of Wordsworth's natural talents, 'grandly imprisoning while it deifies his Attention & Feelings.' In this way the philosophical poem contrasts with 'a sectarian Spirit' which intermittently besets the shorter poems. 'But now he is at the Helm of a noble Bark; now he sails right onward. . . . His only Disease is the having been out of his Element . . .' (*NB* I 1546). Reaffirming these sentiments in a letter to Thomas Poole of the same year, Coleridge expresses his hostility towards 'the plan of several of the Poems in the L. Ballads', and finishes by telling Poole to destroy the letter (*CL* II 1013).

Coleridge's early enthusiasm for Wordsworth's projected philosophical poem anticipates his later arguments for the necessity of poetry. In a letter to Wordsworth of 1803 he told him that his 'Poetry was his . . . Philosophy under the action of strong winds of Feeling – a sea rolling high' (*CL* II 957). Coleridge's enthusiasm has broken out of his original critical metaphor and he identifies the Wordsworthian 'Bark' of genius with the medium, the element it sails in. As he was to claim of diction and metre in *Biographia*, poetic feeling sustains the poet's unifying power and makes his vision entire. It contributes to that happy pun on Wordsworth's name: as he told Southey in the same year, 'Wordsworth's words always *mean* the whole of their possible Meaning' (*CL* II 977). No reason is given for why a full meaning might not also be partisan.

In a letter to Richard Sharp of 1804 Coleridge stated that Wordsworth, more than Shakespeare and Milton, would be regarded by posterity as 'the first and greatest philosophical Poet'. The Wordsworthian virtues listed in support of this verdict culminate in the imagination, as opposed to the fancy, which enables the poet to produce the whole picture through his appreciation of human symbolic procedures in general. Imagination is being used 'in that sense in which it is a dim Analogue of Creation, not all that we can *believe* but all that we can *conceive* of creation.' By expressing this kind of imaginative insight the poetic analogue reveals the potential in different forms of human apprehension without committing us to believe in certain facts. This is the logic behind Coleridge's claim to 'prophesy immortality to his *Recluse,* as the first & finest philosophical Poem, if only it be (as it undoubtedly will be) a Faithful Transcript of his own most august & innocent Life, of his own habitual Feelings & Modes of seeing and hearing.' (*CL* II 1034)

However, this optimism was not to last. Coleridge's disappointment is conveyed to Wordsworth in a letter of 1815, not through a detailed critique of *The Excursion,* but by recalling the expectations he had cherished for a truly philosophical poem: 'not doubting from the advantages of the Subject that the Totality of a System was not only capable of being harmonized with, but even calculated to aid, the unity (Beginning, Middle, and End) of a Poem' (*CL* IV 574).[28] Within his aesthetics, Coleridge's idea of a complete philosophy was symbolized by the unity of a poem. In this letter, as in the *Lay Sermons* and elsewhere, we encounter rapid transpositions from one branch of knowledge to another in the belief that poetry can epitomize the ideal understanding which inspires the progressive method employed in each. Equally, poetic defamiliarization of the 'Totality' of systematic knowledge must lend an extraordinarily impressive shape and structure to the poet's own work. It is this harmonious exchange which explains Coleridge's plan for Wordsworth's philosophical poem. That is why he could remark much later of the ill-fated plan that it was 'in substance, what I have been all my life doing in my system of philosophy' (*TT* II 38).

Wordsworth was to have begun with epistemology by meditating on 'the faculties of Man in the abstract'. Then he was to shift the poetic focus to 'the Human Race in the concrete'. Just as the poetic consideration of epistemology militated against closed systems of philosophy ('Locke, and the Mechanic Dogmatists'), so a poetic review of human development supports a specific view of history and religion. Again, the common factor is not some dogma which the poetry proclaims, but poetry's necessary expression of 'our common nature'. The fall of man, for example, is relevant to a poetic understanding of history because it enriches one form of thought with 'the reality . . . attested by Experience & Conscience' in another. Similarly, the religious hope which Wordsworth was to venture is not described in this letter as based primarily on a particular revelation, but as being a consequence of the openness of poetry, its refusal to be bound by 'clear Images' and 'distinct conceptions' (*CL* IV 574–6). As he remarked in another letter of the same year to Thomas Methuen: 'I do not hold it becoming to bind down Providence, no not even in my fancy, to any particular means' (*CL* IV 580). Wordsworth's poem was to work on a general level, showing that religion was only possible

---

[28]See his letter to H. J. Rose of 1816 (*CL* IV 687), 'I am convinced that a true System of Philosophy (= the Science of Life), is best taught in Poetry as well as most safely.'

under the aegis of a philosophy which did justice to man's progressive nature; this is defined in turn through a prophetic understanding of human history. In this way, by transpositions between different forms of thought revealing a common interest in human potential, 'all that we can *conceive*', the philosophical poem was to disclose 'an insight into the whole Truth' (*CL* IV 576).

After reading a plan of action like this one feels considerable sympathy for Wordsworth. It may be, as Stephen Parrish claims, that Coleridge's programme for the philosophical poet was 'something no mortal could have managed.'[29] But there seems also to have been a misunderstanding between the two poets which made chances of success on Coleridge's terms both more plausible and less likely. Wordsworth worked on *The Prelude* not only as a preparation, but also as a surrogate for the poem he really wanted to write. That was to be a work of surpassing philosophical profundity in comparison with which *The Prelude* was depressingly 'below what I seemed capable of executing.'[30] Yet Wordsworth's own ambitions probably led him further astray than any advice from Coleridge. The failure to write *The Recluse* left a creative vacuum in Wordsworth's work, holding together a circumference of successful poetic outriders. It was these poems, peripheral to the main purpose, which Coleridge continued to value. In starting to write *The Recluse* Wordsworth relied greatly on Coleridge's encouragement,[31] and asked, with increasing anxiety, for Coleridge's 'notes for the Recluse' as Coleridge prepared to depart for Malta in 1804.[33] This dependence on Coleridge continued after Wordsworth knew the notes had been lost. *The Prelude* was pronounced finished in May 1805, and Dorothy reported as early as August of the same year that her brother was eager for the peace and quiet necessary for work on *The Recluse*. However by December the problem was not the distractions of company, but the inability 'to do much more till we have heard from Coleridge.' In August of the

[29]S. M. Parrish, *The Art of the 'Lyrical Ballads'* (Cambridge, Mass., 1973), 57–8.
[30]*The Letters of William and Dorothy Wordsworth*, I, 594.
[31]'Home at Grasmere', Part First, Book First of *The Recluse*, ed. Beth Darlington (Ithaca, New York and Hassocks, Sussex, 1977), 'Introduction', 5.
[32]*The Letters of William and Dorothy Wordsworth*, I, 452, 464.

following year William claimed, 'Should Coleridge return, so that I might have some conversation with him upon the subject, I should go on swimmingly.'[33] Despite lacking Coleridge's advice, Wordsworth nevertheless conscientiously set about philosophizing earlier work for inclusion in what was to become *The Excursion*, the philosophical poem Coleridge wanted. But, as it turned out, the result of these efforts was only to depart further and further from the Coleridgean model on which he thought he was writing. In a letter of April 1815 to Lady Beaumont, which triggered the exchange of views with Wordsworth, it was the earlier poems which Coleridge valued more highly: 'the tale of the ruined Cottage' (which he remembered as a separate poem existing long before the version included in *The Excursion*) and, of course, *The Prelude*.[34] Faced with this misunderstanding we must either judge that Coleridge perversely misled Wordsworth's poetic talent and then launched into recriminations; or else we must conclude that it was the unforgettable experience of hearing and reading these early poems which Coleridge thought was of a philosophical importance which Wordsworth's subsequent work ought to articulate. The only way in which this could be done without a new beginning, without losing continuity with past success, would be for Wordsworth to become a more 'sentimental' poet, conspicuously conscious of his art, its sublime range defined in relation to other forms of thought, and above all keen to make that consciousness an essential part of his poetry. This would have answered the criticisms of Coleridge's letter and fulfilled the hopes of *Biographia*.

To some extent Wordsworth had already achieved this in *The Prelude* of 1805. Coleridge valued this above *The Excursion*, and it is a poem acutely aware of its own genesis, overtly concerned with the relation of the poet's calling to the general education of mankind. And the kernel poem, the two part *Prelude* of 1799, concentrates on expressing the poet's sense of vocation by telescoping passages kept many books apart in the later versions. Wordsworth's questioning of his own feeling of poetic favour — 'Was it for this . . .' — is directly

---

[33]*Ibid.*, I, 617, 664; II, 64.
[34]"The Ruined Cottage' and 'The Pedlar', ed. J. Butler (Ithaca, New York and Hassocks, Sussex, 1979), xii, 34–5.

answered by the art with which he elicits poetic meaning from the experiences recorded as 'spots of time'. The entire poem is Wordsworth's most confident justification of his aesthetic consciousness. Ironically, it is most likely Coleridge's critical response to this poem which inspired his belated theory of what Wordsworth ought to have written subsequently.

THE DIVINE EXAMPLES: SHAKESPEARE AND MILTON

Although Wordsworth finally disappointed Coleridge, Shakespeare and Milton continued to inspire him. Wordsworth's ultimate failure to produce a poetry of the philosophical significance envisaged by Coleridge is measured against the standard set by these two poets. Within Coleridge's literary pantheon, the divinity of Shakespeare and Milton allows him as full a development of his concept of poetry as he could wish.

And, according to a *Table Talk* entry of 1830, they are truly divine: 'Shakespeare is the Spinozistic deity – an omnipresent creativeness. Milton is the deity of prescience . . .' (*TT* I 127). The difference in their godliness, though, does not amount to a division of labour equivalent to the specialization demanded by the writing of *Lyrical Ballads*. Coleridge's thought is full of such dualities in which one member animates natural categories with mental life, while the other fills out the vague shapes of mental entities. This configuration of a philosophy of identity is a recurrent form in his thought. Aristotle and Plato, Bacon and Plato, Shakespeare and Milton, Wordsworth and Coleridge himself – all partly illustrate the complement of real and ideal within this philosophy. But neither Shakespeare nor Milton is ever considered as a mere component of the overall pattern.

Milton's complete vision of man is religious. In trying to understand Coleridge's criticism of Milton and Shakespeare it has to be remembered that eschatology is meant to constitute the point, the direction of poetic language as it moves beyond scientific jurisdiction. Poetry is the only linguistic purchase we have on this extra-scientific realm. Both poets unify a natural category with an ideal category figuring an as yet unrealized but true expectation.[35] Milton imagines an objective existence for spiritual revelation and prophecy. Shakespeare dwells in the present, showing, none the less, the seeds and principles of progress in a characteristically human apprehension of things. To this end he displays his protean ability, much lauded in Romantic commentaries, to range through all the forms of the natural world. Coleridge suggests, in marginalia to Thomas Fuller, that by understanding human faculties to a 'degree . . . far surpassing what one would have thought *possible*' Shakespeare is able to show the helps towards and the obstacles in the way of our fulfilment (*CSC* 470). That is why, for example, he can portray a 'moral necessity' in *Hamlet* (*SC* I 37). Coleridge means that Shakespeare does not merely sympathize with the character of Hamlet he has created: he has a privileged viewpoint from which he can discern a *telos* in relation to which Hamlet's disordered and unbalanced outlook can be measured. In the *Treatise on Method,* Coleridge describes Shakespeare's imaginative insight as first of all retrospective: the depth and thoroughness of his imaginative creation 'gives us the history of minds'. But Shakespeare's poetic openness is also forward-looking. Shakespeare does not only show us how things have happened, how a life has been shaped, he also gives us a sense of the normative, a stronger feeling than we had before of what would be an ideal development of character. This is what is meant by claiming that Shakespeare 'studied mankind in the Idea of the human race' (*TM* 31, 27). His art defamiliarizes human nature by constructing the ideal conditions under which we can see it as it really is.

Coleridge describes the poetry of Shakespeare and Milton as being tendentious without having particular party interests. This view once more uncovers the strengths and weaknesses of his criticism. He insists that great art does not consist in static portrayals, but leads somewhere. However he refuses to allow any historical or political

---

[35]See the description of this identity in *SC* II 129, 'the poet descends from the ideal into the real world so far as to conjoin both – to give a sphere of operations to the ideal, and to elevate and refine the real'; see also Barfield, interpreting Coleridge's 'fine contrast' of Shakespeare and Milton as showing how 'the finite activity of poetry . . . still requires a predominance, however slight, of the one pole over the other', *What Coleridge Thought*, 90.

content to this radical movement, and is content to hint at a covert theodicy. Yet the tensions in his criticism of Wordsworth and in the form his own aesthetic takes have been shown to be shaped by historical pressures and even to grow more interesting on that account. Also, Coleridge's lack of specificity helps explain a real feature of the historicity of literature. The meaning of a work of art varies with the historical perspective of its readers; its greatness lies in its power to maintain its value through many historical exchanges, as each age reinterprets it and claims to recover its 'real' meaning in terms of its own particular historical preoccupations. Coleridge as critic and aesthetician does justice to the sense of timelessness in aesthetic appreciation, the recurring conviction of Shakespeare's contemporaneity, while realizing that this is a quality of the original's open-endedness: that unattached tendentiousness of which we can make ourselves the target. Coleridge describes how 'an Idea is an experiment proposed, an experiment is an idea realised' (*TM* 42). Shakespeare's examination of the human race in its 'Idea' is a perpetually forward-looking study, open to successive historical confirmations. Coleridge's abstract terminology, at first sight unhelpful, translates into an important truth about the historical exchange-value of the great literary work.

It is their different versions of the same activity which explain for Coleridge Milton's 'egotism', and how Shakespeare can seem 'characterless': Milton's 'subjectivity of the poet' and Shakespeare's 'subjectivity of the *persona,* or dramatic character' (*TT* I 127–30). Milton is obliged to give a personal colouring to his otherwise unimaginable subject. The historical character which his poetry gives to things existing only in prophecy requires him to invent symbols for the invisible. Thus, his highly personal renderings of Satan, Death and Sin in *Paradise Lost* display the ingenious resources of a great poet when no observable facts were within his reach, no possible experiences available in which he could, by meditation in the Shakespearian manner, have shown the latency of the prophetic truth. Yet Milton avoids lapsing into that forced kind of allegory deplored in Coleridge's third lecture of 1818 (*MC* 31). He wins our negative faith in the natural existence of his own imaginary character by giving the

workings of his own mind as a substitute for felt experience (*SC* II
138–9).

This egotism, though, this 'subjectivity of the poet', can only be
understood in relation to something of universal application – 'a
revelation of spirit' (*TT* II 241). His prose writings may have been
partisan, but, according to a letter to Daniel Stuart, 'his poetry
belongs to the whole world', appealing to churchman and dissenter,
monarchist and republican alike (*CSC* 471). According to a *Table
Talk* entry of 1832, Milton's politics were a failure to impose his ideal
vision on the mixed and corrupt natures actually existing in the world
(*TT* II 54). But his poetic language, no less than Shakespeare's, is
untranslatable, and offers us no Wordsworthian alternatives. Miltonic language is everywhere adequate; everywhere, Coleridge tells us
in the tenth of his 1818 lectures, we are 'surrounded with sense . . .
every word is to the purpose' (*MC* 169). The fallen angels *are* human
passions. The character of Satan *is* pride and sensual indulgence (*MC*
164, 163). Milton's modifications of the language of real life are in the
interests of a more adequate articulation. In chapter 23 of *Biographia*
Coleridge likens Satan to the character of Don Juan because he is 'from
beginning to end an *intelligible* character'. Milton achieves this not
simply by inscribing Satan in a poetic context which is ideal, but in
one which is '*professedly ideal*' (*BL* II 186–7).[36] Milton's poetry is as
constitutionally self-conscious as Coleridge wanted Wordsworth's to
be.

Shakespeare, on the other hand, seems 'characterless' only because
he is 'characteristic' (*SC* I 82). His poetry shows the possibilities
inherent in any particular historical fact because he feels that
particular to such a 'degree'. He fulfils the requirement for a great
poet to be 'a profound Metaphysician' because of the implications of
this sensitivity. A famous passage from a letter of 1802 to Sotheby
helps to explain this and to gather up the threads of Coleridge's
argument about Shakespeare:

[36]See Kierkegaard's discussion of 'the ideality . . . in the traditional conception' of
Don Juan, in *Either/Or,* trans. D. F. Swenson and L. M. Swenson, with revisions, and
a Foreword by H. A. Johnson (Princeton, New Jersey, 1971), 2 vols, I, 102ff.

a great Poet must be, implicitè if not explicitè a profound Metaphysician. He may not have it in logical coherence, in his Brain & Tongue; but he must have it by *Tact* / for all sounds, & forms of human nature he must have the *ear* of a wild Arab listening in the silent Desart, the eye of a North American Indian tracing the footsteps of an Enemy upon the Leaves that strew the Forest — ; the *Touch* of a Blind Man feeling the face of a darling Child – (*CL* II 810)

In *Biographia* Coleridge praised Shakespeare's 'perfect dominion, often *domination,* over the whole world of language' (*BL* II 19). The poet's sensitivity enables him to run the gamut of the different vocabularies of human apprehension. He transposes between different skills, thus acquiring a more general, open or 'characteristic' view of things through his 'tact', a gift not subordinated to any single sense. The Shakespearean facility confirms in 'tact' what Coleridge the philosopher was seen to be striving for by way of 'logical coherence' in *The Friend* and the *Lay Sermons.* In the *Treatise on Method* it is Shakespeare's 'pursuit after unity of principle, through a diversity of forms' which illustrates 'the Science of Method' (*TM* 25–7).

Shakespeare's divinity lies in the character discernible beneath his seeming characterlessness. He is the 'deity' of the Spinozistic scheme, and not the underlying, dead skeleton, which is how Coleridge described Spinoza's philosophy in a letter of 1815. Shakespeare, as a guide to Coleridge's philosophy, embodies Coleridge's philosophical ambition of bringing that skeleton to life, and lending it 'a glorified Body'. Spinoza's 'majesty of openness' which matches the Shakespearean range of transposition should be neither aimless nor rigidly determined by an 'iron Chain of Logic', but should suggest a prophetic understanding of man (*CL* IV 548).[37] Shakespeare's divinity is therefore his own, the signal of his artistic intervention or 'tact'.

[37]See also *CL* IV 863. For a concise description of the difference between an idealist philosophy of identity and the somewhat similar monism of Spinoza, see G. Lukács, *History and Class Consciousness,* trans. R. Livingstone (London, 1971), 142–3. See also Coleridge's remarks in a marginal note to Hegel on'Το Πρωτον ψευδος of Spinoza's Ethice. He attributes to Determination (= determin*are*) what belongs exclusively to the being determined (= determin*ari*)', transcribed by H. N. Nidecker, *Revue de littérature comparée,* 10 (1930), 168.

Shakespeare's actions as a 'youthful god of poetry' draw attention to the picturesque artifice of his poetry and the conceitful dance of his language which, Coleridge argued in *Biographia,* defamiliarize the objects he describes to his reader's advantage.[38] His ability 'to become by power of Imagination another Thing' is not a total submission to the natural world, but like that of 'Proteus, a river, a lion, yet still the God felt to be there' (*NB* III 3247). The presence of the 'God' is the presence of art.[39] But Shakespeare's personal touch, 'diffusing over all a magic glory', never deviates from the 'regular high road of human affections. . . . He is the morning star of philosophy – the guide and pioneer' (*SC* II 168, I 228). His language unites the real and the ideal categories, or makes them enable each other. He is 'a genuine Proteus', and so he lets us see nature 'as images in a calm lake, most distinct, most accurate, – only more splendid, more glorified. This is correctness in the only philosophical sense' (*SC* I 79). The philosophical importance of imaginative vision derives from its generous, poetic consciousness for which to show things as they really are is inseparable from showing what, potentially, they ought to be.

It is therefore the Shakespearean medium which is philosophically significant for Coleridge: Shakespeare is not a philosopher because he has a set of specific doctrines to propound, but because of the exemplary comprehensiveness of his mode of description, poetic or dramatic. Shakespeare can make 'even folly itself the vehicle of philosophy' (*SC* II 315). Coleridge belittles the importance of his choice of subject in his major plays. He thinks that Shakespeare has the same regard for his subject-matter – the 'story' of Hamlet, for example – as a painter has for his unmarked canvas, 'a mere vehicle for his thoughts'. Similarly, the story of Lear is 'merely the canvas . . . a mere occasion'. This devaluing of narrative is justified with reference to the necessity of poetry, a necessity in which the story does not

[38]See also *SC* I 96; *NB* II 2396; *SC* I 17, 78, 149–50; II 140, 186, 190.
[39]Contrast Schiller's description of the divinity of the naive, and therefore artless poet: 'Like divinity behind the world's structure he stands behind his work: *he* is the work, and the work is *he*', *Naive and Sentimental Poetry,* 106. Schiller would not have thought of Shakespeare as sentimental. Schlegel and, I suggest, Coleridge, would. According to a notebook entry of 1804, nature '*shakespearianized*' illustrates the distinction between an imitation and a copy, 'silk' not 'worsted' (*NB* II 2274).

participate. To Shakespeare, narrative is not 'the . . . *sine qua non* of the incidents and emotions' but is *'accidental'*.[40] This is the corollary of the criticism Coleridge made of Wordsworth's use of history and biography. In creating an 'animated whole', Shakespeare's drama renders history transparent, and we are able in imagination to glimpse a unity in which events become 'the clothing and manifestation of the spirit that is working within' (*SC* I 139). The 'higher order' of historical drama symbolizes 'the Totality of a system' and so achieves the synthesis he desired Wordsworth's philosophical poem more consciously to aim at.

Much of Coleridge's practical criticism of Shakespeare's plays is intended to show that Shakespeare's use of language reinforces the aesthetic awareness Coleridge attributed to poetry in general. The quality of his psychological observation of Shakespeare's characters has tended to distract critics from this basic preoccupation. In the *Treatise on Method* Coleridge describes how 'Shakespeare was pursuing two Methods at once; and besides the Psychological method, he had also to attend to the Poetical' (*TM* 32). Coleridge's criticism gives us a greater feeling of the presence of Shakespeare's text than the criticism of many other critics. He does this not only by his frequently expressed approval or condemnation of editors' readings and by his own suggested emendations, but also by communicating his constant awareness that he is analysing poetic language. His investigations of character, narrative, plot and other dramatic features of the plays frequently collapse into descriptions of the uses, and so of the status, of the language involved. As William Walsh argues, it 'is the activating force of language, Coleridge demonstrates, which is the natural base for a dramatic action in Shakespeare.'[41] Coleridge's criticism exemplifies his belief that, as he says in the seventh of his 1818 lectures, 'the very essence of a play, the very language in which it is written, is a fiction to which all the parts must conform' (*MC* 50).

---

[40]See J. Jones, *On Aristotle and Greek Tragedy* (London, 1962), §I, ch. 3, for a discussion of this characteristically modern interpretation of tragedy, involving the primacy of 'character' over 'action'.
[41]W. Walsh, *Coleridge – The Work and The Relevance* (London, 1967), 59.

In his notes on *Hamlet,* Coleridge charts 'the gradual ascent from the simplest forms of conversation to the language of impassioned intellect' in the first scene, and contrasts this with the immediate, visionary appeal of *Macbeth. Hamlet* begins with the confident use of 'the language of *sensation'*: but the self-sufficiency of the acts of naming weakens and is eroded by 'the broken expressions as of a man's compelled attention to bodily feelings allowed no man.' The need to advance to a more complex and expressive usage presages and prepares us 'for the after gradual rise into tragedy' (*SC* I 20). The 'consequent elevation of the style' results in the dramatic propriety of a ghost which we can believe in. Our dramatic expectations are moulded by the *'credibilizing* effect' of the language with which Shakespeare chooses to establish the linguistic universe of his play. The character of Hamlet himself dramatically embodies this 'credibilizing' success by literally standing midway between the natural and the visionary worlds: supported by a familiar audience he addresses an imaginary being.

The knowledge, the *unthought* of consciousness, the *sensation,* of human auditors, of flesh and blood sympathists, acts as a support, a stimulation *a tergo,* while the *front* of the mind, the whole consciousness of the speaker, is filled by the solemn apparition. (*SC* I 25)

Shakespeare's staging of the scene, the presence of Horatio, Marcellus and Bernardo, the frequency of the ghost's appearances, all combine to make Hamlet's 'impetuous eloquence perfectly intelligible'. The scene holds the poles of human experience, ideal and real, in dramatic equilibrium and so becomes a figure, for Coleridge, of the nature of poetic meaning.

Coleridge thinks that Shakespeare's management of his first scenes displays his dramatic judgement in an especially important and striking manner. He manages, 'by contrast of diction', to give an initial impression of the defining boundaries of his poetic terrain (*SC* I 41–2). These deliberate contrasts persist throughout the plays. Coleridge therefore agrees with and expands Schlegel's justification of the player's speech in Act 2, ii – which Hamlet begins, 'The rugged Pyrrhus, he whose sable arms' – as a 'substitution of the epic for the dramatic, giving such a *reality* to the impassioned dramatic diction of Shakespeare's own dialogue.'[42] Differences in diction create the dramatic perspective for what would otherwise remain a one dimensional world. Coleridge wishes us to recognize 'the exquisite judgement in the diction of the introduced play . . . what if Shakespeare had made the language truly dramatic? Where would have been the contrast between *Hamlet* and the play of *Hamlet?*' (*SC* I 40).

Coleridge, like Schlegel, appears to separate the language of drama from the language of poetry, and to equate the former with the language of nature. Shakespeare's protean ability to take on any character and speak with its 'proper' tongue allowed him to speak 'the very language of nature' (*SC* II 193, 135, 137, 267), and at least one passage in the *Shakespearean Criticism* suggests that there may be a sense in which 'the poet may be said to speak, rather than the dramatist' (*SC* II 137). But it is the necessity of poetry which solicits the negative faith sanctioning dramatic probability. Our belief in the logic of the events taking place on the stage is at one with our appreciation of the artifice necessary for the unity and completion of the artist's imitation. Shakespeare's 'language of nature' remains untranslatable 'poetry' because it must conform to '*a unity of feeling* [which] pervades the whole of his plays', indicative, as poetic passion was seen to be, of the artificial order of the 'whole composition', however natural may be the details of its 'component parts' (*SC* II 193–4, 265; I 42–3).

Any tension between the dramatic and the poetic in Coleridge's criticism of Shakespeare is an extension of the meaning of the plays. In *King Lear* this uniformity comments on the development of Lear's character: the hegemony of the poetic here is not part of a slack Romantic habit of eliding important aesthetic distinctions by calling different things poetry. Coleridge, as noted earlier, thinks that Shakespeare treats his narrative subject as 'a mere *occasion*' for the exertion of his poetic powers. Lear himself becomes 'the open and ample play-room of *nature's* passions' (*SC* I 59, 62). Lear's character

---

[42]*SC* I 27; A. W. Schlegel, *Dramatic Art and Literature,* 406–7.

shows how the poetic language can temporarily dominate the dramatic context. The narrative of the play languishes, and eventually, as Lear's 'imagination' works upon his own 'anguish', his character disintegrates. The pressure of his grief breaks out of any single dramatic role and takes command of the whole play. We find ourselves present at 'a world's *convention* of agonies', listening in Act 3 to 'the howlings of convulsed nature' which 'seem converted into the voice of conscious humanity' (*SC* I 63–6). Nevertheless, this absence of drama through the lack of contrasts between different dictions renders the single language of the play temporarily static, thus portraying Lear's predicament, 'the brooding of the one anguish, an eddy without progression'. As in the case of Macbeth's excessive inwardness there is no longer any forward movement, 'no more prudential prospective reasonings' (*SC* I 65, 77). Shakespeare restores Lear when he lets the poet and the dramatist speak together, uniting the coherence of an imitation with the progressive idea inherent in human nature: 'the whole remaining faithful to the character supposed to utter the lines, and the expressions themselves constituting a further development of that character . . .' (*SC* I 94). Protean 'tact' enables Shakespeare to portray spiritual growth in the particular case. The integrity of the individual in Shakespeare's plays is not a closed definition of the inalienable qualities of a character, but an expression of the unrealized possibilities naturally open to him or her. It is on these possibilities that successive audiences seize, and out of them make their historically interested choices, proving Shakespeare 'the poet of all ages' by finding him prophetic of their own (*SC* II 130).

CHAPTER SIX

Religion, Politics and Criticism

THE ANTINOMY

The form taken by Coleridge's later theological and political thought reflects on the interpretation of his oetics offered so far. The idealist vocabulary in which he thought it safe to present publicly his radical view of poetry eventually obscures its emancipatory impulse entirely. Consolidation of the author's philosophical authority in his specialized terminology translates into support for the established order of the state. The progressive views Coleridge maintains are not allowed to disturb permanent hierarchies in both religion and politics. He supports theological and political systems in a way which helps explain the increasing coincidence in European Romanticism of orthodoxy in religion and conservatism in politics.[1] And since this part of Coleridge's thought was the most influential in his own country after his death, and the most politically expedient, we find another reason for the neglect of his critical theory. The neglect represents a political interest paradoxically encouraged by Coleridge's own formulation. It repeats the contradiction inherent in *Biographia*, and emphasizes the necessity of the historical effort required if we are to allow Coleridge's poetic its voice, in spite of the way in which he has chosen to muffle it.

We have seen how Coleridge could think that poetic expression is not defined by the conditions determining scientific knowledge and

[1]See H. G. Schenk, *The Mind of The European Romantics* (London, 1966), for an accessible compendium of evidence for this view.

so can serve a religious purpose lying beyond the grasp of science. Religion needs poetic expression, and is 'the parent and fosterer' of poetry and the arts in general (*LS* 62). Coleridge's poetic symbols can reflect the unity of human nature in one direction and 'the unity of the infinite Spirit' in another (*LS* 90). However, Coleridge believes that religion yields us knowledge of the truth rather than mere poetic faith in it. He is then led to describe a kind of religious intuition, analogous to sense, which lies beyond the reach of language, but which provides certainty. In a religious context, 'Faith *is* knowledge.'[2] This coexists puzzlingly with his religious patronage of poetic symbols whose purpose is to express within language an experience lying outside the bounds of knowledge. Both sides of the antinomy can exist happily on their own; but contradictions arise when Coleridge tries to bring the two halves together.

In the eighth of his 1811–12 lectures on Shakespeare and Milton, Coleridge began by claiming that it 'is impossible to pay a higher compliment to poetry, than to consider the effects it produces in common with religion.' Both, he says, use man's imaginative ability to go beyond his senses; and both employ the symbolism in which such an effort is expressed. Coleridge thinks that the 'grandest point of resemblance between them is, that both have for their object . . . the perfecting, and the pointing out to us the indefinite improvement of our nature, and fixing our attention upon that' (*SC* II 147). Like Lessing, whose biography he once wanted to write, he describes religion as essentially educative.[3] Religion supports poetry when it takes as wide and radical a view of man as possible, and in so doing draws attention to the transpositions between different activities which we have seen him think necessary to a full and just description of human nature. Religion 'is calculated to occupy the whole mind, and employ successively all the faculties of man' (*LS* 196). Religion is 'a total act of the soul'; and so it is that 'we need not wonder that it has

---

[2]*CL* VI 940. This is a late letter to Thomas Pringle of c. June 1833, but Coleridge writes exactly the same thing throughout the *Lay Sermons*. See especially, *LS* 47, 175–6, 179.

[3]'The Education of the Human Race', in *Lessing's Theological Writings,* trans. H. Chadwick (Stanford, 1967), 82ff.

pleased Providence, that the divine truths of religion should have been revealed to us in the form of poetry' (*LS* 90; *SC* II 148).

Nevertheless, Coleridge's apparently unequivocal confidence in poetry coexists in much of his thought with so strenuous a desire to maintain the certainty and autonomy of the Christian religion that poetry and its methods have to give way to a different kind of experience altogether. According to a notebook entry of 1804, when religion is 'the Friend of Poetry' then 'God, Soul, Heaven, the Gospel, miracles, &c are themselves a sort of *poetry*'; but in an entry of the period 1813–15, Coleridge makes a claim for 'the transcendency of religious Intuitions over Language' (*NB* II 2194; III 4183). The religious *intuition* works on a model which is different from the idea of language which illustrates the rest of Coleridge's philosophy. Yet the theology based on intuition is found embedded in statements juxtaposed to other statements which rely on the idea of language. The contradiction is a real one.

THE CYCLICAL POEM

Coleridge tries to resolve the antinomy generated in his thought by the problem of religious expression in contradictory ways. The first is apparently to abandon his Kantian theory of poetry, and write instead of a poetry which proposes for its immediate object not pleasure but religious truth. The second, diametrically opposed to this, is to claim that we can have an immediate intuition which if it is to be described at all must be described literally, not poetically: 'the words of the epistle are literally and philosophically true' (*LS* 17–18).

If we consider the first of Coleridge's options we find that the notion of poetry as the bearer of religious truth grows out of a venerable tradition going back to Plato's myths. Near Coleridge's own time this way of thinking was found in the work of German philosophers opposed to Kant, such as J. G. Hamann and Herder. This movement culminated in the inordinately ambitious poetic schemes of post-Kantians like Schelling. Hamann, in his criticism of Kant, is more like a Scottish common-sense philosopher criticizing Hume.[4] But he combined a hermeneutical stance in philosophy with

[4]'Without the word – no reason, no world. Here is the source of creation and

a specifically religious orientation in a way that was to prove most influential. Language was the mother both of 'reason and revelation'.[5] History is construed as part of a religious poem. The corollary of this, a conclusion drawn by Hamann's friend Herder, Eichhorn and the 'higher criticism', is that we can read the Bible as a religious poem without prejudicing its claims to be recounting historical fact. The emergent definition of history accommodates both within the idea of poetic truth. Herder's interest in the philosophy of language must have appealed to Coleridge, despite his firm support for Kant in the disputes between the two philosophers.[6] As Elinor Shaffer has shown, Herder's theology certainly attracted him. Coleridge reproaches Herder when he thinks Herder is treating religious truths purely historically; but he shows great interest in the possibility of a poetic reading of biblical history such as that given, at Herder's suggestion, by Eichhorn in his *Commentarius in Apocalypsin Joannis*. In her authoritative study, Shaffer argues persuasively that this is a source both for 'Kubla Khan' and Coleridge's plans for a 'last possible epic'.[7] In *Biographia* Coleridge claimed that to 'give the history of the bible as a *book*, would be little less than to relate the origin or first excitement of all the literature and science, that we now possess' (*BL* I 156). However, the most ambitious schematization of history as God's poem to be encountered by Coleridge was Schelling's; and recent scholarly concentration on Coleridge's abhorrence of the Spinozistic pantheism in Schelling's work has tended to obscure Schelling's perpetual influence on his religious thought.[8]

---

government! What is sought in oriental cisterns lies in the *sensu communis* of the usages of language.' Letter to Jacobi, December 1784, trans. in R. Gregor Smith, *J. G. Hamann 1730–1788* (London, 1960), 250.

[5]Letter to Jacobi, 28 October 1785. *Ibid.*, 252–3.

[6]According to a marginal note on the wrapper of his copy of Herder's critique of Kant's *Critique of Judgement*, *Kalligone*, Coleridge 'never read a more disgusting Work, scarcely so disgusting a one except the Meta-critik of the same Author.' *M* I lxviii. See G. A. Wells, 'Man and Nature: An Elucidation of Coleridge's rejection of Herder's Thought', *Journal of English and Germanic Philology*, li (1952), 314–25.

[7]Shaffer, *'Kubla Khan' and 'The Fall of Jerusalem'*, chs 1, 2.

[8]I am thinking of McFarland's influential work, recently cited by G. Steiner as an exemplary reading comparable to 'any other studies of the stress of influence', 'Critic'/'Reader', *New Literary History*, x, no. 3 (Spring 1979), 452.

Coleridge believed that, as he wrote in the posthumously published *Confessions of an Inquiring Spirit,* 'history must be providential' (*CIS* 6–7). He told H. F. Cary, in a letter of 1827, that the biblical prophecies provide us with 'a magnificent Scheme of *History* a priori' (*CL* VI 689). In his lectures of 1818 Coleridge describes three kinds of history: the merely chronological; the exemplary history which takes its stand 'on some moral point'; and history 'most truly grounded on philosophy'. This final kind tries 'to describe human nature itself on a great scale as a portion of the drama of providence' (*MC* 146). Eliciting a redemptive pattern from history is typical of Schelling, and leads to a scheme which seems unavoidably pantheistic, identifying God with his immanence in history. As late as 1832 Coleridge wrote in a letter that he believed in 'a God who *seeketh* that which was lost, and that the whole world of Phaenomena is a revelation of the Redemptive Process' (*CL* VI 897). Earlier he tried to safeguard from pantheism this religious expression of the *Sehnsucht* of Schelling's Absolute. He claims that it is just *our* poetic way of figuring divine ideas to our imperfect understandings. He writes to Joseph Cottle in 1815:

Doubtless, to *his* eye, which alone comprehends all Past and all Future in one eternal Present, what to our short sight appears strait is but a part of the great Cycle – just as the calm Sea to us *appears* level, tho' it be indeed only a part of a *globe*. Now what the Globe is in Geography, *miniaturing* in order to *manifest* the Truth, such is a Poem to that Image of God, which we were created into. . . . (*CL* IV 545)

Because we do not have a God's-eye-view of the redemptive process of history we must picture it for ourselves in the shape of a poem. For Schelling, as we have seen, poetry does produce knowledge: individual instances of the Absolute's self-consciousness. In the relatively close confines of *Biographia* this contradiction between Coleridge's Kantian and Schellingian allegiances proved disastrous. In the wider field of theology Coleridge attempts an extraordinary synthesis. We have already seen how poetry is impervious to desynonymy, untranslatable because it already expresses figuratively the condition which desynonymy is trying to achieve. Coleridge's attempt to assimilate Schelling's theory of knowledge to 'common life words' through the model of desynonymy has also been discussed.[9] The conclusion invited by these two premises – that Schelling's philosophy will finally reveal the completion of science and the evolution of nature blending together in one vast, indivisible cyclical poem – is one which Coleridge drew but, typically, in an impossibly hybrid form. He tries to have it both ways: a Schellingian scheme in a Kantian poem.

'History,' Schelling had written in 1804, 'is an epic composed in God's spirit'; a theme which had exercised him towards the end of his *System of Transcendental Idealism* where he described how we participate in a poem, 'the Odyssey of the spirit', which appears in the world around us 'only as a meaning does through words.'[10] The 'spirit' needs the world in order to represent to itself its own activity. This is at once its own poetic act and the evolution of nature: the rules of imagination identifying themselves this time literally with the powers of growth and production in the world. This philosophy of identity, understanding nature as the unconscious poetry of spirit or mind engaged in a Homeric journey towards consciousness, shows Schelling's *Naturphilosophie* trying to remedy the deficiency in contemporary mythology diagnosed by Friedrich Schlegel. Schlegel claimed that 'the method of the physicist must be historical – his ultimate aim mythology.'[11] As Coleridge described such a scheme in a letter to C. A. Tulk of 1817, 'the whole process is cyclical tho' progressive' (*CL* IV 769). The impossible ambition of writing this cyclical poem of voyage and return, separation and reunion, was with Coleridge to the end of his life. In his last work published in his lifetime, *On the Constitution of the Church and State,* he declares that it has been to

the ascertainment and enucleation of . . . the great redemptive process which began in the separation of light from chaos (*Hades,* or the indistinction), and has its end in the union of life with God, the whole summer and autumn and

[9]See above, 'Living Words' and 'The Philosophy of Identity', 81–96.
[10]F. W. J. Schelling, *Werke,* ed. M. Schröter (München, 1927), 12 vols, VI, 57; III, 628–9.
[11]Schlegel, *Dialogue on Poetry and Literary Aphorisms,* trans. E. Behler and R. Struc (Pennsylvania, 1968), 81; 'Philosophische Lehrjahre', *Kritische Ausgabe,* XVIII, 154.

now commenced winter of my life have been dedicated. *Hic labor, hic opus est,*
on which alone I rest my hope that I shall be found not to have lived
altogether in vain. (*C&S* 113)

SPIRITUAL POSITIVISM

What of the second way open to Coleridge to resolve the antinomy in
his religious thought? By way of a preface to his theology of religious
intuition we must appreciate another context of intellectual influence. This can be described as spiritual positivism: the claim that
religious truths can be intuited once and for all in a fixed doctrinal
form. We noted that one half of Coleridge's contradictory theological
allegiances is in implicit agreement with Lessing that religion is a
progressive force working for the education of the human race.
Lessing deplored positivism whose doctrinal fixity he regarded as an
impediment to progress. In Coleridgean terminology, he always
supported the 'resistance' of reason to the 'captivity' of any specific
definition of religious truth. He claimed that there existed a logical
gap between the historical component of any doctrine and the
eternally progressive rational destiny religion ought to describe.
Lessing complained of his own inability to leap across this gap;[12] but
Kierkegaard made a hero of Lessing in his *Concluding Unscientific
Postscript* because he was convinced that Lessing's complaint must be
ironical. He did not want the gap to be closed because that would have
made religion positive, fixed in a specific historical mould. Kierkegaard similarly wanted to preserve the gap, the absurd transition
which made the leap of faith necessary. On the other hand, F. H.
Jacobi, whom Coleridge much admired, became convinced that
Lessing's stance was a mask for Spinozism, and that his aversion to
doctrine constituted pantheism. Kierkegaard detected irony in
Lessing's famous, 'half-smiling' remark to Jacobi, quoted by Coleridge in *Biographia,* on the occasion of an inconvenient shower of rain:
'You know, Jacobi, perhaps it is I am doing that.'[13]

---

[12]'On the Proof of the Spirit and of Power', *Lessing's Theological Writings*, 53–5.
[13]S. Kierkegaard, *Concluding Unscientific Postscript*, trans. D. Swenson and W. Lowrie
(Princeton, New Jersey, 1968), 95; *BL* II 113.

For Lessing, opposing religious positivism was perhaps more important than the impending *Pantheismusstreit*. Jacobi was a positivist who argued that religious faith was a kind of intuition; and Schelling, trying to break out of the Spinozistic structure of his own thought, also developed what he called a positive philosophy, making the purely intellectual intuition of philosophy the instrument of a doctrinal understanding of religion. Coleridge, in complete contradiction to those statements in which he is sympathetic to a position like Lessing's, was much influenced in his theology by Jacobi and Schelling. In a marginal note to Jacobi's *Werke* he connects Jacobi's 'mystery', or what he elsewhere calls his 'splendid mysticism', with an 'organ of spiritual truth', in intuitive faculty which, like Schelling, Jacobi developed out of the Kantian theory of apperception.[14] However, if the divine becomes the object of an absolute science, to be intuited directly, what need is there for the symbolic approximations of poetic language? Coleridge's theology when based on the possibility of an immediate intuition of religious truth is a kind of spiritual empiricism. It draws on Jacobi, and also reflects Coleridge's attempt to escape from Schelling's pantheism in a form mirroring Schelling's own attempt to escape from Spinoza. This escape took the form of making the Kantian 'reason' cognitive, but cognitive only of religious truth, the object of a 'higher' reason.[15] But Coleridge, unlike Kierkegaard, is only fitfully aware that he has now isolated an experience quite beyond language. Kierkegaard's achievement was to invent uses of language which do justice to our compelling need to talk about the extra-linguistic.

[14]See J. I. Lindsay, 'Coleridge Marginalia in Jacobi's *Werke*', *MLN*, L (1935), 219, 'And what is Jacobi's mystery? Is it not the organ of spiritual Truth? And what is this but the *real* Ich that shines through the *empirical* Ich – the correspondance of which with the former is categorically demanded'; J. H. Muirhead, 'Metaphysician or Mystic', in *Coleridge – Studies by Several Hands* (London, 1934), 191, 'It has further to be admitted that the idea of reason as endowed with a direct intuition of truth, inherited from Plato and reappearing in Fichte and still more explicitly in Schelling's "intellectual intuition", often deeply coloured [Coleridge's] . . . thought, and that, when in Jacobi he came upon the notion of a special organ appropriate to it, he was ready, as he tells us, to accept it'; compare W. Schrickx, 'Coleridge and Friedrich Heinrich Jacobi', *Revue Belge de Philologie et d'Histoire*, 36, ii (1958), 812–50, for a general discussion of the relations between the two thinkers.
[15]See R. Wellek, *Immanuel Kant in England* (Princeton, New Jersey, 1931), 124–31.

His attempt is worth considering very briefly here because it shows the magnitude of the problems Coleridge never fully faced. Kierkegaard wanted to transcend Lessing's irony. Irony is 'when I say something and do not say anything.' He wanted to say something by saying nothing; or, even better, to improve upon Socrates and Socratic irony by saying the same thing as Socrates, but not nearly as well. Kierkegaard's indirections aim to allow language to participate in the absolute paradox of trying to enunciate alternatives to itself. It can only give shape to this other by tracing its own boundaries, condemned to repeat itself with increasing internal diffidence (therefore 'not nearly as well as Socrates') and a corresponding confidence in a potentially richer alternative (improving on Socrates). The restrictions on what does or does not constitute a meaningful statement can be regarded either as delineating the integrity of language, or as throwing into relief the impinging shape of something utterly different. Yet these opposites are formed by the same linguistic expression: they repeat each other.

The supreme paradox of all thought is the attempt to discover something that thought cannot think . . . the Unknown is the different, the absolutely different. But because it is absolutely different, there is no mark by which it could be distinguished. . . . If no specific determination of difference can be held fast, because there is no distinguishing mark, like and unlike finally become identified with one another, thus sharing the fate of all such dialectical opposites.[16]

Kierkegaard's descriptions of religious experience contribute to a movement of thought which extends through Nietzsche to Derrida. Coleridge's spiritual positivism follows Schelling's swerve away from that new road, and instead reiterates an ancient contradiction.

This is that characteristic of western thought, shared by Coleridge and Schelling, which A. O. Lovejoy pursued through many of its ramifications in *The Great Chain of Being.* There are two Gods or sources of spiritual truth in Coleridge's thought. The first God is approached mediately through inadequate forms expressive of human limitations and aspirations. He is the principle of that growth and

[16]S. Kierkegaard, *Philosophical Fragments,* trans. D. Swenson (Princeton, New Jersey, 1967), 44ff., 55–6.

progress by which we strive to approach him. Such a God matches the absolute activity described in Schelling's philosophy of identity which we have seen it to be the project of Coleridge's cyclical poem to express. The other God is, in Lovejoy's words, 'the Absolute of otherworldliness – self-sufficient, out of time, alien to the categories of ordinary thought and experience.'[17] This is recognizable as that area of spiritual truth to which Coleridge's religious intuition gains access, isolated and immured in 'its own evidence'. In his letter to Tulk of September 1817 he imagines that he can, with consistency, adopt a philosophy which holds matter to be informed by an immanent spirit, and 'teach on the other hand a real existence of a spiritual World without a material', a positive teaching which he says belongs to 'a higher science' (CL IV 775).

In Schelling's work the intuitive relationship with the latter, *ausserweltlichen* God contradicts or makes redundant the progressive disclosure of God in history.[18] Heine deplored the fact that the notion of progress disappears from Schelling's increasingly orthodox religious thought, allowing him to be identified with the forces of political reaction.[19] We shall see how Coleridge's theology comes to reinforce his own conservatism. In his chapter on Schelling's 'intellectual intuition' in *The Destruction of Reason*, Georg Lukács states that Schelling's 'unequivocally reactionary period' begins with *Philosophy and Religion* (1804) and that this 'change consists in the fact that it was now religion and no longer art that was the "organon" of philosophy'. However, one of Schelling's fullest descriptions of the *Iliad* and *Odyssey* of history, a view which Lukács recognizes elsewhere as progressive, occurs in *Philosophy and Religion*.[20] The conclusion to be drawn is rather that Lovejoy's analysis is the correct one: both poem

---

[17]A. O. Lovejoy, *The Great Chain of Being* (Cambridge, Mass., 1936), 394.

[18]See the discussion by P. Tillich, in *Mysticism and Guilt-Consciousness in Schelling's Philosophical Development*, trans. V. Nuovo (Cranbury, New Jersey and London, 1974), 77–80.

[19]Heine, 'Zur Geschichte der Religion und Philosophie in Deutschland', *Sämtliche Werke*, 8/1, 113–15.

[20]G. Lukács, *The Destruction of Reason*, trans. P. Palmer (London, 1980), 155; Schelling, *Werke*, VI 57.

and intellectual intuition exist side by side, contributing mutually opposed approaches to the truth.

THE RELIGIOUS INTUITION

Coleridge's theology of religious intuition returns us to the model of knowledge which existed before those thinkers who had used language as a weapon against empiricist epistemology. An eye of reason uninformed by any human qualities registers with complete impartiality the immediate impressions of the spiritual world. This new spiritual positivism functions in exactly the same manner as the old empiricism, only transposed to a 'higher' plane. Coleridge describes in *Aids to Reflection* how we simply encounter again 'the same thing, power or principle' which we knew through sensuous experience, but now in 'a higher dignity' (*A* 198). The wheel has come full circle.

Coleridge continues to claim, most notably in the 'Preface' to *Aids to Reflection,* that a further refinement of 'the Science of Words' will reveal the intelligible structure of religious language. Yet frequently his description of the means by which he thinks we appropriate religious and spiritual certainties is a description of an experience which escapes from and lies beyond the power of language to symbolize. Coleridge describes the religious intuition as consubstantial with that which it intuits. The immediate intimacy which this form of knowledge enjoys with its object is made possible through an identity of the subject with the object. Side by side with the ambitious 'cyclical' schemes described in the letter to Tulk in 1817 exist contradictory strictures against any attempt to communicate religious truth: 'it is the Intuition, the direct Beholding, the immediate Knowledge, which is the *substance* and true *significance* of all – But to *give* or *convey* to another the *Immediate* is a contradiction in terms –' (*CL* IV 768). There are no questions we can ask about the representation of spiritual knowledge because consubstantiality means that no real relation between known and knower is involved; religious truths are to be understood 'irrelatively' (*CL* IV 806). In a footnote in *Biographia,* Coleridge objects to Kant's 'exclusive' sense of 'the term intuition' which 'denies the possibility of intellectual intuitions' (*BL* I 190n.), and he defines the term as comprehending 'all truths known to us without a medium'. While in a notebook entry of 1810 he describes how language becomes totally irrelevant to religious experience: 'concerning God we can talk neither sense or nonsense'; but he does not think this prejudices spiritual knowledge which 'does not need the medium of words, O! how little does he [the truly religious man] find in his religious sense either of *form* or of *number* – it is the *Infinite*!' (*NB* III 3973).

This exaltation of intuition over language again has its source in Schelling, in whose phrase 'Spirit rises above the Word',[21] and confronts us with an area of experience existing outside the range of language yet within the bounds of knowledge. In *The Great Chain of Being*, Lovejoy shows that Schelling, in his attack on the single-minded intuitionist Jacobi, is aware of the contradiction in believing that God can exist in isolated independence, while also believing in a God who necessarily participates in the world.[22] Access to an isolated God implies the redundancy of any mediate forms of understanding his existence. If we can directly intuit a truth there is no point in trying further to catch at it in approximate language. In the *Aids*, the immediacy of spiritual truth is the fulfilment of Christ's intent 'to "take Captivity captive"' (*A* 398). But this means that, contrary to Coleridge's radical argument, there is no more need for human resistance; no further progress is required, for in Christ human development and growth have reached fruition. Christ's words record intuitions consubstantial with the absolute categories which are their objects: '"My words", said Christ, "are Spirit; and they (i.e. the spiritual powers expressed by them) are Truth"; i.e. *very* Being' (*A* 398). Religious doctrine, on closer examination, turns out to be something to be lived, not spoken: 'Christianity,' writes Coleridge in the *Aids*, 'is not a Theory, or a Speculation; but a *Life*' (*A* 136). The

---

[21]Schelling, *Of Human Freedom*, a translation of 'Philosophische Untersuchungen über das Wesen der menschlichen Freiheit . . .' by James Gutmann (Chicago, 1937), 84.
[22]Lovejoy, *The Great Chain of Being*, 320, 322–3.

sublime understanding of the self in poetry, we remember, was to be spoken, not lived.

In the same work Coleridge does tentatively suggest that there is a connection between a religion which is bound up with moral progress and the '*positive* Insight' which 'belongs to a more advanced stage' (*A* 70). Spiritual positivism is the 'more substantive knowledge' for which '*Religious* Morality' is 'the natural preparation' (*A* 74). But he still does not succeed in connecting the two religions: for, in his descriptions, the sensuous faculty of religious intuition only employs the efforts of the conscience to dilate itself fully (*BL* I 167; *CIS* 60). Religious intuition is not built on previous, intermediate forms of apprehension. Spiritual truths are only spiritually discerned within the closed circle of spiritual knowledge (*A* 399; *C&S* 47n.). As Coleridge wrote in the *Lay Sermons,* and repeated in *Biographia,* 'Reason and Religion are their own evidence' (*LS* 10; *BL* II 215). In the 'rifacciamento' of *The Friend* Coleridge has 'no objection to define Reason with Jacobi, and with his friend Hemsterhuis, as an organ bearing the same relation to spiritual objects, the Universal, the Eternal, and the Necessary, as the eye bears to material and contingent phenomena'. The only clause with which he would supplement this definition draws attention to the consubstantiality of this faculty of knowing and the objects known: 'it must be added, that it [Reason] is an organ identical with its appropriate objects. Thus, God, the Soul, eternal Truth, &c. are the objects of Reason; but they are themselves *reason*' (*TF* I 155–6).[23] The spiritual senses and the ideas which they sense are the same substance; the circle cannot be broken. Religious symbols are therefore 'tautegorical' rather than 'allegorical', expressing 'the *same* subject but with a *difference*' rather than progressively extending or elaborating the meaning in 'a different subject but with a resemblance' (*A* 198–9).[24] The difference

[23] J. S. Lyon traces Coleridge's supplementation of Jacobi back to Plato and Plotinus, in 'Romantic Psychology and the Inner Senses', *Publications of the Modern Languages Association,* 81 (1966), 251.

[24] See the distinctions between symbol, allegory and metaphor in the eighth of Coleridge's 1818 lectures (*MC* 99), and in his marginalia to the seventeenth-century divines, Donne, Fuller and Leighton (*CSC* 174–5, 238, 255). On symbol and

in sameness of tautegory is certainly nearer the idea behind Kierkegaardian repetition, and correspondingly different from an educative poetic. But Coleridge's repetition does not seem intended to suggest the extra-linguistic plenitude Kierkegaard describes, but asserts the fixed, doctrinal authority annexed by spiritual intuition.

Despite Coleridge's complacent juxtaposition of the two kinds of religious thought throughout his writings, religious intuition remains isolated and independent of any poetically mediated approach to the truth. What John Coulson has described as Coleridge's 'fiduciary' use of language with regard to religion helps define further the antinomy in his religious thought. A 'fiduciary' usage can mean taking the words on trust in the sense that we allow poetry to symbolize for us thoughts and feelings to which we have no other means of access. Then, in Coulson's words, 'understanding religious language is a function of understanding poetic language.'[25] But, as Coulson goes on to argue, religious statements are different from poetry in that they claim to describe the truth. Religious statements are thus 'fiduciary' in a sense different from poetry where they ask us to take words on trust as standing for a set of facts. For Coulson, 'religious assertions . . . can be paraphrased into *true* statements of what is the case.' However, we saw that Coleridge's idea of the necessity or autonomy of poetry established its untranslatability. Coleridge's religious intuition does allow for a religious experience existing outside language, approachable by doctrinal assertion, not poetic appreciation. The trouble for his interpreters always arises when they try to account for his inconsistent poetic support for religion on other occasions.

---

consubstantiality, see Barth, *Coleridge and Christian Doctrine,* 20, 86–7. Wellek observes that Coleridge's symbols are not the product of metaphor but a kind of synecdoche, a 'figure of contiguity', while metaphor is 'a fragment of an allegory'. 'The Romantic Age', 174. P. de Man, in 'The Rhetoric of Temporality', disentangles some of the contradictory demands the Romantics made of the idea of symbol, and argues persuasively that in fact allegory rather than consubstantial symbol supports the art of Romantic poetry. *Interpretation and Practice,* ed. C. S. Singleton (Baltimore, 1969), especially 190–1.

[25] J. Coulson, *Newman and the Common Tradition* (Oxford, 1970), 4, 11–12.

POLITICS AND CRITICISM

The immediate intuition of spiritual truths through religious symbols is irreconcilable with Coleridge's poetics. Coleridge's ideas on desynonymy were meant to show that language is an 'instance and illustration' of our growing body of knowledge stirred to progress by the symbolic example of poetry. Language is not similarly active within Coleridge's scheme of religious symbols because he thinks we intuit spiritual truths immediately. The consubstantiality of religious reason with its intuited object eliminates the need for an interpretative medium. Coleridge's religious symbols use words to reflect truth directly in accordance with a fixed doctrinal scheme of their own. When Coleridge does enlist poetic support for his theology it is the progressive, historical revelation of religious truth which poetry encapsulates, not some isolated realm of spiritual certainty.

This paradox is carried into Coleridge's political theory where his notion of an educated class, the Clerisy, is intended to enrich and inform the fabric of society but is described in *On the Constitution of the Church and State* as something separate from the actual functioning of the state. The state is formed by two estates of the realm, landed and mercantile, providing for the permanency and the progressiveness of the nation respectively. The Clerisy is not bound to either of these interests but aims 'to secure and improve' the harmony of both (*C&S* 44). The Clerisy is part of the nation and not of the state, although it is in the state, the practical realm, that its benefits are to be reaped. At first this seems a plausible idea for a university, making room within a political theory for a class of people representing Schiller's aesthetic state – people whose duty it is to educate the rest into a sense of their own radical possibilities and so elicit 'the harmonious development of those qualities and faculties that characterize our *humanity*' (*C&S* 42–3). But this progressive idea is illusory because the Clerisy only educates people to an extent commensurate with their already existing 'rights and duties' defined in relation to the social class to which they belong. Because the Clerisy and its values exist outside the political arena, not contesting established political forms, the progress to which they contribute has no critical substance. The corollary is that because people's ideas of what constitutes their own humanity and how they should cultivate it are derived from a realm explicitly dissociated from real political intervention they would never dream they might discover their potential by effecting a radical change in their social status. It is only in this way that Coleridge can hope to secure permanent and progressive interests within the constitution of his Church and state.

This is only the logical conclusion of what was seen to happen in the earlier writings, especially in *Biographia*. In that work Coleridge urged the writer never to pursue literature 'as a trade', but instead to enter the Church where leisure and a steady income were guaranteed. Removed in this way from an economic interest in the means of literary production the writer need never question 'that loyalty which is linked to the very heart of the nation by the system of credit and the interdependence of property' (*BL* I 142–3). Coleridge also suggested in *Biographia* the radical stance of poetry as the standard of adequacy, while remaining nervous of its practical implications in the poems of Wordsworth. But he tried to deduce rules of criticism *ex cathedra,* from above, in a specialized, borrowed vocabulary, promoting his role as a prescriptive, authoritarian philosopher in possession of a consciousness which 'cannot be intelligible to all, even of the most learned classes' (*BL* I 168). He distrusted politically the shared, public language out of which his new critical distinctions were first generated in chapter 4, and repressed the original theory of desynonymy which rationalized them. That theory fostered a different kind of consciousness altogether – 'a certain collective, unconscious good sense working progressively to desynonymize those words originally of the same meaning' – which would have challenged the critical truce which he imposed between a progressive culture and a permanent social hierarchy.[26]

The intellectual sleight of hand which has neutralized the

---

[26]B. Knights, in *The Idea of the Clerisy in the Nineteenth Century* (Cambridge, 1978), shows comprehensively how 'The paradox of the idealism that attracted the proponents of the Clerisy is that, while it urges the primacy of spirit over matter, and hence the possibility of human freedom, its allegiance is to a static order of truth', 20.

progressive idea, harmonizing it with Coleridge's conservatism, is revealed when the ideas which are the foundations of the Clerisy's education of society are described. They turn out to be those of immediate intuition.

That is, of knowledges immediate, yet real, and herein distinguished *in kind* from logical and mathematical truths, which express not realities, but only the necessary forms of conceiving and perceiving, and are therefore named the *formal* and *abstract* sciences. Ideas . . . correspond . . . to objects whose actual subsistence is *implied* in their idea, though only *by* the idea revealable. (*C&S* 47n.)

These ideas, which 'constitute . . . humanity', obviate the need for political praxis in the same way that we have seen them dispense with Coleridge's poetics. Once we possess them, innovation through political action or education by poetic example are redundant. The antinomy of immediate intuition and poetic expression created a contradiction when they were brought together in Coleridge's theology; but in his political theory this inconsistency only supports his political conservatism. In 'the *fontal mirror* of the idea', a favourite phrase of Coleridge's, the educated citizen can contemplate his baptism into Coleridge's political orthodoxy (*C&S* 58, 70, 219).

Perhaps the best parallel here with Coleridge is Friedrich Schlegel. His early belief, under Schiller's influence, in a self-conscious 'progressive, universal poetry' is certainly matched by and may have influenced Coleridge's poetics.[27] He also ended up a theological positivist and a political conservative. The 'spiritualism' of Schlegel's *Philosophy of Life* fosters 'an inward experimental science of a higher order', an empiricism in complete contrast to his earlier poetic articulation – 'all theology is poetry' – of his religious thought.[28]

---

[27]Schlegel's most famous description of 'progressive, universal poetry' is found in 'Athenäum–Fragment' 116, *Kritische Ausgabe,* II, 182–3. Coleridge's copy is not annotated, see *M* I 980.

[28]Schlegel, *Philosophie des Lebens,* trans. A. J. W. Morrison, in *The Philosophy of Life and The Philosophy of Language in a Course of Lectures* (London, 1901), 61; see also *Literary Notebooks 1797–1801,* 1664, and the youthful Schlegel's claim that 'Every God whose concept is not *made,* i.e., fully produced, by a man for himself, but is given to him, is – however sublime [*sublimiert*] this concept may be – a mere idol,' *Prosaischen Jugendschriften,* ed. Minor (1882), II 105; trans. H. Eichner, *Friedrich Schlegel* (New York, 1970), 107.

Coleridge's contradictory philosophical tolerance also prefigures that identity of incompatible interests, radical and conservative, discerned by Raymond Williams within nineteenth-century concepts of the 'organic' unity of culture.[29] Coleridge's attempt to have it both ways conceals a crucial separation which removes the conclusions of his radical philosophy to an isolated, immediate domain whenever they threaten his conservative interests in existing institutions. Aided by John Stuart Mill's interpretation of Coleridge, this was eventually to culminate in the disengagement of the idea of culture and art from the motor forces of social change. Writing in 1831, Mill felt, as Coleridge had done, that the progressive character of the age undermined the possibility of 'a large body of received doctrine, covering nearly the whole field of the moral relations of man.'[30] Later, in his essays on Bentham and Coleridge, Mill saw Coleridge's philosophical effort as an attempt to restore this 'received' common category.[31] But Mill's interpretation significantly presents Coleridge's understanding of the importance of culture as something to be reconciled with Bentham's radical idea, not as something productive of change itself. With considerable effort the spirit of the age has to be persuaded to find a place for aesthetic values to humanize a progress whose real impetus comes from another source. Arnold's compliment of describing an aesthetic or cultural value as 'timeless' in fact ensures that it cannot be a historical agent. The gradual sequestration of the aesthetic realm, from Arnold onwards, arises out of the need to combat the radical qualities which art had accrued in the poetics of Romantics like Coleridge.

Arnold's repeated desire for that effort he thought to be typical of the European intellect, 'the endeavour, in all branches of knowledge, theology, philosophy, history, art, science, to see the object as it really is',[32] takes up the Coleridgean idea of criticism by transposition,

[29]R. Williams, *Culture and Society 1780–1950* (Harmondsworth, 1963), 146. See Wilkinson and Willoughby on the differences here between Schiller and Coleridge, *On the Aesthetic Education of Man,* clv–clvi; and Knights, *Clerisy,* 23, 51–3.
[30]J. S. Mill, *The Spirit of the Age* (*The Examiner,* 6 January 1831; 29 May 1831), ed. F. A. von Hayek (Chicago, 1942), 32.
[31]*Mill on Bentham and Coleridge,* ed. F. R. Leavis (London, 1950), 100.
[32]M. Arnold, *The Complete Prose Works,* ed. R. H. Super (Ann Arbor, 1960–74), III, 258.

a defamiliarization accomplished by the 'free play of the mind upon all subjects'.[33] But how this is to be justified, what underlying philosophical method is involved, we are not told. Despite complaining that the Romantic movement in England had been immature, that the Romantics had not known enough, Arnold never philosophizes in detail, never engages in the hard labour of trying to explain how there can be a humane basis to all the sciences. He does not have to do this, but he is therefore not entitled to disparage Coleridge's efforts in the same field, 'to lay bare the real truth of his matter in hand, whether that matter were literary, or philosophical, or political, or religious . . .'.[34] Arnold quotes from Wordsworth's 'Preface' as though it were poetry, and conveniently regards metaphysics as a disguised form of poetry unimportant in its own right.[35] He makes no attempt to understand the theory which has established literature at the centre of things; he merely assumes the authority it has provided. A good example is in his lecture 'Literature and Science', which he originally delivered in Cambridge, but later took to America and repeated many times. He therefore must have remained consistently untroubled by the indadequacies of the following:

But how, finally, are poetry and eloquence to exercise the power of relating the modern results of natural science to man's instinct for conduct, his instinct for beauty? And here again I answer that I do not know *how* they will exercise it, but that they can and will exercise it I am sure.[36]

All he can do is record successes. The esteem in which he holds the literary language leads him to try to educate us by quotation, by the 'timeless' example of his 'touchstones'. The trouble, however, is that the critical thought behind his selection is also a quotation, pressed into rhetorical service.

Carlyle, like Arnold, shows the masterly use of a suasive vocabulary in giving to us the feelings accompanying the successful conclusion of an argument rather than the argument itself. His opposition of

[33]*Ibid.*, 268.
[34]*Ibid.*, 189.
[35]See L. Trilling, *Matthew Arnold* (London, 1949), 358; W. A. Madden, *Matthew Arnold – A Study of the Aesthetic Temperament in Victorian England* (Indiana, 1967), 148.
[36]Arnold, *Works*, X 68.

dynamism and mechanism in 'Signs of the Times', and his insistence on the prophetic vocation of the poet in his lecture on 'The Hero as Poet' are good examples. He also argues by transposition, whether under the aegis of the 'Philosophy of Clothes' in *Sartor Resartus,* or in his claim, anticipating Pater, that if we see deep enough we 'see musically'.[37] Carlyle inherits features of Coleridge's thought, but unlike both Coleridge and Arnold he does not cite the nature of a literary language, its manner of symbolism, as the clue to poetry's philosophical significance.

George Eliot, a writer who believed that 'aesthetic teaching was the highest of all teaching', wrote novels acutely conscious of the radical implications of their own aesthetic status.

> But my writing is simply a set of experiments in life – an endeavour to see what our thought and emotion may be capable of – what stores of motive, actual or hinted as possible, give promise of a better after which we may strive – what gains from past revelations and discipline we must strive to keep hold of as something more sure than shifting theory.[38]

But those who write literary criticism have chosen to express themselves in 'shifting theory' rather than through poetic effect. At the perpetual risk of being reductive, critics must produce diagrams of the novelist's picture rather than more pictures if they are to preserve the autonomy of their own activity. It is uninformative, for example, to say as a recent critic does of Gwendolen Harleth that she 'is one of those great characters in fiction whose vitality comes off the page like a blast of life.' Appropriating the novelist's own categories in this way can, at best, only produce an impression recognizably parasitical upon that of the work of art itself. The claim to 'life' assumes without explanation the successful transparency of the novelist's conventions. Coleridge's 'ideal' poet need not know how his work gains its peculiarly 'sure' grasp on life; but Coleridge believed that the poet must unavoidably possess a modern, sentimental awareness that ironically it was only through an artificial detachment that such control over life could be achieved. This self-consciousness

---

[37]T. Carlyle, *Works,* ed. H. D. Traill (London, 1896–99), 30 vols, V 84; XXVII 83.
[38]*The George Eliot Letters,* ed. G. S. Haight (New Haven and London), VI (1956), 216 (To J. Payne, 25 January 1876).

constituted a defence of poetry for the critic to develop. This was as true of the 'exquisitely artificial' diction of Shakespeare and Milton as of the successes of Wordsworth. The opacity, not the transparency of convention is important here: its ideal pretensions expose the normally hidden assumptions behind our definitions of the real. A critical understanding of the immediacy of a poem's engagement with life depends on the ability to situate oneself historically in relation to the latent theories such immediacy implies. Much recent structuralist and post-structuralist criticism has concentrated exclusively on the foregrounding of literariness, but seems tempted into extravagance by the vacuum in English literary theory created by the post-Romantic dismissal of Coleridge as a philosophical critic. A theory so neglected is perhaps too easily revived as original. In their eagerness to deconstruct unreflective critical orthodoxies some of the new theorists tend to act as if under no historical constraints themselves.

The modern critical consciousness mediated by Coleridge was born of specific historical constraints. In the 'Preface' to the first edition of *The Critique of Pure Reason* Kant wrote that 'our age is, in especial degree, the age of criticism, and to criticism everything must submit.'[39] This sounds impressively uncompromising, coming from the Kant in whom Heine and Marx would like to believe. But in *What is Enlightenment?* Kant also wrote that the

public use of one's reason must always be free, and it alone can bring about enlightenment among men. The private use of reason, on the other hand, may often be narrowly restricted without particularly hindering the progress of enlightenment. By the public use of one's reason I understand the use which a person makes of it as a scholar befoore the reading public. Private use I call that which one may make of it in a particular civil post or office which is entrusted to him.[40]

This is full of strategic compromise, and floats the notion of a disinterested, educated class whose deliberate investment of their critical power in political causes would eventually be described as betrayal – 'la trahison des clercs'. Coleridge inherited this ambiguity in the Enlightenment concept of the critical activity and leaves

---

[39]Kant, *Critique of Pure Reason*, A xi n.
[40]Kant, *What is Enlightenment?* (1784), trans. L. W. Beck (Chicago, 1950), 287–8.

Arnold to be decisive between its political choices. Criticism is separated from the radical idea, and Arnold is helped in his formulation, as we have seen, by Mill's presentation of Bentham and Coleridge as intellectual opposites. Mill's Coleridge is the bearer of a cultural tradition complementing the progressive view of society which comes from another, Benthamite direction. In our century Leavis seized on this polarity; and as a result practical criticism has frequently appeared in a reactionary, anti-theoretical form which slights its original radical potential. The literary autonomy for which Leavis was fighting increasingly became a championing of his own profession — academic literary critic — rather than a vindication of the best literature of his time. In his later works it is criticism, not poetry, which Leavis takes it upon himself to defend against the encroaching explanations of other forms of thought. Literature is refused a wider theoretical significance in the interests of preserving the purity of the critical approach.[41]

Leavis wrote that Coleridge as a critic 'was very much more brilliantly gifted than Arnold, but nothing of his deserves the same classic status of Arnold's best work.'[42] But it is just this disparity between Coleridge's general importance and his individual achievements that is so revealing of the historical dilemma he had to cope with in his work. He was a radical lacking in political confidence, deeply distrustful of the political shape which the progress urged by his radical theory of poetry might take. Hence his suspicion of the particular examples through which Wordsworth chose to make felt the pressure of aesthetic education. From this also stems his repression of his theory of desynonymy which, before it was smothered in specialized borrowings, threatened to use the common means of social

[41]See Williams, *Culture and Society*, 248, 'Of course Leavis is right when he says that many of the "subtlest and most perishable parts of tradition" are contained in our literature and language. But the decline from Coleridge's allegiance to all the sciences is unfortunately real.' See also recent critiques by I. Wright, in *Culture and Crisis in Britain in the Thirties*, ed. Clark, Heinemann *et al.* (London, 1979), 37–67, and Francis Mulherne, *The Moment of Scrutiny* (London, 1979), especially his conclusion. On the other hand, Walsh detects a Coleridgean conclusion to Leavis' work, in *F. R. Leavis* (London, 1980), ch. 8.
[42]F. R. Leavis, 'Coleridge', in *Scrutiny*, IX (1940), 69.

communication as the model of philosophical discovery. As early as 1803 Coleridge wrote: 'Seem to have made up my mind to write my metaphysical works, as *my Life*, & *in* my Life – intermixed with all the other events/ or history of the mind & fortunes of S. T. Coleridge' (*NB* I 1515). *Biographia* is incomprehensible except as such a mixture of theory and history. In our own time, when theory appears to be losing its historicity, and historicism is declaring the poverty of theory, the Coleridgean mixture seems perversely exemplary. Coleridge participated in a historical movement of thought initiated by Kant and developed by Schiller, Friedrich Schlegel and others which increasingly attributed the importance of a work of art to the constitutive role played by its awareness of its own aesthetic status. In Coleridge's original work, the close reading and practical criticism of poetry leads to this philosophical principle which becomes more than abstract by defining poetry's radical stance in relation to other forms of thought. The twisted shape this argument takes in *Biographia,* going against the grain of its transcendental project, registers the force of particular historical anxieties on Coleridge's theory. To dismiss *Biographia* as simply confused, or to exonerate it as an ironic success, is to ignore this historical component which is present in the expression of any critical theory. We need a criticism which can explain the educative importance of literature, and Coleridge, for all his weaknesses, gives the English tradition the modern formulation of the problem. In the details of its recovery, the 'history of the mind & fortunes of S. T. Coleridge', are to be found the self-defining range of interest criticism needs to encourage, and the shaping spirit of historical engagement it needs to understand.

Index

28

Due 28 Days From Latest Date

MAR 2 8 1984			
MAY 21 19			
		WITHDRAWN	